D1707666

ROMANTICISM, NATIONALISM, AND THE REVOLT AGAINST THEORY

DAVID SIMPSON

ROMANTICISM, NATIONALISM, AND THE REVOLT AGAINST THEORY

THE UNIVERSITY OF CHICAGO PRESS

CHICAGO AND LONDON

David Simpson is professor of English at the Univeristy of Colorado
at Boulder.

The University of Chicago Press, Chicago 60637
The University of Chicago Press, Ltd., London
© 1993 by The University of Chicago
All rights reserved. Published 1993
Printed in the United States of America

02 01 00 99 98 97 96 95 94 93   5 4 3 2 1

ISBN (cloth): 0-226-75945-8
ISBN (paper): 0-226-75946-6

Library of Congress Cataloging-in-Publication Data

Simpson, David, 1951–
    Romanticism, nationalism, and the revolt against theory / David
Simpson.
        p.   cm.
    Includes bibliographical references and index.
    ISBN 0-226-75945-8. — ISBN 0-226-75946-6 (pbk.)
    1. English literature—History and criticism—Theory, etc.
2. Great Britain—Civilization—European influences.   3. Criticism—
Great Britain—History.   4. Romanticism—Great Britain.
5. Nationalism—Great Britain.   I. Title.
PR21.S55   1993
820.9—dc20   92-27447
                                                            CIP

♾The paper used in this publication meets the minimum requirements of
the American National Standard for Information Sciences—Permanence of
Paper for Printed Library Materials, ANSI Z39.48-1984.

FOR MARGIE AND SUSANNA

CONTENTS

ACKNOWLEDGMENTS

The Humanities Research Center at the Australian National University gave me a fellowship to begin this project. My thanks to Ian Donaldson, to the staff and other fellows of the center, and to Michael Holquist and Katerina Clark for showing us their Australia. A University of Colorado faculty fellowship gave me a year to do most of the reading, much of which was done in the Butler Library, Columbia University, and in the New York Public Library. My thanks to both these institutions and to the Columbia English department for its most generous hospitality. Over the years innumerable conversations and writings have contributed to this study. Among many, I particularly thank John Barrell, Colin MacCabe, and Geoffrey Hartman. Geoffrey Hartman first made me conscious, even against my will, of a peculiarly British hostility to theory, which at the time I shared all too glibly. It is a satisfying circularity that finds him as one of the latest readers of this manuscript, along with Mary Poovey; both of them produced extremely helpful reports. Martin Meisel gave me a key word for my title, proving that the top of his head could do better than the darker reaches of mine. I thank my students—especially Jean Lehman, Alfred Lutz, Steve Martinot, and Julia Sawyer—for sharing their own ideas and helping me express mine. I owe to Margaret Ferguson the most generous and most critical reading and talking through of everything here and much else besides: a companionship and common concern that is only the more cherished as time goes by. To her and to Susanna, our pilgrim soul, this book is dedicated—romantically, practically, and theoretically.

INTRODUCTION: A HISTORY
FOR THEORY

Theory has not yet been blamed for the Gulf War or for the destruction of the ozone layer, but it may be only a matter of time. In the United States, in this summer of 1991, the most macrocosmic social, intellectual, and educational calamities are being attributed by conservative commentators to an outbreak of "ideology" appearing in the classrooms as a new consciousness of gender and ethnicity and organized by the deeply bunkered command post known as "theory." On this topic, mere intensity seems to guarantee an interview, while paranoia produces at least an article. Lest we be tempted to relax our vigilance with the end of the Soviet menace and collapse into another age of good feeling, we are now told that there is an evil empire within, one working, in the words of George Will (but their name is legion), to erode "the common culture that is the nation's social cement" by imposing "collective amnesia and deculturation." Will specifies the technical method of such deculturation as "deconstructing" or "politically decoding."[1] The strong spin that Paul de Man and Jacques Derrida put on "theory" in the United States made it, for a time, identical with "deconstructing," and apparently much more threatening than it had been for the readers of Wellek and Warren, whose *Theory of Literature* sponsored a certain technicality, but one seemingly less likely to bring about the end of the American way of life or, as is often suggested, the fall of Western civilization (a phrase that does ambiguous duty as the description of a popular humanities course and as a definition of several hundred years of history).

Ironically, no one eschewed political reference more fastidiously than did Paul de Man, and no one complicated it more compulsively than did the vintage Derrida. Nonetheless, politics and theory have come to be identified once again, and even against their will, as public enemy number one, and those who would defend us against them are

regular guests on the television talk shows and inevitable contributors
to the magazines and journals. Daniel Harris finds that "postmodern
academic theorists have become ruthlessly appropriative, trying their
hand at everything from nuclear disarmament to apartheid, from
physics to MTV," with the result that everything is often reduced to
"innocuous generalities."[2] Harris's article might be taken as well inten-
tioned in that it upbraids ACT UP, the imaginative and activist AIDS-
awareness group, for its failure of radical effect, but in so doing it
repeats complacently all the old saws concerning the inevitable difference between theory and practice, as if what is theoretically articulated
could never be practically effective, even when it is at its most practical!
Harris cannot prove that ACT UP, with its apparently academic inspirations, has not done helpful things for the "real" politics of AIDS
activism; he merely assumes that because it has a theorized position, it
cannot possibly have done so.

The antitheoretical bandwagon is rolling with particular impetus in
the United States right now. In Britain it has mostly rolled at a more
stately pace, but with greater continuity and inevitability. Britain has an
even deeper tradition of fetishizing common sense and a less autonomously "professional" academic culture, so that it would be only slightly
melodramatic to declare that the vigilance against theory has hardly let
up since at least the 1650s. In the United States recent demographic
shifts and an increasingly acute economic division have made the established cultural and political interests more visibly nervous about their
futures; and theory has often been a great leveler (though this can no
longer be taken for granted, as we will see). In Britain what we may
loosely describe as "class consciousness" and "class struggle" have been
permanent rather than occasional components of the national discourse. (I am not, of course, saying that America is a classless society,
merely that it has often managed to describe itself as such.) This has
meant that the (mostly) generalizing habits of theory and method have
fairly constantly been taken as subversive of the national settlement,
along with the Scots, the Irish, the Welsh, and the trade unions.

But it has not always been so. There have been times, as in fashionable academic circles in the 1970s and early 1980s, and especially in
America, when theory was all the rage, more prepossessing as cocktail
party conversation than adultery or even salaries. Branford Marsalis
once said that he took up the saxophone to meet more girls—the
clarinet just wasn't doing it. So it was with theory, which was at once a
masculinist (at first) and a critical subculture. All this has now changed
dramatically. It is now fashionable to be against theory, not only on the

right, which is traditionally against theory, but also on the liberal left, which has traditionally resorted to what is called theory for a rhetoric of demystification and critical distance. The defenders of common sense have never had any time for methodized procedures; now, even consciously countercultural postmoderns can be suspicious of theory, with its apparently inevitable appetite for assertions about what is normative, schematically elegant, and describable by acts of pure intellection. Theory now, in many ways, is against itself.

I will return to these questions and to the contemporary situation in more detail in my concluding chapter. For the book that follows is not principally an account of modern critical theory, though its analogues and indeed its motivations clearly reside there. It is the product of the usual slow accumulation of evidence and argument over a number of years, and I could hardly have predicted at the beginning of this project that the question of theory would be a headline item in 1991. I was interested in why the British habitually and the Americans often have been hostile to theory, and curious about how the anglophone national traditions have constructed and perpetuated this particular phobia. I was also exercised by the importance of understanding these traditions at a time when, as I have said, the hitherto egalitarian and even radical associations of method and theory were coming under attack from the left itself as symptoms of the problem rather than the solution, as instances of elitism, masculinism, Eurocentrism, and a merely instrumental reason.

Hence, in my view, the importance of beginning a history for this theory. But not in order to produce a fraudulently neat model of absolute continuity. I hope I will not be caught saying or even implying that nothing is original to X in 1991 because it is all there in Y in 1791. There is no more depressing tactic of academic reification than the claim that everything happening now has already happened, and that there are no surprises. This fantasy places the scholar-analyst in absolute control both of history and of him or herself, but it serves no intellectually useful function. At the same time, motivated by having grown up in a culture whose apologists yodel belligerently at the mere attempt at systematic thought outside the sciences (Britain), and having already lived through both the glamorization and demonization of theory within another culture (the United States), I cannot but be impressed by the considerable coherence between past and present, and by the (somewhat depressing) persistence of certain rhetorics of disbelief. The contemporary situation is not at all a direct replication of the discourses of Romanticism and the debates over the French Revolution, but nei-

4 INTRODUCTION

ther is it clearly independent of them. The past is neither a prison within which the present can only passively subsist, nor the object of a merely antiquarian interest for its own sake.

One significant explanation of the continuity is that the revolt against theory that took place in the 1790s, contested by the "Jacobin" left but unsuccessfully so, was effectively proposed and identified as a quite natural and proper emanation of the British national character. Antitheoretical rhetoric thus became a central motif in the definition of a nationalism whose ramifications went far beyond the 1790s, and far beyond the immediately urgent debates in political theory carried on between Burke and his antagonists. This nationalist mythology continues to be available even today for the articulation of a British (and, with some differences, an Anglo-American) way of doing and seeing things, one based on common sense, on a resistance to generalized thought, and on a declared immersion in the minute complexities of a "human" nature whose essence is usually identified in an accumulation of mutually incommensurable details rather than in a single, systematized personality. Such a personality, indeed, is widely accepted as inhuman and has been imaged as the consequence, at various times, of the scientific spirit, of communism, and of German culture, among other "undesirable" forces.

This modeling of human nature along nationalist lines has not just supported a distinct mode of investigation in aesthetics and literary criticism. It has also functioned as the rationale for a political system—or rather, for a series of political practices, habits, and traditions. It is visibly alive in Britain, and most of all in England, where it is frequently deployed to legitimate the hegemonic role of England within Great Britain and Northern Ireland. Its career in the United States is more complex for a number of reasons, which include the more highly developed ethic of professionalism in American graduate schools (bringing with it a respect for special practices) and a more evasive and ambiguous attitude to a national culture that not only has an ostensibly constitutional (and hence theorized) base but also maintains a declared commitment to pluralism as a means of composing that culture by way of a laissez-faire assembly of different interests. For these reasons, among others, the American academy has seemed to offer a warmer welcome to "theory" than has its British counterpart. At the same time, the generalist and humanist countercurrent against both theory and the tradition of professionalization in America has often been more energetic than it appears to have been in Britain, perhaps because it is a countercurrent rather than a relatively complacent orthodoxy or received way of doing things. Those who argue the case for this generalist reaction are seldom comfortable invoking a national character as something already in place; more often, they propose such a character as the goal of their efforts, thus tapping into the common fantasy of some educators and politicians about a single, mutually intelligible and culturally coherent "American people," one nation under one language, one middle-class ethic, one intellectual tradition, and, perhaps, one god.

There is a connection, then, though it is neither simple nor unmediated, between the mythology of the British national character, with its contempt for theory, and the debate in the United States about that same theory. And, indeed, federalist America worked almost as hard as conservative Britain to keep out the contamination of French ideas in the 1790s and early 1800s. There is enough common history to make the substance of the present study important to an understanding of the contemporary educational polemics in both cultures.

But the career of method and theory through the nineteenth and twentieth centuries makes up only a part of the total picture. There is a definite risk that any account of that part that goes into sufficient detail to command some level of assent is going to look and sound like an image of the whole: as if the British national character, and then British history, were entirely described in terms of the revolt against theory. At risk of laboring the point, let me make clear what I have already suggested: I do not believe in the power of discourse or ideology to exercise any absolute power over the course of history, while I do believe that they contribute, along with other technological, economic, and material determinations, to that history. One cannot, then, compose a history simply by transcribing the history of an idea, or even of an idea-in-practice. Such accounts as tend toward this assumption risk forgetting that culture itself is seldom if ever uncontested from within, by various class and subcultural interests, so that the paradigm available for description is not so much a fixed unit as a continually self-adjusting and self-defending series of forces and energies evolving at uneven rates and reacting often unpredictably with various influences. The agglomeration of cultures may produce the image of a whole *culture,* which thus looks like a normalizing medium, and this image may be employed to project and defend a rhetoric of wholeness and continuity. Those of us who write about culture—for instance, those of us who have a professional interest in the humanities—often seem to take this rhetoric at face value or as a kind of shorthand, and it is often filled out by reference to a dominant attitude or worldview. In the 1790s the majority of commentators on both left and right pronounced that the French Revolution was principally the result of ideas. The right found those ideas dangerous; the left saw in them a means for bringing about utopia. Both reproduced the fallacies of taking the part for the whole, and ideas for events.

There is another error of extremity, though one less likely to be incurred by anyone writing about the past from a literary-theoretical perspective: that of a merely occasionalist history. If ideas do not simply "make" history, they remain an important part of it, and they do effect continuities that are as good as empirical. History is not just the collision of unpredictable forces, even as the element of unpredictability remains large. The model of occasionality, or complete contingency, remains the preference of some conservative historians who are anxious to head off the claims to credibility of all theoretical or general descriptions. Edmund Burke, in making his case for the power of habit and custom, suggested that without the guiding hand of intelligent patriarchy mere traditions could not alone defend us from the chaos of such contingency.

The most convincing historiography, then, is imprisoned by neither ideas nor disconnected events, but remains aware of the play and possible relations between them, and aware also of the field of other determinations that must be reckoned into any satisfactory model of the past. As we look back at the debates of the 1790s, we find everywhere the figure or image of Burke, as the hero of the right and the demon of the left. A different Burke is recalled in the memoirs of Joseph Pearson, the doorkeeper of the House of Commons: "He never rises but I have directly to open the door to let the members out."[3] The figure who was nationally syndicated as the heroic defender of the national interest was also likely to send his regular listeners straight to the nearest coffee-house. We have to imagine a world wherein Burke had not one or the other of these effects, but both.

A history of theory, then, is only a part of a theory of history. I have lodged these preliminary and perhaps apparently abstract qualifications because I am setting about a history of theory, and in taking the topic very much on its own terms I might otherwise be taken as endorsing its effects on history as more important than any others. In taking the argument back to Ramism and Puritanism, as I do in chapter 1, I risk producing a long-view model of the emergence of nothing less than modernity itself. Within the terms of this model, one can trace a fairly continuous association of method and theory with aspirations to political and educational equality. But the same Puritan "method" that has been related to scientific discovery and to a measure of democratization coincided with and perhaps enabled Cromwell's unprecedented expansion of the English navy and accompanied major developments in colonialist control of the Caribbean. No one would argue that there was much of the spirit of liberation involved in that process, though it provided the economic base for the modernization of Britain. My account, by limiting itself to the languages transcribed within the nation-state, cannot but underemphasize that whole dimension of modernity, of which the magisterial work of Eric Williams, among others, should be a constant reminder.[4] The same Ramist and then Painite method whose politically liberating functions are described in this study cannot be divorced from the technologism whose negative effects we are more and more aware of today. Lucien Goldmann aptly sketches the working assumption among the philosophes that

the mission of man, which gives meaning to his life, lies in the effort to acquire the widest possible range of autonomous and critical knowledge in order to apply it technologically in nature and, through moral and political action, to society.[5]

This same autonomous critical knowledge, in the light of the shifts articulated by feminists and postmodernists, themselves reflecting a recognition of a massive global crisis (both economic and environmental), now has a bad reputation: it is masculinist (as "theory" itself is often said to be), exploitative, and Eurocentric, and it is received equally critically by the poststructuralist left whether it emanates from classic capitalism or classic Marxism. From within the Enlightenment, Condorcet's case against the liberal relativism of Montesquieu came from what was then recognized as the left; today the language of universal method is itself suspected by a left that identifies all such aspirations as repressive fantasies produced by a rationalized masculine imagination.

This is a major shift, and one not comfortably contained by the genealogy of method and theory that, I suggest in this study, describes much of the debate around those terms through the middle of the twentieth century. And yet perceivable continuities remain. It is, for example, under the banner of theory that the postmodern left attacks method, thus reintroducing a separation between two terms that had been rhetorically if not definitionally synonymous for much of the past two hundred years. In the early chapters of this book, "method" will be the principal focus. This is the term used to specify the radical element in Ramism and in Puritan and Methodist doctrine. It suggests not so much a finished, totalized system (though this may be implied or projected) as a way of doing things according to a progressive procedure. The debate about method is most often a debate about the relation of such procedures to the true order of things in the world, and about the transferability of any one procedure from one area of the world to others. "Theory," on the other hand, tends to describe a more speculative or

hypothetical mental projection, perhaps gesturing toward a point that
the executive capacities of method cannot reach, or have not yet
reached. Rationalism held the two together, for within the rationalist
ideal the projections of theory must eventually be in accord with the
conclusions of method. Orthodox Baconians, on the other hand,
claimed method but abjured theory. In the British reactions to the
French Revolution, we can see the two terms coming to be identified as
either in themselves synonyms or effectively so in the dangerous confusions put about by the French politicians. Here the belief in method,
in the progressive application of mental techniques to practical-political
ends, comes itself to be regarded as a wild and visionary delusion—a
delusion of "theory." After this conjunction, analyzed in detail in this
study, the polemical negation of all schemes and models, whether they
emanate from theory or method or both, becomes a key motif in the
mythology of the British national character and serves to diminish the
reputations of rationalists, utilitarians, and Marxists alike.

Increasingly the critical antithesis came to be that between "theory"
and "practice," with the orthodox Baconian tradition now aligned
clearly with the second, and with the term "method" tending either to
drop out of the lexicon or to survive in less controversial contexts (we
tend to be somewhat friendlier toward a methodology than toward a
theory).[6] Thus it is "theory" that has survived as the term used to challenge the empiricist and positivist methods designated as central to the
Anglo-American tradition, and it is "theory" that is reciprocally deni-
grated by that tradition as impractical and merely speculative. Even
when the theory stands against rationalist or totalized paradigms (as it
does in so many of its postmodern formulations), even when it stands
against method, it still remains "theory" in the eyes of those anxious to
resist the claims of all generalized thought.

These semantic evolutions and revolutions are examples of the
degree to which the debates about theory and method are variable and
even different within a tradition that is at the same time somewhat continuous. Hence the word *revolt* in my title, which conveniently implies
(as does the older sense of *revolution*) a turning back to as well as a turning away from something already in place. It thus refrains from attributing any complete originality to 1789, which was a major moment
but not the only component of the debate. I begin with Ramism in order to explain some of the preformations that made 1789 register upon
British observers in the way that it did; at the same time, I mean to confirm that 1789 did refigure the terms of the argument, an argument
subsequently refigured again by (at least) utilitarianism and poststructuralism.

And so to the French Revolution. I begin with two moments of recognition, of self-congratulatory history-making. Here is the first:

> I have been too long a farmer to be governed by any thing but events; I have a constitutional abhorrence of theory, of all trust in abstract reasoning, and consequently a reliance merely on experience, in other words, on events, the only principle worthy of an experimenter.

This is Arthur Young, the card-carrying English yeoman, in 1793, getting in his licks at what he calls, in a prophetic phrase, "French theory."[7] Take out the reference to farming, along with the shrewd displacement of the political by the bodily-intuitive sense of "constitutional"—an exact address to the semantic conflicts of the 1790s—and one might here be reading the transcript of any one of a number of debates in the universities throughout the 1970s and 1980s about what was also called "French theory," or just theory in general. Young was not writing for the academy but for a general readership that would have recognized the familiarity of his position, one that had become a commonplace after Burke's infamous attack on the French Revolution as the terrible product of a misguidedly systematic philosophy.

Here is the second moment:

> Talkers who lack ideas—and there are a few of this sort—drone on and on with nonsense about what they call the importance of practice and the uselessness or the perils of theory. Only one point need be made in reply: imagine any sequence of the most wise, useful and excellent facts possible. Well! do you believe that there is no corresponding theoretical sequence of ideas that exactly corresponds to your practical sequence of facts? If you are a rational creature, this sequence of ideas will follow you, or, to be more correct, it will precede you. What is theory, pray, but this corresponding theoretical sequence of truths which you are unable to see until put into practice but which, nevertheless, someone must have seen unless we are to assume that people had been acting without knowing what they were doing.[8]

This is the Abbé Sieyès, one of Burke's principal targets, writing in 1789, even before Burke has attacked him. His response, by anticipation, closely prefigures the responses of those modern literary theorists who stand accused of an implausible faith in system and structure. Everyone, says Sieyès, lives and acts by theories: the only difference is that some of us are aware of it and some of us are not.

These are but two of the many possible citations that visibly connect the debate of the 1790s with that of the recent past and the present. But, as I have said, the pleasure of recognition must not lead us to ignore the complex mediations that come between the language of the 1790s and that of the generation responding to the events that we know in shorthand as "1968." The narrative is neither one of decline nor of world-historical continuity. It is very tempting to look upon the enemies of literary theory as farcical reincarnations of the titans of the 1790s: they had their Burke and a possible European revolution, while we have only Professor X arguing against some or other change in the curriculum as if it were prophetic of the end of civilization. Much more implausible is the narrative of continuous identity, much in vogue in the late 1980s, which accepts Professor X as indeed the defender of civilization (usually civilization "as we know it") and looks to him as our last hope of preventing its collapse.

The more interesting and useful account, as I have been implying, is somewhere between these two extremes, and it is difficult to ponder because it is not a clear and distinct narrative. In so declaring I must, I suppose, appear to be replicating a good old British predilection for finding the truth between two extremes, and thus myself wielding the very ideology I am proposing to critique. But I do not mean to imply that *a* truth is going to be found there, and simply by definition, by virtue of *being* between two extremes; rather there is, more basically, a great deal of work to be done to allow any useful posing of the question. If this book of mine does anything more than to rearticulate a truism—that the British, and to some extent the Americans, don't much care for theory—then here is where it will do its work. One of the definite legacies of 1968 is the awareness that the universities were and are more a part of the public sphere than the besetting image of ivory towers would have us believe. They are neither a place to hide nor a rostrum from which the tide of events may be viewed with mandarin disinterest. Those academicians who are aware of this legacy feel the need to remain curious about how what they do in print and in the classroom relates to a larger model of history, whether local, national, or international. In addressing this question now it is important to avoid extreme inferences from two major trends of recent decades: one saying that what we do has no consequences and can be described and justified in microinstitutional terms (the training of a profession or the reproduction of a tradition), the other countering that what we do is of absolute importance, as the inevitable and total reflection of a single ideology or (the obverse) of a pure revolutionary imperative.

This question is so difficult that it has hardly yet been addressed.[9] And it seems important to set about that address after a year like 1989, a year that gave rise to a plethora of conferences, essays, and editorials on the essence and afterlife of the French Revolution. The most frequently repeated conclusion of these various gatherings and publications may be summarized in one pithy phrase: "la révolution est finie"—the Revolution is over. This argument, most prominently presented in the writings of François Furet, now the most widely read historian of the period, makes the case that the recent realignments in French political life—and in particular the decline of the Communist party—have finally freed France from the terms of a debate laid down in the years after 1789 and not substantially refigured for a century and a half thereafter. This message of new beginnings (on roughly liberal free-market principles) is a selective rendering of both the French and the international political scene, but it has proven popular both in the United States, where Furet spends much of his time, and to some extent in a Europe whose ruling interests look forward to a prolonged period of federation free from such traditional embarrassments as class struggle and class consciousness. While it may make sense to describe some of the institutional and even psychological or cultural legacies of 1789 as "over," it does not seem sensible to reify either the Revolution itself or its legacies as open to any conclusive historical subsumption (unless one is a certain kind of Hegelian), without presuming also a world in which the events and languages of that earlier period can no longer, and by definition, offer any provocations for the imagining of a future. Obvious imbalances within the developed nation-states, not to speak of the relations between those states and others less developed, would at least suggest that we are some way from such a situation.

To return to the question of theory, and by analogy: we cannot divide up the exponents and opponents of contemporary theory into the same relatively explicit political camps that characterized the debate about theory in the 1790s, but neither do we discover that there are absolutely no connections between then and now. For Tom Paine and his followers, as for their Enlightenment precursors, rational method was a liberating and demystifying energy, a way beyond the illusions of social, political, and religious conventions, which it exposed as just that: illusions. The dissemination of method would occur through the power of print, which would solve a problem of persuasion conceived as entirely and merely empirical: the naturally reasonable mind had only to be shown the truth for the truth to spread and prevail.

We are now a long way from such idealisms, but the negative position against theory still finds a use for such ideas within the rhetoric of vilification. When the Cambridge English faculty, in the early 1980s, was trying to head off the challenges of more or less everything, it was "structuralism" that was most often invoked by the old guard of all ages as the representative bogeyman. Even though the conjunction of Marxism, psychoanalysis, and poststructuralism clearly constituted the real challenge, "structuralism" remained a useful term of abuse, not least for its connotations of bloodless rationalism and theoreticism, and its reputation for murdering by and for dissection. This redefinition of the problem enabled the defenders of the faith to ignore (or at least pretend to ignore) the political and libidinal dimensions of the crisis in their discipline, and allowed them to academicize the rather complex interaction between institutional, national, and indeed global determinations that impinged upon local dissent, as if it were all simply a matter of literary sensitivity and interpretive tact. Even the dreaded structuralism, moreover, had at its heart, in the emergent image of bricolage, a whiff of the postmodern, and a willingness to cope with a ruined metaphysics not just by abstract methods but by opportunism, approximation, and to-handedness.[10]

As I have said, the rationalist ideal is now defended by hardly anyone on the left. In extreme cases—in some of the work of Foucault, in the Frankfurt School critique of instrumental reason, and in the postmodern critique of totality and the resulting preference for dislocation over connection—rationalism is itself identified as the blatant beast of the modern condition, and made responsible for such undeniably historical phenomena as genocide, nuclear weaponry, sexism, racism, and ecological brinkmanship, as well as for the more quotidian punishments of bureaucratic discipline. Across a wide range of academic practices, a common pattern has emerged whereby the urge for or belief in anything that looks like Enlightenment rationalism is identified negatively with such belated subcultures as blinkered scientists, old-style Marxists, and political reactionaries. Hans-Georg Gadamer's influential hermeneutics, for example, takes as its antagonist precisely the deluded social scientist who believes in objectifiable models for human behavior. His emphasis on the linguisticality of all forms of human understanding is directed against our "naive surrender to the experts of social technology" (though it is also an attempt to head off the more radical possibilities attendant upon a recognition of history and tradition as embedded in temporality).[11] Among humanists at large as well as among historians of science, Thomas Kuhn's *The Structure of Scientific Revolutions* has been enormously influential for its argument that the illusion of atemporal objectivity can only be preserved during periods when the research establishment is devoting its energies to "normal science"—to the fine-tuning and application of previously devised paradigms. And Paul Feyerabend, in his boldly titled *Against Method,* has argued not only that the conventional scientific education "cannot be reconciled with a humanitarian attitude," given its repression of "imagination" in the pursuit of "enlightened conformism," but also that science itself can only proceed and succeed by anarchistic gestures:

"Even a law-and-order science will succeed only if anarchistic moves are occasionally allowed to take place."[12]

So dominant are these voices, and others like them, that it now seems impossible to maintain a countercultural or oppositional posture by trying to defend any version of Enlightenment rationalism. The kind of "theory" that shook the establishment in the 1790s is now, in other words, itself the target of radical critique, and imaged as the ideology of the ruling interests. We can hardly lament this situation, even if it does put into question the whole attempt at devising objective terms for social or aesthetic analysis, since there is no way back to the discursive configurations of two hundred years ago, unless it is the way of fantasy. Today's radical intellectuals, notwithstanding their commitment to particularities and their distrust of system-producing speculation, are not at all the successors of Edmund Burke and Arthur Young. The terms of the debate have changed, so that its contemporary participants cannot be reduced to mere shadows of a heroic or villainous past. The postmodern suspicion of the rationalist paradigm does, after all, articulate itself as a commitment to democracy—the very concept defended by the rationalists themselves in earlier generations.

It is the model of that democracy that has changed. It is no longer envisaged as a collectivity of normative subjects, all thinking and behaving alike when freed from restraint. It is now supposed that a properly egalitarian social contract must be premised on the recognition and acceptance of irreducible differences. Rational uniformity is now seen as the myth of a privileged class-gender subgroup, so that the degree of true democracy comes to be measured by the computation of the maximum available number of alternative subject-formations.

This ethic of absolute tolerance has inevitably raised, for both proponents and critics of the postmodern attitude, some critical questions. If power remains in the hands of the few, then tolerance, precisely as an ethics, becomes a mystifying rationale for the preservation of the status quo and for a purely laissez-faire evolution of political entities. Attitudinally, everyone is recognized, but power remains exactly wherever it happens to be. This position is reasonably open to criticism as the ideology rather than the critique of contemporary capitalist culture. On the other hand, those who extend the recognition of difference to a call for the empowerment of differences can justifiably claim to be offering a radical imperative. The debate about the politics of postmodernism must concern itself with these two extremes, and these two possibilities. Because the terms of the argument inevitably shift with the different contexts and occasions encountered, we cannot decide the politics of postmodernism in the abstract, as if there were a stable affiliation to something called "postmodernism." We cannot know in advance if "it" is really the rhetoric of late capitalist alienation or that of radical critique, because the argument looks quite different in different situations and with different participants. By the same token, we cannot know in advance whether what comes to us labeled "theory" is the signifier of a subversive energy or of a practically conservative instinct. "Theory" now describes many things, from the consciously interventionist to the merely technocratic. Even what looks like the same theory has different consequences and implications when it "travels," as Edward Said told us some time ago.[13] Things are now inescapably more complicated than they were in the days when the defenders of Burke tilted at the followers of Paine.

There is, then, work to be done. I will return to the questions attending contemporary theory in the conclusion to this study. For now the whole aspiration to knowledge is itself under interrogation. We can no longer convince ourselves that patience and diligent inquiry, along with an openness to a variable play between item and system, are enough to guide us toward something acceptable as truth. Many of us believe that to seek patiently in the light of an effort at self-consciousness is the best we can do, and we may even believe that we do find something truthful thereby. But there is always attendant a skepticism that is much more than the ghost of a doubt; it is the awareness that all acts of understanding are premised upon incompletion or even misdirection. In his magisterial description of the framework within which the modern condition is experienced and expressed, Michel Foucault has specified this syndrome as the constitutive moment of the "sciences of man" and of a subjectivity positioned within the "analytic of finitude." For him the very condition of our expressive existence involves an awareness that expression itself emanates from a synthesis of temporal determinations, cultural and biological, that is "man," and that is indescribable in "objective" terms, because inescapable. Whenever we speak, we speak from within this condition, and what we speak can never tell us the difference between mere expression and the analysis of that expression.[14]

For the historian or literary critic who would (who must) acknowledge the problems of interest and motivation in all attributions of meaning, the acceptance of Foucault's diagnosis of necessary indeterminacy has proven either terrifying or euphorically liberating, and sometimes both. Either one embraces the inevitable indecisiveness as the appropriate permission for saying one's piece—by definition no less defensible than anyone else's piece—or one is possessed by a declared agnosticism, confident of nothing. It remains open to us—and I think this is the right response to an awareness of the "analytic of finitude"—to explore the incompleteness of all constructions of meaning within interim formations, in time and place, that explain those meanings as more than simply personal. Here we have to try to articulate such determinations as those of class, gender, ethnicity, occupation, and subculture, within which we are subjectively implicated in an objective way. These explanations are difficult, not only because they are themselves subject to hermeneutic skepticism (there is no position outside finitude), but because the terms themselves change, even unpredictably, in relation to an unpredictable number of other determinations. Class, gender, occupation, and other apparently local syndromes are not immune from interaction with such spasmodic agencies as war, climate, and the whole international political-economic sphere. They do not simply reproduce themselves in identical forms, and they are further redefined by individual contributions, themselves variable along a spectrum from biological accident to conscious will.

In other words, we no longer live in a world likely to accept the application of a simple theory or method as the key to all our mythologies. But this admission need not entail a collapse into mere worship of detail or an acceptance of that strand of the postmodernist rhetoric specifying all pursuit of totalities (as explanations) as totalitarianism (in practice). The stone-kicking rituals of ordinary life have appealed to some neo-pragmatists as a way out of some of these dilemmas, but these are in my view part of the problem and never the solution. Conversely, the celebration of absolute idiosyncrasy can provide only a personal epiphany. Perhaps it is the model of problem-solving itself that needs reconceiving, as we move away from atemporally objectivist to temporally objectivist paradigms, arguable and explicable as efficiently determining for now but not forever. It is the Marxist tradition, viewed as a complex and contested evolution and not as a polemically reduced facsimile in the service of a cold-war ideology, that has most consistently maintained a commitment to the methodological priority of temporality in relation to (and not simply at the expense of) an aspiration toward some workable or possible objectivist component. And it is this tradition that has perhaps the most to offer to those interested in the analysis of theory in its modern and postmodern identities.

The schematization of the contemporary situation for "theory" given above sets out a series of problems that I cannot hope to solve in this study, even by an extended redefinition of what it is to "solve" (though that is surely the task before us). Here, I am engaged in a history of an important part of the career of method and theory in the Romantic period. I have suggested that such a history neither confirms nor denies a definitive relation between the Romantic and the modern

and postmodern situation, but that there are significant and determining continuities. The debate of the 1790s, in other words, does not
give us all the terms required for an understanding of the 1980s, but it
remains relevant to its composition and articulation. There is no ideological predestination, but neither can we ignore the evidence of strong
continuities, especially when, as I have claimed, they are maintained by
the powerful ideology of nationalism. In his pathbreaking essay of
1968, "Components of the National Culture," Perry Anderson remarked that "the British bourgeoisie had learned to fear the meaning
of 'general ideas' during the French Revolution: after Burke, it never
forgot the lesson."[15] My entire study can be read as an exposition of this
remark, and a documentation of its various expressions and implications. In 1799 a repentant Sir James Mackintosh, whose *Vindiciae Gallicae* had been one of the earliest defenses of the Revolution, lectured at
Lincoln's Inn Fields to the effect that "simple governments are mere
creatures of the imagination of theorists, who have transformed names
used for convenience of arrangement into real politics. . . . As constitutions of government approach more nearly to that unmixed and uncontrolled simplicity they become despotic, and as they recede further
from simplicity they become free."[16] Mackintosh, like Burke before
him, had come to think that too much theory would ruin Britain.
Napoleon declared himself convinced that a similar excess had produced everything bad that had happened to France.[17] John Stuart Mill,
in his *Autobiography*, would be quite clear that something very like what
we might call "theory" had almost ruined him; and the same antitheses
between thought and feeling, analysis and intuition, reason and imagination, reappear throughout the nineteenth century, in the "two cultures" debate of the twentieth century, and again in the arguments for
and against literary theory. There is indeed a history here, and an important one.

    And what of "literature"? If method and theory are, in the Romantic
period, the property of the radicals and then of the utilitarians, and are
simultaneously imaged (as they are) as the antagonists, in the aesthetic
and psychological sphere, of the literary, then we can predict a tendency for literature itself to assume an alliance with a conservative social agenda. This conjunction does, as we shall see, hold good as the
symptom of a general tendency, though it has been by no means an om-
nipotent determination. The concomitant feminization of the literary
made available the language of the erotic, which proved able to present
a different kind of challenge, one not always containable within the mythology of a customary common sense even though it too denied the
authority of rationalism. Although criticism has recently been pre-

pared to explore explicitly its relations to the erotic (in the work of
Roland Barthes and of Julia Kristeva and other feminist critics) it has
made use of that language less commonly than of a modified or pro-
totypic theorizing that does not put too much strain on the patience of
the national character.

   These considerations, and others like them, provide the motives for
the present study, which hopes to convince its readers that, even if some
of the legacies of 1789 might now appear irrelevant, it cannot be proposed in any serious sense that the Revolution is "finished."

1

THE POLITICS OF METHOD

Peter Ramus, Martyr

Edmund Burke made a late career out of his opposition to the methods of philosophical and scientific logic, whose procedures he continually imaged as cold, abstract, and heartless. In the transports of his own impulsive and inspirational prose he tried to make them seem this way as if by negation. He proclaimed the rights of immethodical thought and expression, presenting them as the rhetorical incarnation of a free and liberal society itself imagined as uniquely British—a society that could tolerate no restrictively exact definition and must frustrate any desire for a merely rational predictability. Burke saw himself not only as the apologist but also as the very voice of this English political-stylistic cornucopia: "I beg leave to throw out my thoughts, and express my feelings, just as they arise in my mind, with very little attention to formal method."[1]

Some thought that Burke protested too much. "Radical John" Thelwall, in *The Rights of Nature,* tried to expose what he saw as an artful order behind the appearance of disorder:

Hence, if you want to know the whole meaning, and real object of this master of political controversy, instead of following him through the regular succession of pages and paragraphs, we must seek for the leading traits and positions of his work, and then, putting together the disjointed parts of the syllogism so artfully divided, we must extract the enveloped conclusion for ourselves.[2]

Burke, in other words, is a logician through and through. He is naturally given to rational and systematic expression, as Thelwall imagined all human beings to be, but he disguises the terms of his argument in a deliberately disorderly prose to prevent us recognizing the presence of the syllogism, the logician's mark of Cain. To recall an earlier Burkean preoccupation, we might say that he fires up the smoke screen of the sublime to inhibit any perception of the order and stability of nature as participating in the balance and harmony of the beautiful, and to pre-

19

empt the suspicion that things might, after all, be left to themselves. A belief in symmetry and simplicity in the natural and political order had by the 1790s became the signature of radicalism. Capel Lofft, another of the many critics of Burke's *Reflections,* described the ideal political system as being exempt from "unnecessary, disconnected, unduly united, or disproportioned parts."[3] And Thomas Paine himself, in *The Rights of Man,* praised the French Declaration of Rights because its first three articles comprehended "in general terms" everything that came after them.[4]

I doubt that any of these writers—Thelwall, Lofft and Paine—or the many others who declared similar preferences had the name of Peter Ramus even at the back of their minds. But they were all reannouncing or reinventing Ramist doctrine, and repeating the terms of an intense debate in the sixteenth- and seventeenth-century academy generated by Ramism's perceived attack on the received pedagogic practices. Generations of scholars have managed to render this conflict into a dry-as-dust chapter in the history of ideas, but it was much more at the time. Ramus ended his life a Protestant martyr, murdered on St. Bartholomew's Day 1572. He had been a reformer both in the limited but visible world of the university and in the wider sphere of printed books. He wanted to revivify higher education by replacing private disputations with public lectures and by abolishing sinecures; he wanted more books printed in the vernacular; and he radically revised the contents of these books, both typographically and by abbreviating the received logic into a ready and easy manual potentially available to all who could read their native language and were possessed of a modicum of natural reason. Academics in the sixteenth- and seventeenth-century universities fought even more violently over Ramism than have their modern successors over Derrida and others like him. And, while the determinations and applications of modern literary theory remain variable and even ambivalent, the implications of and reactions to Ramism were much clearer. In fact, wherever one encounters the argument over Ramist method in post-Renaissance Europe, one picks up the scent of political dispute and declared social crisis. It is not hard to see why. Any system purporting to describe human behavior along autonomously rationalist lines tends to entail an assault on habits and on the credibility of customary laws and institutions. More radically, it may suggest that such institutions are positively pernicious. This is the threat that Burke sensed from the radicals of the 1790s. As soon as human nature is imaged as in itself essentially progressive, out go monarchs, aristocrats, placemen, and the entire apparatus of class discipline—all the attributes of what Burke thought of as old England, but what Paine preferred to characterize as Old Corruption.

Thelwall's critique of Burke's style follows the method set down in Ramus's 1543 *Dialecticae Institutiones* (fol. 48):

When you have cut out from the parts of the continuous discourse the many syllogisms therein (after having found them, for they are often concealed), take away all the amplifications, and, after making brief headings to note the arguments used, form into one syllogism the sum total of the discourse, this sum total being ordinarily self-evident, although it may be swelled to undue proportions by accumulation of ornaments.[5]

Ramus's Scottish translator and adaptor, Roland MacIlmaine, saw this method as both an epitomizing and demystifying technique. The abolition of all "tautalogies and vayne repetitions" meant that the sense of a passage could be condensed "into a little rome." In a passage that strikingly anticipates later criticisms of Burke, he asks:

What shall we say then of those, that in teaching and writing (to the greate hurte of the memorie) dothe put as it were the tayle formest, having no regard how euery thing is placed, but euen as it chauncethe to come into their Mouthes, so lettethe it go. Dyd euer Plato or Aristotle so? no in deede.[6]

Ramus himself had recognized that a poet or orator might reasonably expect to surprise and delight his audience by a degree of deliberate confusion, employing the "cryptic" method. In his rendering of this section of Ramus's logic, MacIlmaine chose to translate *De Crypsis* as "Of the craftie and secrete methode" (p. 100). His somewhat sarcastic advice to those who would employ it is to omit or obscure definitions, divisions, and transitions, to digress as much as possible, "but mostly chiefly see that in the begining thou inuerte thy order, and place some antecedentes after there consequentes" (pp. 100–101).

MacIlmaine's title page announced Ramus as a Protestant martyr, and one may suggest a pattern whereby the British Ramists maximized the Puritan potential of his arguments for a critique of eloquence and of the high style. The Ramist enterprise was from the first committed to making its methods available to more people than could be educationally enfranchised by the inherited scholastic traditions grounded in the classical languages and in complex renderings of Aristotle. Ramus had based his work on the notorious "single method," a simplifying procedure that governed both inquiry itself and the presentation of its results. The assumption behind the single method was that its proper exercise reflected not just the order of the mind but also the order of things in the world. Alexander Richardson, another British Ramist, put it thus: "Method makes all things one, and we remember all things as one: & therefore it is that the world is one, namely, by method." Again: "For if all things are made one by the rule of method, though there are many things in the world, then there cannot be more methods, for then there should be more worlds."[7] Where modern philosophers find themselves having to take seriously the question of "more worlds," both as emanations of antithetical subject positions and in the literal post-Copernican sense to which Richardson may here be alluding (ironically or otherwise), the Ramists firmly believed in one, at least as governs the affairs of this planet. The mind, once stripped of its false sophistications and accretions, would naturally reproduce the single method and a single world. Ramist method was in this way radically egalitarian and progressive. Where traditional humanist pedagogy functioned by accumulation and example, tending not to gather particular instances under general procedures, Ramism presupposed complete logical coherence and thus perfectibility.[8] In the words of the Ramist Claude Mignault (Claudius Minos), the *unica methodus* was a "star to light our way across the ocean of the liberal arts and an Ariadne thread to lead us out of the labyrinth of confusion."[9]

Ramus was not engaged in what modern philosophers would recognize as an epistemological argument, and there is some disagreement about the degree to which he was a fully committed realist.[10] It is, however, clear that he was perceived as a popularizer and as challenging the restricted educational franchise of his times. The star and thread that Mignault found in the Ramist method were ones that all might follow, regardless of how much conventional education they had received. In declaring the need to begin with the clearest proposition in order to work toward the more obscure, and to proceed "from the most generall to the speciall and singuler" (MacIlmaine, *Loglike*, p. 94), Ramism might now seem trivially commonsensical. But it was exactly the commonality of Ramist sense that appealed to its exponents and appalled its antagonists. MacIlmaine offered the "naturall method" of his "lytle booke" as equivalent to four years' study of Plato and Aristotle (p. 14). He promised that any reader with "quicknes of spirite" could master it "almost by thy self" in "the space of two monthes" (p. 15). Robert Fage's 1632 adaptation of Ramus began with a poetic preface declaring an explicitly populist agenda:

> God reason taught, and man he did inspire
> With faculties, which Logicke doth require.
> The matter precepts, forme Methodicall,
> The end is reason's use, to teach th'unlearned all.[11]

Fage's very title promised to make Ramus's method, already received as a simplification, even more simple, "for the more facility of understanding." Yet more explicitly, William Bedwell's translation of *The Way to Geometry* (1636) addressed itself to tradesmen and artisans rather than to university men, declaring itself "not for the deepe and Iudiciall, but for the shallowest skull, the good and profit of the simpler sort, who as it was in the Latine, were able to get little or no benefite from it."[12]

This popular and even populist broadening of educational opportunity, and of the definition of intelligence itself, did not pass without notice. Dudley Fenner, one of the Cambridge Ramists, argued that this was quite proper: since "men in generall" had "sowen the seede of these artes, why should not all reape where all have sowen?"[13] We do not have to cast Ramus as a conscious revolutionary to understand the force of the alternative that Ramism represented. Even if he intended nothing beyond the forwarding of the interests of the Protestant entrepreneur class, as has been suggested, then this was taken very seriously in the early seventeenth century.[14] The alliance between Ramist method and Puritan social and theological doctrine in Britain further enhanced Ramism's image as a harbinger of democratic upheaval. Marlowe's *The Massacre at Paris* has Guise describe Ramus as a "peasant" and Anjou remark that "ne'er was there collier's son so full of pride."[15] Abraham Fraunce satirized the orthodox Aristotelian response in terms that seem the less hyperbolic the more one reads of this debate:

Ramus rules abroad, Ramus at home, and who but Ramus? Antiquity is nothing but Dunsicality. . . . Newfangled, youngheaded, harebrayne boyes will needes bee Maysters that neuer were Schollers; prate of methode, who neuer knew order; rayle against Aristotle assoone as they are crept out of the shell. Hereby it comes to passe that euery Cobler can cogge a Syllogisme, euery Carter crake of Propositions. Hereby is Logike prophaned, and lyeth prostitute, remooued out of her Sanctuary, robbed of her honour, left of her louers, rauyshed of straungers, and made common to all, which before was proper to Schoolemen, and only consecrated to Philosophers.[16]

Fraunce has his answer, and it is in the voice that has been the voice of British radicalism from Langland to the present: "Coblers bee men, why therefore not Logicians? and Carters have reason, why therefore not Logike?" With this faith, Fraunce set out to discover reason and logic in the body of English common law, which he found to be rational *because* common, because it was the unplanned but spontaneously ordered accumulation of reasonable practice.

In the passage just cited, Fraunce's Aristotelian images the transgression of class and educational boundaries as a breach of sexual propriety. This is an association that will appear again and again as we follow the career of method through the eighteenth century and into the aftermath of the French Revolution. It seems unlikely that Ramus himself, or the early Ramists, had any clear intention of challenging the gender codes to the point of specifying women readers as among the beneficiaries of the new pedagogy. Here learning is personified *as* a chaste woman, and not as the property *of* women. At the same time, intellectual and sexual democracy were often seen to go together in the radical movements of the seventeenth century, whether in the language of their advocates or in the hostile reports of those who repressed them. And there were some incentives to this association in the early Ramist texts. Alexander Richardson glossed the last phrase in Ramus's famous definition of logic, *ars bene disserendi*, as "to sow asunder," and Perry Miller cites another English Ramist's description of the logician as one who "disperseth his seed in divers places.[17]

These are images of male sexual freedom and sexual access, scarely feminist in even the most restricted contemporary sense. Moreover, Ramus's educational reforms were aimed at the universities, where they would have applied only to young men. Here he deplored corruption and the wasting of money on feasting and regalia and argued for public lectures in place of private disputation.[18] None of his proposals in any way directly affected the condition of women in relation to educational opportunity. But Ramus's texts were *printed*, and as such were open to a wide and unpredictable readership. They were radical documents not only in what they said about the commonality of rational intelligence, but also in their very format. As an author, Ramus practiced the simplification that he preached. The *Dialectique* of 1555 was the first philosophical work written in French, and it further introduced a new typographic convention whereby foreign or illustrative material was set off by commas or italics. This had the effect, according to Antoine Compagnon, not only of challenging the image of the text "as the model of the voice" but also of "preventing the citations becoming arguments based upon authority."[19] The format now projected the presence of different authorities and various sources. Ramus also introduced the convention of the table of contents, thus dramatizing the status of the book as an artefact, and proposed a new phonetic typography in an attempt to disambiguate the representations of cognate sounds. Thus *j* and *v* came to be known as "the Ramist consonants," introduced to distinguish them from *i* and *u*, which had hitherto been printed in the same characters.[20] Ong has located these developments as part of a general reorientation in epistemology occurring with the passage from manuscript to print culture and from spoken to written communication, so that "the printer's font corresponds to the locus of the topical logics, and the printed page to methodized discourse."[21] It is perhaps hard for us to imagine the first appearance of the table of contents and of the new typefaces as dramatic events, even gestures of *Kritik*, and certainly of rational intellectuality. The emphasis on spatialized representation, on a simplified "seeing at a glance," appears also in the Ramist predilection for charts, diagrams, and analytic tables—a preference that would be shared by Joseph Priestley and Jeremy Bentham, among others. MacIlmaine (and/or his printer) observed the Ramist convention of distinguishing narrative from illustrative matter, using three different typefaces, though the Ramist consonants were not incorporated. He also maintained the commitment to the vernacular, both in principle and in print. All his classical citations were Englished, in declared despite of those who thought it "not decent to wryte any liberall arte in the vulgar tongue, but woulde haue all thinges kept close eyther in the Hebrewe, Greke, or Latyn tongues." After all, Hebrew, Greek, and Latin were the "vulgar" tongues of Moses, Aristotle, and Cicero: "Shall we then thinke the Scottyshe or Englishe tongue, it not fitt to wrote any arte into? no in dede."[22] The aim of those who seek to restrict publication to the learned languages can only be "to roote out all good knowledge & vertue, and plate [plante] mere ignoraunce amongest the common people" (p. 16). This "common people" would, as we shall see, more and more come to be seen as including women of all ranks as well as men of the middle and lower orders.

The Method of the English Revolution

So far I have been arguing for an exemplary rather than an empirical relation between Ramism and the debate about method and theory in the 1790s. I have not, in other words, meant to suggest that Thelwall or Paine or anyone else ran to his bookshelves for a well-thumbed Ramist logic with which the better to confute the text of Burke's *Reflections*. On the other hand, it should not be assumed that there were no decisive continuities between the Ramist controversy and the crisis in political discourse in the late eighteenth century. Even after the original Ramist texts ceased to be objects of attention, and well after what Ramus called "logic" no longer occupied the center of the educational experience, the ambitions of Ramism and the tensions around it continued to reappear in variously mediated and differently emphasized ways in a range of disciplinary languages: philosophy, science, politics, and education. In the most general sense they were activated as part of the process sometimes called "class struggle." This concept has been subjected to

recent critical interrogation by those social historians who have assimilated the poststructuralist suspicion of all kinds of essentialism and who
have taken issue with the more reified Marxist interpretations of class
identities.[23] But we do not have to give the paradigm of class struggle a
fixed definition, least of all one based in a reading of nineteenth-
century social history, in order to find it useful. In the time of Ramus
himself, and well into the eighteenth century, the records of the con-
tests between social groups suggest a general campaign by the middling
sorts for access to literacy and social-educational opportunity. But there
were also more extreme claims, more radical demands from the common people for a more comprehensive redistribution of land and
wealth. Historians argue over how representative and how general
these claims could have been: witness, for example, the debate over
whether there "really was" a Ranter movement, as distinct from a few
writings by a few people (this is discussed briefly below). But they were
certainly perceived as threatening enough by the established interests,
surely in part because the language of method and general statement is
a universal language, so that it is no sooner invoked as support for the
interests of one social group than it threatens an application to all others. The politicians of the first French republic also discovered this
when they promulgated the rights of man and at once found themselves adding restrictive clauses about who might properly or conveniently be admitted to those rights.

The continuity between Ramism and the 1790s is not, then apparent
as the autonomous coherence of a single set of principles marching in
good order through different times and places. But there is continuity
nonetheless, perhaps most significantly mediated through the experience and memory of the conflicts of the English Revolution of the
1640s that were so important to Burke and Coleridge and others in the
later crisis. To the extent that the two crises of the 1640s and 1790s concerned theory and method, it is indeed proper to suggest that their
legacies are with us still, not least because the nation-states that have
employed antitheoretical mythologies are also still with us and continue
to employ ideologies related to those of earlier centuries.

So how was the debate about method "sown asunder" in seventeenth-
century England? Orthodox Ramism fell out of favor after the Restoration, but even before that many of its tenets were challenged by both
scientists and philosophers. Its reliance upon the syllogism and upon
arrangement by dichotomies, along with its apparent confidence in a
relation of simple correspondence between mind and world, rendered
it apparently archaic in the face of those developments in experimental
science (though we should not assume the self-evidence of their suc-

cesses) associated with an inductivist method. Bacon was the most famously invoked founding father of the new philosophy, and Bacon
hated Ramus, whom he described as "that man of bold disposition, and
famous for methods and short ways which people like, " and who popu-
larized the fantastic notion that any mere logic could be "subtle enough
to deal with nature." Bacon's own method was explicitly antagonistic to
what he saw as the Ramist dream of reason: "For God forbid that we
should give out a dream of our own imaginations for a pattern of the
world."[24]

According to Christopher Hill, and despite the strong Ramist component in Puritan thought, it was Bacon and not the martyred Ramus
who was the most important philosophical icon for the parliamentary
movement in the seventeenth century.[25] Even the rationalist Descartes
was no mere Ramist, though he took over and modernized essential elements of the method. He too proposed a single method, one governed
by the "natural light of reason," and he frequently repeated the Ramist
strategy of reducing complex problems to a serial sequence of simple
deductions. He too was committed to writing and to graphic form as the
medium of education: "Nothing that does not require to be continually
borne in mind ought to be committed to memory, if we can set it down
on paper."[26] Descartes also wrote philosophy in the French language.
But he was much more an exponent of the geometrical paradigm than
his predecessor, and quite skeptical about the usefulness of the syllogism. In fact he thought it tautological, only verified when its users
"have first secured the material out of which to construct it," and useless
unless "they have already ascertained the very truth which is deduced in
that syllogism." As such it is no good for investigating "the truth of
things." Human reason finds its proper first principles in intuitive
rather than deductive perceptions and should rely on "the light of nature alone" in comparing two or more things together.[27]

John Locke, relying upon a similarly titled *lumen naturae,* moved the
consensus even further from the Ramist legacy as well as away from the
rationalist paradigm.[28] *An Essay Concerning Human Understanding* disclaimed any ambition for universal knowledge in favor of a more limited reliance upon utility and probability. His admission that there may
be things to which "our Understandings are not suited," and the general humility of his rhetoric about a priori claims, made him the natural
voice of the emergent national (and nationalist) philosophic identity.[29]
For Locke, clear and distinct ideas were few and far between, and no
"single method" would produce more of them. His modification of the
Cartesian vocabulary shows in his preference for the terms "*determinate*
or *determined,* instead of *clear* and *distinct*": we are out of the sphere of

rationalist self-evidence and into the now habitual problem of cause and effect, with all its attendant mechanical and linguistic options. Locke agreed with Descartes mainly where Descartes had disagreed with Ramism, and he further diminished the prestige of the syllogism. Men can reason "exceeding clear and rightly without it," for

> God has been more bountiful to Mankind then so. He has given them a Mind that can reason without being instructed in Methods of syllogizing: The Understanding is not taught to reason by these Rules, it has a native Faculty to preceive the Coherence, or Incoherence of its *Ideas*, and can range them right, without any such perplexing Repetitions.[30]

The syllogism is now an artificial form, rather than the simple setting out of the operations of natural reason. Locke here represents a trend that would displace the syllogism even from its special place in theories of logic.[31] As probability came to be seen more and more as the proper business of the understanding, the syllogism's perceived dependence on the already known made it redundant except for teaching the already known, and helpless in predicting what might yet be known. But Locke, in the passage just cited, is nonetheless professing a faith in something he calls a "native Faculty" of understanding, a God-given fit between mind and world. For him this is not a rationalist entity, and it is far from a simple appeal to a "reason" lodged in the common mind, in the manner of the Puritan radicals whose claims so much of his own work was designed to repudiate. Locke's *Essay* transcribed the epistemology of compromise. It acknowledged a "short natural plain order" that "every one may see" (pp. 673–74) but it embedded this intuitive integrity into a highly complex set of relations among qualities, ideas, and words, completely displacing any simple realist accord between mind and world in the explanation of experience. This relation is instead adjudicated by a gradually developing and self-testing consensus (Locke never declares himself a strict nominalist), one removed from both autocracy and democracy. The stylistic analogue of this self-verifying exposition is a declared subservience to contingency and repetition rather than to order and epitome, the same sort of "discontinued way of writing" (*Essay*, p. 7) that Edmund Burke would later invoke as most appropriate to his *Reflections*.[32] It is a deliberate alternative to the Puritan (and English Ramist) commitment to plain speaking; or, more exactly, it claims a different kind of plain speaking, one affiliated with skeptical self-fashioning and nuanced reflection rather than with propositional self-confidence. As such it is a retreat from the forthright claims of "method" and from the political causes with which method was associated.

If the political application and implication of the *Essay* is relatively esoteric, as befits its topic and its assumed audience, then in *The Reasonableness of Christianity* (1695) Locke is quite explicit in his claim that "the vulgar, and mass of mankind" cannot be expected and should not be encouraged to follow "the long and sometimes intricate deductions of reason." Like Coleridge after him, Locke proposes that "the greatest part cannot know, and therefore they must believe." Those employed with "the plough and the spade" cannot be expected to follow the processes of "mysterious reasoning."[33] The very force of Locke's negations might lead us to suspect that the argument allowing right reason to the wielders of plough and spade was by no means extinct.

Thus far I have described the response of the "high" philosophical and scientific traditions to Ramist doctrines, which has been largely a negative one. Even here, the conventional narratives of the history of ideas may have overemphasized the unanimity accompanying the emergence of Baconian science and British empiricism.[34] And the major upheaval of the seventeenth century was of course not in the discourses of science and philosophy but in the more comprehensive sphere of the events of the English Revolution, events that were of the first importance in persuading Locke to a "discontinued way of writing." The extraordinary outpouring of idealism and discontent that marked the middle years of the century remains the subject of considerable debate among historians, not least because of the obviously divisive political and historiographic alternatives available to them. The debate is less melodramatically public than that among French historians about 1789, partly because it concerns a more distant time, and one less visibly implicated in the emergence of modernity, but also and perhaps most of all because of the beguiling invention of a "Glorious Revolution" for 1688, a semantic lightning rod that has successfully attracted the attentions of school and university syllabus-makers and of so many of the scholars they eventually produce. For many of us who have been through the English education system, the 1640s were identified as the years of a "Civil War" in which befeathered cavaliers defended a good cause against humorless Puritans whose deviations were corrected by common sense twenty years later.

Despite the obfuscations of hindsight, one may trace a concern about the implication and interpretations of the 1640s and 1650s throughout the eighteenth century, although after 1789 some of the anxiety could be more conveniently focused on the French and thus treated as a symptom of undesirable otherness. Some modern historians have argued for the primary importance of this period for the evolution of English social and political culture. In terms of this study of mine, it could be said that the mythology of the national character that is in various ways the subject of the next three chapters was developed very much as a placebo to be administered against the propensity for further revolutions. I have no right to an opinion on such questions as "how democratic were the Levellers" and "how real were the Ranters," but it is clear enough that the tendencies represented by these movements and others like them were very important in the cultivation of subsequent British hostility toward theory and method.[35] Christopher Hill has said of the twenty years or so after 1641, when there was more or less no censorship of the presses, that "for a short time, ordinary people were freer from the authority of church and social superiors than they had ever been before, or were for a long time to be again."[36] This freedom produced a perhaps unprecedented volume of writings conflating political, social, and sexual radicalisms, each expressing itself in terms of the others, and even more widely accused of so doing. This was no Enlightenment feast of reason. The relaxation of the censorship certainly produced far more almanacs and prophecies than popular logics, and there were many more astrologers than men of method in the ranks of the army radicals.[37] But the outpouring of what we might call the "irrational" was accomplished by a regular recourse to "reason" on the part of those excluded from Cromwell's commonwealth. Indeed, we can see in the responses to these radical initiatives the same association of method with madness that would characterize the criticisms of Methodism and then of Jacobinism. The combination of reason and sensibility was already perceived as powerfully threatening to the projected authority of common sense.

Richard Overton and the other authors of the Leveller pamphlets made frequent reference to a "naturall radicall principle of reason" in their arguments for annual parliaments and for the reopening of the enclosed common lands—causes that would be articulated in similar ways in the 1790s.[38] A Remonstrance of Many Thousand Citizens (1646) denounced the much-vaunted Magna Carta as nothing more than a "beggarly thing," and did so in the language of reason:

Yee know, the Lawes of this Nation are unworthy a Free-People, and deserve from first to last, to be considered, and seriously debated, and reduced to an agreement with common equity, and right reason, which ought to be the Forme and Life of every Government.[39]

The Digger leader Gerrard Winstanley argued for "reason" as pervading the whole universe while dwelling particularly in human nature. He thought it the proper term for, rather than an antithesis to, "conscience." Indeed, he thought it a better term than "God," "because I have been held under darkness by that word, as I see many people are."[40] In this spirit Winstanley invoked a "great Creator Reason" who was a radical egalitarian, a figure who spoke "not one word . . . that one branch of mankind should rule over another" and whose coming to earth had yet to happen.[41]

Although the Puritan radicals were very different from their Enlightenment successors, professing an excess of faith rather than any skepticism or atheism, they are employing a similar language for similar ends: the rights of the common man under the rule of reason. In their middle-class or common identity, the Puritan radicals were perhaps even more threatening than the aristocratic, high-philosophical personalities who came after them. But the later reception of the likes of Voltaire and Helvétius was mediated through the memories of the 1640s, as well as through a recognition of the ongoing populist traditions that carried those memories: Methodism, dissent, and democracy. The Puritan character was imaged by both friends and foes as the product of extraordinary self-discipline and methodical single-mindedness, and it had produced a major empirical incarnation in the New Model Army. As Michael Walzer has suggested, this citizens' army was both a secular and a sacred entity:

Puritanism . . . made revolution available to the minds of seventeenth-century Englishmen as it had never been before. It trained them to think of the struggle with Satan and his allies an extension and duplicate of their internal spiritual conflict, and also as a difficult and continuous war, requiring methodical, organized activity, military exercise, and discipline . . . permanent warfare was the central myth of Puritan radicalism.[42]

The New Model Army was efficient enough to defeat a king, and volatile enough to destroy itself. By the late 1640s the cause of the army had come to be identified with that of the poor and the dispossessed.[43] In a hostile commentary of 1649 Clement Walker accused the army radicals of a methodical attack on the enabling mysteries of authority that was also, among other things, an attack on the political uses of what would soon be called "the sublime," as it would reappear in the crafted obscurities of Burke's prose:

They have cast all mysteries and secrets of government . . . before the vulgar (like pearls before swine), and have taught both the soldiery and people to look so far into them as to ravel back all governments to the first principles of nature. . . . They have made the people thereby so curious and so arrogant that they will never find humility enough to submit to a civil rule.[44]

Walker's play upon "civil" is a timely one: it defines the nature of the positive law, and it implies the code of politeness, of civility, that would

thereafter be so often invoked to defend it. The prospect of the vulgar
raveling back government to first principles echoes some of the terms of
the Ramist debate.

But Puritan radicalism's recourse to nature included an element that
had not figured in the original disputes over logic and method: the element of sexual liberation. Abraham Fraunce's Aristotelian spoke, as we
have seen, of knowledge as a chaste woman to whom only the favored
few should have access. The threat of Ramism was perceived as a threat
to pedagogic patriarchy. During the turbulent years of the English Revolution, the threat might have appeared about to be made good.
Christopher Hill has argued that even mainstream Puritanism worked
ultimately to further the idea of equality between men and women,
though it was in no sense committed to sexual liberation.[45] But the radical sects went much further, and they were the principle object of the
conservative critique. Abiezer Coppe's *The Fiery Flying Roll* claimed that
even "rogues, thieves, whores, and cut purses" could be "every whit
as good" as the great men of this world, and the Ranter Lawrence
Clarkson wrote that "what act soever is done by thee in light and love, is
light and lovely, though it be that act called adultery . . . if that within
thee do not condemn thee, thou shalt not be condemned." Typically, in
1657 Thomas Collier accused both Ranters and Quakers of having "no
Christ but within . . . no ordinances, no law but their lusts, no heaven
nor glory but here."[46] A title like Robert Barclay's *The Anarchy of the
Ranters and Other Libertines* (1676) tells much about the terms of the
negative reaction to the Puritan radicals. Denial of sin, rejection of
church marriages, and celebration of erotic love were powerful principles when allied with radical social and political motivations. In the
seventeenth century the word *libertine* invoked both the original Latin
sense of "one manumitted from slavery" and the now more familiar
usages describing any antinomian or free-thinking person, in both political and sexual contexts. As the red ribbons worn by the army radicals
in 1647 prefigured the red caps of 1789, so Blake's vision of rejuve-
nated women "naked and glowing with the lusts of youth" and of the
opening of "the Brothels of Paris" harked back to the 1640s.[47] The
most important mediating element for these ideas, in their variously
and considerably modified forms, was the Methodist movement, to
which we may now turn.

John Wesley, Methodist

It is now perhaps clear why the term "Methodist" might have seemed
both apt and threatening in naming a body of enthusiastic Christians

who never declared an absolute disaffiliation from the Church of England but who nonetheless aroused versions of the same opposition that had gathered to defeat and discredit the radicals of the 1640s. The titles of the Methodist tracts criticized by George Crabbe in the preface to *The Borough* (1810)—titles like *Forty Stripes for Satan* and *The Naked Bow of God*—were visibly continuous with those of generations before, such as *The Covenant-Avenging Sword Brandished* and *Babylon's Ruin, Jerusalem's Rising* (both published in 1643).[48] Leigh Hunt attacked the Methodists as followers of Bunyan, whom he saw as the sponsor of their literary simplicity and moral self-righteousness.[49] No Methodist ever articulated a social and political program that was as radical as those of the Diggers and the Levellers, but there were many more Methodists than there had been Diggers and Levellers, so that any perceived continuity at all, however diluted, must have seemed threatening. Many in the eighteenth century claimed to see in Methodism the most likely origin of another English revolution.

The naming of the movement itself has remained something of an etymological puzzle. The name "methodists" or "methodics" had once been applied to physicians who "put their patients under stringent regimens," as did Wesley and his followers in the service of a spiritual cure.[50] Early commentators did identify the Methodists with rigorous personal discipline, and with the habit of accounting exactly for all the small routines of daily life.[51] Halévy derives the name of the movement from the ritualism of Wesley's Oxford "Holy Club," wherein there was "no sound piety without the 'method' and 'rites' prescribed by ecclesiastical tradition."[52] Wesley himself seems to have endorsed this explanation, while Ong, true to his interests in the history and influence of Ramism, points to the possible importance of Wesley's having written *A Compendium of Logic* (Bristol, 1750), which, while not itself avowedly Ramist, did echo the Ramist commitment to simplification and to the needs of a general reader.[53] Again, the first edition of *Encyclopaedia Britannica* (1771) specified the "Methodists" among the ancient physicians as those who "reduced the whole healing art to a few common principles or appearances."[54]

Without some critical discoveries of the sort now probably unlikely to be made, we will never know for sure whether the movement got its name from only one or from a number of these associations working together. Etymological obscurity indeed befits a movement that was characterized as much by contradiction and eclecticism as by any simple coherence. Despite the strict personal discipline supposedly exercised by Methodists in their private lives, their preaching was criticized for its emotionalism and anti-intellectuality. In this way they were the antithesis rather than the embodiment of Enlightenment reason. In *The Borough* Crabbe tried to prove a close connection between craft and hypocrisy and this same enthusiasm, and he was especially critical of the Calvinistic Methodists, the followers of Whitfield, for their anti-intellectuality—"No worldly learning can these points discuss"—and their abuse of logical sequence. For Crabbe, the rhetoric of this kind of Methodist is "all unconnected, void of limbs and joints," convincing its hearers by "fierce, bold words" rather than by rational demonstration.[55] Earlier critics had similarly found Methodism guilty of an "utter contempt of reason" and of going beyond "Reason and Common Sense."[56] So little of any recognizably philosophic reason did the Methodists employ that Southey, in his *Life of Wesley* of 1820, was able to propose Wesley as England's answer to Voltaire, steady and pious at those points where the Frenchman was ephemeral, irreligious, and evil. Hazlitt too accused the Methodists of indulging in the obscurities of the sublime at the expense of clear and distinct ideas:

They are dull and gross in apprehension, and therefore they are glad to substitute faith for reason, and to plunge in the dark, under the supposed sanction of superior wisdom, into every species of mystery and jargon.[57]

Thus those who are "either unable or unwilling to think connectedly or rationally on any subject, are at once released from every obligation of the kind, by being told that faith and reason are opposed to one another, and the greater the impossibility, the greater the merit of the faith" (p. 60). Again, while Crabbe deplored the Methodist contempt for what was preserved and discussed in books, Samuel Johnson (at least as reported by Boswell) regarded the "inward light" as an authority "utterly incompatible with social or civil security." Accountability can only be expected and preserved "when a person professes to be governed by a written ascertained law."[58]

Johnson's reported remark gives us an important clue to the perceived personality of Methodism in the eighteenth century. Even though Wesley himself has been deemed by E. P. Thompson to have been nothing less than a "high Tory" in his political principles, the mode of Methodist preaching and the nature of the audience for it were enough to cause it to be received as a breach of general decorum—social, spiritual, sexual, and stylistic—and thus in the broadest sense "political."[59] The denial of tradition and hierarchy and the emphasis upon validation by grace became almost as inflammatory for Wesley's opponents as it had previously been for Luther's. Crabbe caught the point perfectly:

> Alas! could we the dangerous rule believe,
> Whom for their teacher could the Crowd receive?

And Leigh Hunt complained that "Among the Methodists every body teaches, men and boys, learned and unlearned," with no respect shown for "the regularity and distinctness of a cultivated mind."[60] It is Hunt's account, about which he or his market felt strongly enough to sponsor an expanded reprint as *An Attempt to Show the Folly and Danger of Methodism* (1809), that is clearest about the implications of Methodist teaching and preaching for the business of interpretation:

> We see how all the tilting sects of religion arm themselves with their own texts, close their vizors upon contradiction, and rush furiously against others quite as well armed as themselves. If A produces a passage in his own favour and takes it literally, B explains it away; if B produces his literal passage, A explains that away; every text which favours a sect is literal and has no other meaning than it presents to the most literal comprehension; every text which opposes a sect is a manifest allegory, a mysticism, a shadow, a way of speaking, an Eastern idiom, a text that it is impossible to . . . a sort of . . . as it were . . . something, which puts the disputer in a passion to see it so abused.[61]

Hunt fears the implications of being told that "the word *faith* has four meanings in Scripture, and the word *grace* fourteen," at the same time as the adjudication of these meanings is placed in the hands of the uneducated in some assumed relation to the "inward light" of grace. Indeed, it was the threat of this kind of interpretive license that inspired Coleridge and others like him to insist on the importance of the Church of England and the pulpit as the arbiter of all such questions. I have argued elsewhere that Romantic aesthetics in general was responsive to a pressure to invite its readers to be makers of their own meanings, or at least to participate actively in the recreation of an authorial meaning to the degree that they might feel the pleasures and responsibilities of discovering it for themselves.[62] This aspect of Romantic aesthetics might be seen as an absorption or analogue of the Methodist imperative toward recognizing the imaginative and interpretive rights of ordinary people, whether or not (to use Wordsworth's phrase) "in a state of vivid sensation."[63] Perhaps it was also a displacement or a heading off of some of the social energies of Methodism, for many Romantic writers were insistent that the kind of ordinariness of which they approved could only be regained by strenuous efforts, efforts likely to prove too much for the majority of general readers. There is something of this paradox in Wordsworth's rather tortured allowance that even the "most inexperienced reader" may judge "for himself," while warning us that if poetry has not been a subject on which "much time" has been bestowed, then the judgment will be "erroneous."[64]

Methodism, as we can now see, was imaged as at once disciplined and irrational, methodical and uncontrollably enthusiastic. At the end of the eighteenth century the extreme of sensibility was deemed just as dangerous and essentially un-English as the extreme of rationality that the philosophic radicals had championed. The combination of the two in a single personality, all extremes and no middle, would become the signature of the "Jacobin" character, as it had been of the Methodist. The figure of British liberty was always located in the middle ground, too wise and prudent to tolerate the excessive development of any one or two from among the many human faculties and temperaments. The Methodists managed to occupy both ends of the spectrum of the nationalist demonology. Their methodical private lives made them seem intolerant, gloomy, and vain, while their enthusiastic public performances laid them open to criticism as sensualists and even lechers. Smollett's *Humphry Clinker* handles the sexual associations of Methodism in a manner that is none the less typical for being very funny. Clinker, whose very name is obscene, is first noticed for his "bare posteriors," an apt intimation of the Methodist principles that lead him to anticipate a time when "there will be no distinction of persons."[65] His enthusiasm first converts all the women of the household, from the bottom to the top of the social scale: first Win Jenkins, then Lydia Melford and Tabitha Bramble. The frisson of having masters educated by servants is mediated by the comic providence of Clinker's being revealed as Matthew Bramble's long-lost illegitimate son, so that Smollett ultimately purveys the fantasy of a declassed society. Clinker's otherwise threatening sexual energies are similarly accommodated by having him marry and promise a "whole litter" of children (p. 315).

Smollett is here finessing a conjunction between the social and the sexual implications of Methodism that caused some more earnest and more punitive response from other observers. E. P. Thompson, while making a famous case, following Halévy, for the ultimately conservative functions of Methodism as unifying rather than dividing the masters and the working class, is at the same time emphatic about the sexual nature of the energies that Methodism was exploiting—energies that seemed to many contemporaries not at all displaced or repressed.[66] There was widespread concern about the much-publicized "love feasts" where men and women gathered together to receive the word of God. The same conjunction between the spiritual and the erotic that had informed Puritan radicalism and the reactions to it appeared again in the relations between Methodism and the established church interest.

When they were not being spoken of as lower-class opportunists looking for an easy living, the Methodists were denounced as lechers operating behind the veil of religion. Leigh Hunt, once again, was eloquent on this subject, calling them "a sort of religious debauchees," not only addressing God as a "mere lover" on the authority of that "indecent eclogue" known as *Solomon's Song*," but also addressing each other in terms quite inappropriate to religious experience. Hunt expressed typically cynical concern over "what an infinite number of rapturous females there are in comparison with the men."[67]

The most famous event in the sexualizing of Methodism's reputation perhaps came some years before Hunt, with the publication of Martin Madan's *Thelyphthora; or, a Treatise on Female Ruin* (1780), answered by William Cowper and at least a dozen other pamphleteers aroused by what seemed to them to be a defense of polygamy according to a reading of divine law. Blake's *Book of Thel* was a late entry in this war of words. Madan, who was a Methodist, had at heart the welfare of abandoned women, who had under the prevailing statutes no legal protection and no claims against their seducers. He appealed to the potent triumvirate of "*scripture, nature* and *reason*" to argue that the mischiefs of polygamy are far fewer than those resulting from the abandonment of "fallen" women. He invoked scriptural law to the effect that a man should "keep, maintain and provide for . . . the women he *seduces*."[68] A radical antinomian, Madan regarded human laws and their basis in custom and convention simply as self-interested departures from the one true law: the law of scripture, which could be interpreted without ambiguity thanks to a realist theory of language applicable uniquely to Hebrew. According to this law, marriage had nothing to do with civil contracts or ceremonies but occurred whenever there was a "*union* of the *man* and the *woman* as *one body*" (1:21). All sexual partners are therefore married in the sight of God, while no unconsummated civil marriage can possibly be valid. Madan, like some among his Puritan predecessors, was a literalist rather than a libertine. He believed that adultery should be punished by death, as the Bible says it should. So he found himself in complete opposition to the laws of the land. Where they condoned adultery but denied common-law marriage, he did the opposite, and on strict biblical authority. The God of the Bible was of course a male God, who had no intention of encouraging women to have more than one husband. Female polygamy could thus be roundly dismissed as "too abhorrent from *nature, reason,* and *scripture,* to admit of a single argument in its favour, or even to deserve a moment's consideration" (2:75n.). But for men it is "*expressly allowed,* and that by GOD *Himself*" (1:95). A recognition of this fact would, thought Madan, work as a corrective among the present immoral generation, so that "those of rank and fashion could not simply abandon the women they seduce to ruin, as they presently do" (1:404).

Blake's rather obscure inquiry into the psychology of female virginity in relation to nature and culture in *The Book of Thel* has to my knowledge not yet been explained in terms of its obvious allusion to Madan's treatise; nor will I attempt that task here. But its place in the debate should serve as a reminder that the narrative passage from Winstanley to Wesley was probably not seen in the years around 1800 as simply, if at all, one of a decline in radical potential, if only because of the numbers involved.[69] Bernard Semmel relates the widespread fear of Methodism after 1789 to the fact that it was "the only body of the 'people' who were so organized as to be capable of making a revolution."[70] Indeed, the sight of a committee of one hundred (a suspiciously Jacobinical round number) in relatively direct connection, through the chapels, with over a hundred thousand people, must have been an awesome one to many of the defenders of Edmund Burke's England.[71] The most politically radical of the Methodists, Alexander Kilham, took with him only about 5 percent of the membership when he broke away in 1796 to form the "New Connexion." But the existence of his movement was enough to occasion a fear of the "Tom Paine Methodists."[72] This association could only have been strengthened by such careers as that of Robert Wedderburn, successively Methodist and Spencean radical.[73] While much of the negative reporting of the Methodist movement must be deemed to have been exaggerated for the purposes of justifying various kinds of domestic repression, there was clearly enough fire behind the smoke to command some belief.

I have tried in this opening chapter to argue for a narrative, necessarily a diversified and mediated narrative, holding together the established culture's responses to method as it appeared in the pedagogic and systematic reforms of the Ramists, in the appeals to a common "reason" made by the seventeenth-century radicals, and in the etymologically sanctioned organizational (and inspirational) abilities of the Methodists. Although Britain did not have a second and unglorious revolution after 1789 and in the manner of 1789, we can imagine why some might have feared the onset of such an event. Even more clearly we can see how the hyperbole of the English reaction to the French Revolution appealed to prejudices and traditions that had been made very familiar through the ideological labors of previous generations who had already determined that the English were too commonsensical to be led astray by theories and methods founded in rational abstractions. They perceived in theory and method, as many still do perceive, a dan-

gerously leveling tendency, one critical of a merely customary social order. This legacy does not completely explain the British response to the
Declaration of the Rights of Man, for no political culture simply reproduces the inheritances of a different series of histories. The career of
"theory" in Romanticism has to be understood as a negotiation between
various rhetorics and determinations, both received and immediate.
But we must understand the legacies of the politics of method as a component in that negotiation. It also included an evidently nationalized
language of alternative methods, to the elucidation of which we may
now turn.

2

THE CULTURE OF BRITISH COMMON SENSE

Us and Them

In the second section of *The Friend*, subtitled *On the Grounds of Morals and Religion*, Coleridge echoes Wordsworth's judgment on the French Revolution as typified by "a dreary want at once of books and men" and looks back to the English revolution of the 1640s for a favorable alternative.[1] In those days, he says, even madness contained the seeds of some or other truth. For that "ferment of a chaos" was activated by Englishmen, and only by Englishmen. The truly "speculative" mind of William Sedgwick, author of *Justice Upon the Armie Remonstrance* (1648), is contrasted with that of the "practical schemer" subsequently suggested by the invocation of that term (p. 414).

Coleridge's recourse to the language of the 1640s is of course selective and deliberately domesticated; it has the comforts and even the hypocrisies of considerable hindsight. But its function here is preparatory; it allows Coleridge to lead us toward an elaborate discrimination among the national characters of England, France, and Germany. The German mind is typified by genius, talent, and fancy, in that order; the English by genius, sense, and humor; and the French by cleverness, talent, and wit. The "forms and effects" of these faculties are, in Germany, idea, totality, and distinctness; in England, law discovered, selection, and clearness; and in France, theory invented, particularity, and palpability. Finally, each of the three countries demonstrates a nationally specific attitude to time. Germany is preoccupied with past and future, England with past and present, and France with the present (pp. 421–23).

Coleridge's writings are commonly punctuated with such comparisons. In *Biographia Literaria*, for example, we are offered a complex definition of the "gentleman" (whose "*antipode* . . . is to be sought for among the Anglo-American democrats")and told that this figure is "frequent in England, rare in France, . . . while in Germany the character is almost unknown."[2] In 1795 he had proposed a course of lectures comparing the "English Rebellion"—Coleridge preferred that word—to the "French Revolution."[3] As far as we know they were never delivered, but we may assume that they would rapidly have moved behind and beyond the merely phenomenal events of history into an analysis of underlying causes, and that those causes would have included detailed accounts of the national characters of France and England. In touching these chords so frequently and tellingly, Coleridge was carrying on a commonplace Enlightenment habit. Even the magisterially philosophic mind of Kant, when off duty from the critical writings, saw fit to engage in extensive reflections on the differences among the English, the French, and the Germans, with some briefer remarks on Italians, Spaniards, and others.[4]

It requires no great originality to suggest that these preoccupations with definitions of national character must be seen as rationalizations of the various political processes whereby the nation-states of Europe were trying either to come into being, to maintain themselves, or to extend their territories and their imagined moral superiorities. Each defines itself in terms of, and usually at the expense of, the others. In England this process took exemplary form after the Restoration of 1660 and continued throughout the eighteenth century, not least in the spheres of literary and philosophical writing. British self-esteem, already considerable in itself, was further indulged by those foreign commentators who looked to England (and to its perceived commercial successes) as a model of what their own countries might be in the hands of a representative government. Montesquieu and Voltaire were only the most famous among the numerous visitors and observers, from France and Germany especially, who took this line. Mme de Staël, in the concluding section of her study of the French Revolution, is endorsing a century-old tradition in looking to England (but only after 1688) as the single European example of "sound political ideas spread through every class," so that the "English nation seems, if we may say so, one entire body of gentlemen."[5]

The Enlightenment construction of models of national character was not, however, the same as the one that displaced it in the Romantic period and thereafter. Herder, for instance, was adamant that there is only one human race and a single human reason: climate and geography largely determine such differences as are enshrined in the various national cultures.[6] There can thus be no innately privileged cultures, and no nations whose citizens are more fully "human" than others. This is Enlightenment cosmopolitanism, an internationalism of imagination

that inhibits rather than encourages the development of nationalist ideologies. This cosmopolitanism is what the Romantic preoccupation
with localism and patriotism so often displaced. The transition can be
traced even within Kant's *Anthropology* (pp. 174–82), where the social-
historical determinations that we now know as "culture" are seen to
produce national characters that are as good as innate by virtue of their
strength and endurance, reproduced for instance in language, and especially in words that cannot be efficiently translated into other languages. Kant's account also transcribes the Eurocentrism that would
become generic for later theorists of national and racial identity and remains commonplace to this day.

But, as Kant himself observed, the cosmopolitan ideal was always
rare enough in England, where post-Restoration writers and intellectuals were consistently busy about the task of establishing how much
luckier they were than their European peers.[7] Hume, for instance,
made the ingenious argument that the very lack of a national character
was the triumphant concomitant of Englishness. He contended that oc-
cupational and subcultural rather than national or geographical determinations were of the first importance in forming the personality. Thus
the English traditions of mixed government and political and social tolerance had produced a culture of individuals rather than of types. British liberty is in this way argued as working against the emergence of
national character, and such character then becomes itself the symptom
of oppression.[8] Kant's not unreasonable response to this argument was
to suggest that an English national character was indeed in existence
and consisted precisely in "contempt for all foreigners" and "*arrogant
rudeness*"[9]

Coleridge, as we have seen, has a rather more flattering definition.
The qualities he finds in England (he does not, be it noted, refer to Britain, although Wales, Scotland, and Ireland were all by this time politically incorporated with England) are genius, sense, and humor (as
intellectual faculties); law discovered, selection, and clearness (in the
application of those faculties); and a concern with past and present
(as attitudes to history). "Genius" is what the French seldom or never
have, the originating faculty that "*adds* to the existing stock" of power
and knowledge through an "originality in intellectual construction."
"Sense" is "that just balance of the faculties which is to the judgment
what health is to the body," operating "without any consciousness of the
mechanism by which the perception is realized."[10]

Coleridge does not explain "humour" but we may interpolate a
definition that partakes of the other two qualities listed with it, genius
and sense. Humor is that which gives the air of ease to genius, and of

lightness to sense. It is deeper and richer than "wit," which is what the French have, and more solid and self-affirming than "fancy," the pre-disposition of the Germans. The application of these English national faculties in "law discovered" speaks for a satisfaction with things as they are, with "the contemplation of ideas *objectively,* as existing powers" (1:422). "Selection" and "clearness" must then speak for a sort of em-pirical contentment, a habit of dealing perspicuously with what is given. Hence the English are focused on the achievements of a past and the satisfactions of a present, and not on an imaginary future.

Coleridge's Englishman, then, is not prone either to flights of vision-ary fancy, like the Germans, or to calculated system-mongering, like the French. He does evince some apparently negative traits—a "con-temptuous nationality," an "inward pride," and "zealotry" (1:422)—which may make him seem less instantly sympathetic than the German with his "cosmopolitism" and "craving for sympathy," though always more so than the Frenchman. This relatively nuanced positioning of the English character, as somewhat close to the German (which also possesses "genius") but always a long way from the French, is more or less typical of the Romantic construction of the national ideology, even among those who are not on the political right. The general consensus about the negative traits of the French made it difficult, as we shall see, for anyone to argue a positive case for the benefits of system and theory, repeatedly defined as French obsessions. Method and theory were not simply provocative of philosophical reservations by the followers of Bacon and Locke but also explicitly un-English. The antimethodical tradition has been described in the previous chapter in terms of the ten-sions between the different elements in the social order—class tensions, and occasionally class struggles. Analogous and perhaps even reflective symptoms can be traced in the scientific and philosophic languages, to which I now turn.

Sticking to the Facts

The most commonly invoked godfather of English common sense in the exercise of science and philosophy was undoubtedly Francis Bacon. His influence, as we shall see, even extended to the very French tradi-tions against which he was positioned, by his British disciples, in such violent opposition. As we have already seen, Bacon hated Ramism for its short and easy method and for its propensity to displace the com-plexities of nature by the simple figments of the mind. Bacon was the major authority cited by British intellectuals in their campaign against system and theory, and the founding father of what we now tend to des-

ignate as "Anglo-Saxon empiricism." Contrasting his own method with
that of the logicians, Bacon observed:

I, on the contrary, dwelling purely and constantly among the facts of nature,
withdraw my intellect from them no further than may suffice to let the images
and rays of natural objects meet in a point, as they do in the sense of vision. . . .
By these means I suppose that I have established a true and lawful marriage
between the empirical and the rational faculty, the unkind and ill-starred divorce and separation of which has thrown into confusion all the affairs of the
human family.[11]

There is at least a double function to Bacon's rhetoric here. On the one
hand it adopts a profound humility, a reverence for nature and the
world as beyond the "little cells of human wit" (p. 21). On the other
hand it makes a massive claim for accuracy of understanding, for seeing
things "simply as they are" (pp. 32–33). There is at once a radical limitation placed on the mind's intuitive apprehensions—for whatever it
"seizes and dwells upon with peculiar satisfaction is to be held in suspicion" (p. 60)—and a radical endorsement of the mind's ability to gain
an accurate understanding of the world through patience and the discipline of inductive method. This twofold formulation, wherein absolute
self-discipline promises absolute rewards, goes to the heart of Bacon's
"Puritan" identity and helps to explain his appeal *to* the Puritans, who
were, according to Christopher Hill, willing and able to declare themselves Baconians as well as Ramists.[12] Baconian method, produced to its
extreme conclusion, seemed to promise nothing less than a healing of
the breach between man and nature that was the legacy of the fall. *Labor
vincit omnia.* But not, of course, for all. Bacon was clear that patient humility alone does not give us the keys to nature's treasures. He was no
"begetter of handy manuals" after the manner of Ramus.[13] James
Stephens has in fact argued that he "devoted his career as a philosopher
to the preservation of essential knowledge from the masses" and "gave
up much of his time to devising strategies of communication which
would weed out unqualified readers without alienating the potential
'man of science.'"[14]

Induction alone, which could be supposed available to all given a
modicum of patience and application, was not enough to produce correct understanding in Bacon's terms. The principle of social exclusion
resides in experiment, which is proposed as a corrective for the vagaries
of mere sense perception, and should be entrusted only to the qualified
few. Since "the minds of men are strongly possessed and beset" rather
than innocently receptive, experiments must be "skilfuly and artificially
devised" to correct their explanations. Without this correction, the
mind "mixes up its own nature with the nature of things."[15] The induc-

tive method, which promises a "gradual and unbroken ascent" from particulars to generals (p. 50), can only produce truth when it is managed and directed by those able to devise experiments to compensate for the illusions of the "false mirror" that is the human mind (p. 54). The simple accessibility of Ramist method has now been replaced by a system of divided labor, whose benefits may in principle extend to all, but whose implementation can only be permitted to the experts.

With the chartering of the Royal Society in 1662 Baconian method took on a definite and distinctive institutional incarnation. By 1667 Sprat was already writing its history, and already he was attributing its successes and its glorious prospects to the national character, to the "general constitution of the minds of the *English*."[16] Their "sincerity" and "simplicity" placed them in an ideal middle position between the roughness of the northern and the subtlety of the southern nations. These qualities, along with the "universal modesty" of the English, made them the natural practitioners of "*Experimental knowledge*" (p. 114). In Sprat's view the Restoration of 1660 had made possible a scientific ministry of all the talents, not just "an *English, Scotch, Irish, Popish* or *Protestant* Philosophy, but a Philosophy of *Mankind*" (p. 63). Mere logic is no guide to this philosophy of experiment, and no single method can "circumscribe" its procedures. Members of the Society must

keep themselves free, and change their course, according to the different circumstances, that occur to them in their operations; and the several alterations of the Bodies, on which they work. The true *Experimenting* has this one thing inseparable from it, never to be a *fix'd* and *settled Art, and never* to be *limited* by constant Rules. . . . *Experimenting* is . . . never wholly to be reduc'd to *standing Precepts.* (Pp. 89–90)

Rules are a restraint upon the experimenter's openness of mind, just as they would come to be defined by Burke as restraints upon political and stylistic liberality. Overzealous attachment to "*Speculative Opinions*" (p. 118) stood in the way of the ancient philosophers and prevented them from achieving any truly progressive knowledge. The "*methodical*" education by "*universal rules*" is nothing as compared to teaching by "*Practise* and *Experiments*" (p. 329).

Sprat's celebration of the achievements and future potential of the Royal Society artfully performs the gesture of rhetorical inclusiveness that must have seemed especially urgent in the wake of revolution and restoration. No single mind, or faction, is to be allowed any privilege of place: "By all those we have already been deluded" (p. 73), and "*single labours* can be but on a prospect taken upon one side." Scientific advance must be a corporate effort, a "*union* of *eyes,* and *hands*" (p. 85). Nor is this any mere conglomeration of technical talents, as possessed by mere artisans. The society must admit some of these, but only while maintaining a majority of "*Gentlemen, free, and unconfin'd*" (p. 67). Anyone who had made it through almost four hundred pages of the *History* would have found Sprat being perfectly frank about the society's social constitution:

The *Tradesmen* themselves, having had their hands directed from their Youth in the same *Methods of Working,* cannot when they please so easily alter their custom, and turn themselves into new Rodes of Practice. Besides this, they chiefly labor for present livelyhood, and therefore cannot defer their *Expectations* so long, as is commonly requisit for the ripening of any *new Contrivance.* (Pp. 391–92)

Those living "freer lives" may make more mistakes, but they will be generous and creative ones, "which very faults, and wandrings will often guid them into new *light.*" For "*Invention* is an *Heroic* thing," not for the "low, and vulgar," whose "*generosity*" of spirit has been "clogg'd by constant *toyl*" (p. 392). A traditionally aristocratic liberal-mindedness and insouciance is here reinvented for the chosen members of the upper middle ranks gathered together in a *royal* society. If the new wave of experimental science did indeed have its origins in the patronage of the Puritans, no trace of that ancestry is to be found in the official history.[17]

The Baconian method's already apparent social and intellectual selectivity was thus given a further spin by the policies of the Royal Society, and together they defined the institutional character of British science and philosophy at the turn of the eighteenth century, even if they did not entirely govern its practices—for the presence of Sprat's history has perhaps led us to overemphasize the Baconian component of contemporary scientific work. Historians of ideas have noted that the British scientific establishment professed a much purer Baconianism than it ever performed. Barbara Shapiro, for instance, finds that not even Bacon's inductivism was allowed to assume the status of a single method: by the end of the seventeenth century, the mathematical paradigm was becoming much too persuasive to be ignored.[18] At the same time, the expressed ideology of scientific method traded heavily in Baconian rhetoric, in order to maximize the image of the establishment Englishman at the expense of such figures as Descartes and Hobbes. The British claimed to be doggedly empirical, even when they were not.

Similar ideological work has done with the public image of Sir Isaac Newton. Of the various models that might have been derived from Newtonian mathematics, the favored one in England depended upon a conformist-experimental Newton who was a friend to the established church and a generous source of arguments against Hobbes and the freethinkers. Through the Boyle lectures, Lockean theory and Baconian tradition met Newtonian mathematics in a harmonious tribute to British common sense.[19] The famous war cry "I make no hypotheses" was what most nonspecialists heard and took over from Newton. Newton's remarks, in English, in the last sections of the *Opticks,* seemed completely consonant with the Baconian inheritance. His declared commitment to "making Experiments and Observations, and . . . drawing general conclusions from them by Induction, and admitting of no Objections against the Conclusions, but such as are taken from Experiments, or other certain Truths," was as good as received doctrine.[20] His contention that "hypotheses are not to be regarded in experimental philosophy" could have been fitted verbatim into Bacon's critique of the idols of the mind, and his determination to progress from "particular Causes to more general ones, till the Argument end in the most general" (p. 404), repeated the classic objections against the Ramist logicians. In his popularization of Newton, translated into English in 1738, Voltaire did indeed speak of the "equal Right" of all men to share in these great discoveries, but what he showed them was the superiority of Newton over the rationalist Descartes, who did base his ideas "only upon Hypotheses" and was seriously misled by his "Systematical Spirit, or Fondness for System." Even Voltaire's deistical Newton is, then, a friend to Baconian method. The possibility that "all Things in Nature have secret Relations" will only ever be vindicated by rigorous induction and patient experiment.[21]

We may isolate various kinds of typicality within the mainstream British philosophical tradition in the eighteenth century, but none endorses a rationalist method or allows a major role for theory. Shaftesbury, for instance, was the most immethodical of gentlemanly thinkers. He found the "methodic or scholastic manner" best suited to a "dry and rigid" rather than a "fruitful imagination." It can at best produce "firm conclusions and steady maxims," but one false step leads it into absurdities, and it is always "apter to tire us than the metre of an old ballad."[22] The epistemological opportunities of the miscellaneous mode were clearly, for Shaftesbury, dependent upon a social entitlement: " 'Tis the unbred rustic orator alone who presents his clownish audience with a divisible discourse." The gentlemen is motivated "less by form than humour," unlike the "precise and strait-laced professor in a university." Shaftesbury specifies his own method as the method of nature and, prophetically, that of the poets:

And 'tis in this that the very worst of poets may justly be preferred to the generality of modern philosophers or other formal writers of a yet more specious name. . . . They follow Nature. They move chiefly as she moves in them, without thought of disguising her free motions and genuine operations, for the sake of any scheme or hypothesis which they have formed at leisure and in particular narrow views.[23]

Shaftesbury's miscellaneous and diversified style is intended as a gesture of freedom against the constraints of form and system, tendencies he seems to have intuitively identified as the property of an emerging bourgeoisie. When Burke sets out to echo this style, it is marked by the excesses of hyperbole and pastiche, as befits Burke's less assured social identity.[24] Shaftesbury makes clear that it is the vulgar and middling sort who have most to gain from methodical procedures, while the gentleman can follow his instincts, give free rein to his wit, and allow himself such "deviations and excursions" as seem fit.[25] It is one of the ironies of English social and intellectual history that the very bourgeois orders that appear to have had a use for the methodical manner were more anxious to identify themselves with the immethodical habits of their social superiors; the history of aesthetics in the eighteenth and nineteenth centuries (and beyond) is marked by the politically disenfranchised middle class projecting itself into an imaginary posture of gentlemanly disinterest.

Shaftesbury's aristocratic methodological license can hardly be described as "sticking to the facts," in the sense applied to the inherited Baconian tradition. But it presupposes the middle-class prudence and patient attention of that tradition in according itself the alternative permission to range freely *across* the facts. Both the elite and the middle-order methodologies, then, share a disdain for rationalist paradigms; both are anxious to claim for themselves a method that excludes whoever is below them in the social-intellectual hierarchy. A similar emphasis can be found in the more subtle and strictly philosophic naturalism of Hume, which represents a second kind of eighteenth-century typicality, albeit one that was emergent rather than dominant in the eighteenth century itself. Hume too stands against rationalism. Quantity and number are the only things capable of demonstration; everything else is a matter of fact or existence, and whatever is may also not be.[26] However, we live quite comfortably with the little that we know; neither skepticism nor rationalism can withstand the claims of nature, which are "always too strong for principle" (p. 160) In the moral sphere above all, "direct tendency or instinct" governs our behavior, and this immediate determination "comprehends not any scheme or system" (p. 303). Utility is the major factor in the dissemination of ideas: "Truths which are *pernicious* to society, if any such there be, will yield to errors which are salutary and *advantageous*" (p. 279). There is no place here for reason, or even for a Benthamite calculus of effects. Hume was no democrat. Should equality ever appear upon earth its effects, he thought, would be "pernicious" (p. 194). Politicians are to be judged not by whether they obey some notion of universal principle but only by whether they benefit or disadvantage their own national interests, for "nature has implanted in every one a superior affection to his own country," and this is moreover much more useful than "any loose indeterminate views to the good of a species" (p. 225). Nationalism is here prescribed as a natural and not a merely cultural attitude.

A third and much more popular component of the eighteenth-century philosophical tradition is typified by the writings of Thomas Reid. Reid has been described as the first major philosopher "to take Newton's opinions on induction, causality and hypothesis seriously," and as the founder of a "common sense" school identifying Bacon and Newton as co-workers in the cause of an extreme inductivism made more and more synonymous with empiricism and tending to "conflate the terms theory, hypothesis and conjecture and to attack them indiscriminately."[27] This conflation did indeed become pervasive in the popular as well as the philosophical consciousness. Reid's declared determination to "try every opinion by the touchstone of fact and experience" would become a commonplace, if not one already.[28] In his *Inquiry into the Human Mind,* first published in 1764, Reid argued that only mechanics, astronomy, and optics could be developed according to rules that "universally obtain"; any attempt to devise similar rules for the behavior of the mind must result in "darkness and perplexity." Descartes (as Voltaire had also admitted) had been led astray by the desire of "reducing things to a few principles," and even Newton was tempted by similar ambitions: "Both were misled by analogy, and the love of simplicity."[29]

Reid's profession of the narrow limits within which progressive knowledge can be expected leads him to common sense rather than to skepticism as a way of explaining the satisfactory conduct of everyday life:

If there are certain principles, as I think there are, which the constitution of our nature leads us to believe, and which we are under a necessity to take for granted in the common concerns of life, without being able to give a reason for them; there are what we call the principles of common sense; and what is manifestly contrary to them, is what we call absurd.

Reid is fond of attributing these certainties to our mental and physical "constitution."[30] This is the term that will emerge as the most contested item in the debate between Burke and Paine and their followers.

Perhaps enough has been said to make clear that the British way of doing things was predisposed, well before 1789, against the claims of system and theory and in favor of a mythology of common sense, including within it an "aristocratic" component of freedom of maneuver and a more quotidian dimension of inductivism. However far British science ranged from the exercise of a pure Baconian method, the rhetoric of national character would always claim for it that very purity. Especially after 1789 any deviation from this rhetorical tradition was likely to be perceived as a failure of patriotism. Much of Joseph Priestley's writing identified him as recognizably within the British tradition, but he was enough of a theorist—and a friend to "liberty"—to attract widespread persecution and contempt. He believed in perfectibility and in government according to first principles, but the "unbounded improvement" he predicted for the human race was much less rationalist than millenarian, in the typical tradition of British radical Christianity.[31] But Priestley was also a scientist, and it was in science especially that he saw "a quicker progress toward perfection then ever" (p. 131). In 1768 his case against "the unnatural system of rigid unalterable establishments" (p. 142) was inflammatory enough, but it became more so after 1776 and, especially, after 1789. Like many among the moderate radicals, Priestley saw the American and French revolutions as arising from "the same general principles," and thus as evidence of a force working through history toward perfection, liberating "all the powers of man from that variety of fetters, by which they have hitherto been held."[32] An internationalist, he looked forward to the displacement of particular by universal interests, and to the end of empire and war: "The empire of reason will ever be the reign of peace" (p. 150). The way to universality and peace was the way of system and method. Burke's refusal of "*definitions,* or *axioms*" (p. 56) was a denial of right reason, and his assertion that what might be "*metaphysically*" true" could be "morally and politically false" (p. 25) was an outrage against the integrity of the human mind. Like Ramus before him, Priestley was a lover of charts, simplified, graphic representations of complex processes that could be taken in at a glance with more exactness, and in much less time, than could have been done by reading:

I should not hesitate to say, that a more perfect knowledge of this kind of history may be gained by an hour's inspection of this chart, than could be acquired by the reading of several weeks.[33]

Here again is the ready and easy way, and Priestley saw it getting even easier: the chart of our future history would not be as "intersected and disfigured" (p. 20) as that of the past. This chart was advertized as cre-

ated according to Newtonian principles (p. 7), but its tendency to simplification and epitome was not Newtonian, nor was its application to
human affairs rather than merely to mathematical physics. Priestley
here typifies the radical use (or invocation) of Newton, which took
Newton's own paradigms beyond the contexts in which Newton had
himself contained them. Newton "arranged his facts—and then rose,
like a philosopher, to a general principle. What then forbids that we
should be capable of forming the *laws of mind*, as well as the laws of *nature* in *general*?"[34] Children begin with disconnected facts, and it is "nature" that teaches them to "abstract, or generalize" their ideas (p. 22).
There is nothing artificial about the process. What Priestley calls for is
exactly what orthodox Newtonianism had denied—the extension of
physico-mathematical models to a description of human history and
the human mind: "I have asserted that there are *fixed laws* for the *mind*,
equally with the revolution of the heavenly bodies, or the descent of a
stone, when thrown from your hand" (p. 57).

Priestley was, then, a man of method. He told Jacob Bryant, in the
same terms in which he would later respond to Burke: "You have Ora-
tory, I have Logic."[35] The doctrine of philosophical necessity he defended had, by the end of the eighteenth century, come to be known as
a dominantly French invention, while his commitment to simplicity and
epitome placed him directly in the tradition of the English Ramists. Being "*methodical*," for him, was essential to the credibility of any "*elementary treatise*."[36] In his early critique of the "new empire of common
sense," Priestley had reinvented the Ramist belief in a transparent order of things:

The great business of a philosophy is to reduce into classes the various appearances which nature presents to our view. For by this means we acquire an easy
and distinct knowledge of them, and gain a more perfect comprehension of
their various natures, relations, and uses.[37]

These were among the signals that placed Priestley on the eighteenth-
century left, despite his committed Christianity and his preference for
1688 over 1642 as the high point of British liberty, and despite his
avowed preference for the "patient and gentle" rather than revolutionary treatment of social injustice.[38] He published against Paine but in
qualified praise of Hobbes.[39] His recommendation of Hobbes's "proper
doctrine of philosophical necessity" as "no small honour to this country" was hardly in tune with the prevailing specifications of national distinction.[40] Nor were his consciously Frenchified locutions, his habit of
declaring himself a "citizen" and of referring (albeit well before
Robespierre) to the "Supreme Being." Hobbes was no Enlightenment

radical, but his writings were, as Margaret Jacob has said, consistently received as "a grave moral threat to the fabric of social relations and hence to order and stability."[41] His ruthlessly demystifying analysis of the norms of social life made him a threat to those wishing to propose the velvet glove of a mixed constitution rather than the iron hand of absolutism as the solution to the deviations of human nature. Like many others who sought to restrict the claims of rationalism, Hobbes saw geometry as the "only science that it had pleased God hitherto to bestow on mankind."[42] But instead of proposing custom or common sense as the means of filling the gaps, Hobbes saw a solution only in the right use of words and in the ultimate supervision of all conventions by an absolute authority. In the course of arguing against egalitarianism, he deduced the consequences of inequality in such extreme terms that he could not but have embarrassed the apologists of the 1688 settlement by revealing their calculated ambiguities as founded upon policy rather than nature. Universalist reason and absolute monarchism were both threats to the maintenance of the rhetoric of common sense.

The Trials of Reason

The radicals of the 1790s inherited the disadvantages of a nationalist tradition already firmly set against system and theory (as was Baconian inductivism) and often against the entire possibility of method (as was Shaftesbury's cultivated liberalism). As in government, so in argument and experiment the English idiom was hostile to hypotheses, schemas, and prescriptive constitutions. So pervasive was this idiom that it affected even writers apparently on the left. The most important English populist of the Romantic period, William Cobbett, was also violently anti-French and doggedly antitheoretical. More than a little of the same patriotic worship of the profuse impinges on the more coherently radical poetry of William Blake. Many of those in opposition to establishment politics were radical Christians rather than atheistic rationalists, and thus reluctant to ally themselves with the antireligious associations of the systematizing philosophes. This predicament committed the English radicals to a certain insecurity of image and self-image, at a time when their opponents had behind them over a century of patriotic propaganda reinforcing their contempt for the theoretical mode. A month or so before the storming of the Bastille, Arthur Young noted among the Parisians a lack of solid political sense and a penchant for the "ideal and visionary rights of nature." Declaring the practice of political economy to be far more important than any theory about it, he began his *Travels* with a broadside against "the love of system, and . . . the vain theories that are to be found in the closets of speculators alone."[43] Debating the merits of a narrative style as against those of an analytical, tabular format for the presentation of his findings, Young opted for a blend of the two—a mixed style for a mixed subject. Even James Burgh, considered by many as the founding theorist of American constitutional liberties, had declared himself a "true independent Whig" with no "design to form a system of politics" and no faith in the notion that political behavior could ever be governed by "reason."[44]

The radicals thus often found themselves obliged to compete for a vocabulary that had already been convincingly possessed by the nativist ideology. Sir James Mackintosh, in *Vindiciae Gallicae,* declared his explicit faith in the powers of "analysis and method" for leveling "on the intellectual field the giant and the dwarf,"and he wholly approved the "systematic whole" that the French constitution offered for imitation. Nonetheless, his argument for rational reform still pays homage to a Baconian vocabulary:

The rights and nature of men are to the Legislator what the general properties of matter are to the Mechanic, the first guide, because they are founded on the widest experience. . . . EXPERIENCE IS THE BASIS OF ALL. Not the trammelled and puny experience of a *Statesman by trade,* who trembles at any change in the *tricks* which he has been taught, or the *routine* in which he has been accustomed to move, but an experience liberal and enlightened, which bears the testimony of ages and nations, and collects from it the general principles which regulate the mechanism of society.[45]

Here it is the highlighted customary and Baconian terminology of "experience" that is used to insinuate the case for a radical, theoretical endorsement of "general principles."

The opponents of French revolution and English reform thus inherited the discursive high ground in their dismissal of theory as inappropriate to an authentically British aesthetic or political practice. The *Anti-Jacobin*'s contrast between "sound reasoning and useful philosophy" and the "sophistical ingenuity, or visionary theories" of the French was a cultural commonplace, and it worked to reduce into a single doctrine the entire range of French Enlightenment and post-revolutionary thought.[46] In his anonymous *Pursuits of Literature,,* T. J. Mathias satirized the modern "MAN OF METHOD" as a libertine, a democrat, and a francophile, a conflation of attributes that frequently marked conservative rhetoric through the 1790s.[47] The radical commitment to what *The Patriot* called "the clearest method" and "clear and honest definitions" proved hard to market against the in-place ideology of patriotism.[48] But the attempt was made. Various of Burke's critics, besides Tom Paine, deplored his want of "judgment and science" and his failure to observe "the strict discipline of mathematics."[49] Joel Barlow agreed that physics was no model for political science, but he sought to turn the tables on the usual interpretation of that argument in suggesting that *only* in physics do we have to restrict ourselves to "the slow process of patient and positive experience." Political truths, in contrast, are as "perceptible when first presented to the mind, as an age or a world of experience could make them." The great political "experiment" now under way must determine once and for all whether *"Theory and Practice,* which always agree together in things of slighter moment, are really to remain eternal enemies in the highest concerns of men."[50]

Barlow pushed the populist heritage of Ramism to an extreme, and beyond the Ramist focus on literacy, in proposing that the "general revolution" surely at hand would come not from the educated elite but from a "much more important class of men, the class that cannot write; and in a great measure . . . those who cannot read. It is to be decided by men who reason better without books, than we do with all the books in the world." *"Thinking"* rightly is not dependent upon "writing and reading."[51] More usually this natural methodicality was projected as what would be called forth by the power of print. As George Rous explained, the reading experience allowed for the contemplation of arguments "without passion." Rational truths would thus convince the reading class, whose "general assent" would then command the "concurrence of the multitude."[52] In this way, as Mackintosh in turn explained it, the substance of the "great works . . . which cannot be read by the people" would pass "through a variety of minute and circuitous channels to the shop and the hamlet," in a process inevitable enough to be compared to "the process of nature in the external world."[53] Production and consumption both, in this fantasy of reason, come to be imagined as subject to inevitable laws and immune to the reinterpretations of different reading communities and conflicting ideologies.

The vocabulary of theory, then, was almost inevitably specified as the language of the left, so that it was always a fairly vain effort that the left itself mounted to convict its opponents of having theories of their own. The author of *Temperate Comments upon Intemperate Reflections* pronounced Burke himself "like a theorist" in "devoting himself entirely to a favourite hypothesis"; James Parkinson, as "Old Hubert," set out to show that the reactionaries were just as guilty as the radicals of forming associations and passing resolutions, theirs being in favor of the rights of placemen and pensioners; and Thomas Cooper also found that Burke had a system and a theory—he was the "systematic opponent of every Species of Reform" and he espoused the "THEORY of *Privileged orders.*"[54] But these writers, like so many who have come after them, found it very difficult to make popular headway against the nationalist ideology. They found only a little more support than did Thelwall in his demonstration (discussed in chapter 1) that Burke was no child of nature but a logician skilled in the cryptic method.

The associations of theory with cold-blooded mathematical exactitude were actually exemplified in few if any of the British radicals, but they suffered from such assumptions nonetheless. One might compare the way in which "ideology" is used by twentieth-century liberal and conservative critics to describe the views of anyone *outside* the governing consensus, in a precise reversal of its foundational Marxist sense. After 1793 especially, everyone with any tolerance for system or theory was branded a Jacobin, and writers sympathetic to a reformist cause were often all the more cautious. Godwin's *Enquiry* declared itself all for the "methodical and elementary way" of presentation and for a government "in the utmost degree simple." It endorsed "abstraction" as "inseparable from the existence of mind" and "generalization" as "implied in the very notion of a thinking being."[55] Godwin saw knowledge as progressive and mankind as rational and perfectible. But his book was too expensive to incur the opposition directed at popular radicalism and too complex to be amenable to pamphlet reproduction. So extended, indeed, is Godwin's account of all the impediments in the way of the dissemination of right reason that it almost becomes, in passages, a rationalization of the status quo.

Thomas Paine was much more threatening, though he was relatively unpopular among the middle-class, dissenting reformers who feared his atheism (real or apparent) and did not fully share his acute critique of the rhetoric of patriotism.[56] Paine's belief in an ideally simple or only minimally mediated relation between natural and civil rights, and his idea of a "constitution" as either clearly defined or nonexistent, were rendered coherent by an extraordinary faith in the single method.[57] Government, properly conducted, must display its procedures transparently to the average reasoner, who can then see "the *rationale* of the whole system, its origin and its operation" (1:338). Paine reinvented the Ramist correspondence of mind and world, and the utopian faith of the Puritan radicals, in proposing the new principles of government as a "renovation of the natural order of things" (1:342). The established political systems are the real deviations from the truth, and they have only come into being because of our ignorance of "method":

It was the want of some method to consolidate the parts of society, after it became too populous, and too extensive for the simple democratical form, and also the lax and solitary condition of shepherds and herdsmen in other parts of the world, that afforded opportunities to those unnatural modes of government to begin. (1:369)

If Paine did not invent "the Age of Reason" as the definition of his times (or, otherwise, of the times before 1789), he certainly gave it popular currency (1:449). Like the Ramists and Puritans before him, he promised a harmony of mind and world that was nothing less than an overcoming of the consequences of the fall. He showed no concern for the pitfalls of any of Bacon's various "idols": "Man cannot make principles, he can only discover them" (1:488). These principles have "no connection with time" (2:483), and they possess an energy that can overcome anything that governments and nations might put in their way. In *Agrarian Justice* Paine attributes metaphysical omnipotence to a properly deployed method:

An army of principles will penetrate where an army of soldiers cannot; it will succeed where diplomatic management would fail: it is neither the Rhine, the Channel, nor the ocean that can arrest its progress: it will march on the horizon of the world, and it will conquer. (1:622)

Paine was neither logician, mathematician, nor scientist, but he imaged a world where the distinctions among them, and between them and all other people, would hardly matter. In this sense he was easily indentifiable with the French republicans with whom he indeed came to share citizenship.

The British radicals—Paine, Godwin, Price, Priestley, and others like them—were persuasively grouped by the establishment press as bloodless arithmeticians. Burke scored a very palpable hit in his ridicule of the new political organization of France along apparently mathematical lines.[58] William Belsham and Joseph Priestley were only two among those who tried to point out that he had overstated and even misrepresented the case, in his zealous contempt for the "geometrical and arithmetical constitution" (*Reflections*, p. 144). Priestley objected that "the actual divisions of the country" were "no more squares than our counties."[59] Sieyès's plans for the creation of the new *départements* in fact made provision for elaborate local consultation and modification, but they were mathematically self-conscious enough to offer a target for the British press.[60] Isaac Newton, after all, the greatest English mathematician, had been rendered (as he surely rendered himself) a friend to the establishment and an ally of the Baconian method. Descartes and his countrymen, conversely, were theorists and speculators. Britain did not adopt a decimalized currency until 1970, although in 1656 Robert Wood had proposed exactly such a scheme to "lessen the Labour & ease the paines of Men" by a "short and ready way for the extraordinary Facilitation and Dispatch of RECKONINGS."[61] His manuscript, sent to Hartlib, apparently remained unpublished, even at a time when so much was published in a society temporarily free from censorship laws. This was England, after all.

Burke, Coleridge, and the Method of Nature

We have seen that Burke was by no means the originator of the British predisposition against theory and system, which probably took on its exemplary form in the seventeenth century as doing double duty against the Puritans and the French. Burke's countryman Jonathan Swift, among many others, had made the connection between rational method and Satanic transgression that would serve the opponents of the French Revolution so well:

> For, what Man in the Natural State, or Course of Thinking, did ever conceive it in his Power, to reduce the Notions of all Mankind, exactly to the same Length, and Breadth, and Height of his own? Yet this is the first humble and civil Design of all Innovators in the Empire of Reason.[62]

Burke's very lack of originality indeed afforded him the resources of a tradition and made his voice all the more powerful: it was Paine who was obliged to invent (or reinvent) a language. At the same time, Burke's *Reflections*, written before the regicide and the Jacobin hegemony, spends a relatively small measure of its invective on the philosophes, when compared with the later writings. Those who would soon become familiar compound demons—Voltaire, Rousseau, Helvétius, and Condorcet—are largely unmentioned or undiscussed. In 1790 Burke seems more concerned about the lawyers and financial speculators he sees to be in control of French political life: his frequently expressed hostility toward "jew brokers" and "money-jobbers, usurers, and Jews" renders his argument rather more consistently anti-Semitic than antiphilosophes.[63] Burke makes energetic rhetorical capital out of the fact that the English radical dissenters were in the habit of meeting at "Old Jewry" (e.g., pp. 165, 180). He looks back (like Coleridge, with the comfort of considerable historical distance) to the 1640s and to an English radicalism that "bore no sort of resemblance to your present reforming doctors in Paris" (p. 258), at the same time as he focuses on 1688 as an essentially English and positive "revolution." Richard Price is Burke's principal target. It is Price who reminds Burke of the English regicides, who offends against the "spirit of moderation" (p. 94), and who departs from the conventions of a "national character" properly marked by "cold sluggishness" and a "sullen resistance to innovation"—

qualities Burke means positively (p. 181). Theory and method are quite simply inhuman and inhumane, the offspring of "cold hearts and muddy understandings" (p. 171). Burke prefers "untaught feelings" (p. 183). Those who are "so taken up with their theories about the rights of man" have "totally forgot his nature. Without opening one new avenue to the understanding, they have succeeded in stopping up those that lead to the heart" (p. 156). Burke's preferred method is the "method of nature," one that is neither simple innovation nor conservation but a complex and above all imperceptible and unpredictable balance of continuity and change, one suited to a "permanent body composed of transitory parts" (p. 120).

If there is "method" here, then we hardly notice it, as it works through different shapes and forms through place and time. Burke here sets out to capture a language of method that had, before Bacon, been associated with clarity and self-consciousness and often with a leveling tendency or ambition: "It is one of the excellencies of a method in which time is amongst the assistants, that its operation is slow, and in some cases almost imperceptible" (p. 280). Instead of being a ready and easy way that speeds up mental and social processes and economizes on human energy, Burke's "method" is almost identical with the slow passage of recorded time. And at each moment there is a watchdog, both within the intelligent self and, even more important, in the shape of the patrician class, to supervise its formation:

By a slow but well-sustained progress, the effect of each step is watched; the good or ill success of the first, gives light to us in the second; and so on, from light to light, we are conducted with safety through the whole series. (P. 281)

Burke goes on to describe this supervisory principle in terms that exactly prefigure a famous Coleridgean definition of the imagination:

We see, that the parts of the system do not clash. The evils latent in the most promising contrivances are provided for as they arise. One advantage is as little as possible sacrificed to another. We compensate, we reconcile, we balance. We are enabled to unite into a consistent whole the various anomalies and contending principles that are found in the minds and affairs of men. From hence arises, not an excellence in simplicity, but one far superior, an excellence in composition.[64]

In this way, Burke says, the principle governing the state may be compared to a "plastic nature" (p. 282). It is not to be entrusted to "the metaphysics of an undergraduate, and the mathematics and arithmetic of an exciseman" (p. 299). Burke offers his experience of "near forty years" (p. 180) as the alternative to that metaphysics and mathematics.

It has taught him that "the rights of men are in a sort of middle, incapable of definition, but not impossible to be discerned" (p. 153). This had been the rhetoric of the membership of the Royal Society, as reported by Sprat.[65] In place of axiom and proof, Burke looks to the heritage of a "mixed system of opinion and sentiment" (p. 170) and finds it in a "mixed and tempered government" (p. 227). Throughout the early 1790s Burke kept up and indeed stepped up his campaign against "the surfeit and indigestion of systems" and "the fashion of wild, visionary theories" and "new theoretic language."[66] With unerring polemical intelligence he specified the most dangerous of all revolutions as that "in the national spirit," and he both identified and excoriated the tendency in the theoretical mind toward internationalism. As the Jacobins ceased to be "local or territorial" and took over France, so France itself aspired to a "universal empire."[67] Events certainly assisted Burke in gaining conviction for his conflation of democratic ideology with classical imperialism, and in his associated denigration of the British radicals. According to Burke, Paine and Robespierre were the new Ramists, with their "short revolutionary methods" and (Paine's) claim to rehearse in "six or seven days" the wisdom of "six or seven centuries."[68]

Perhaps I need not labor the obvious point: Burke's image of the nation as a self-adjusting system aligns the supervisory functions of a patrician class together with a laissez-faire rhetoric of natural evolution into a powerful conservative rationale. His emphasis wanders as it needs to, and as it must do if it is to disguise the authoritarian element that is at its heart. To pass from Burke to Coleridge is to discover what happens when this ambivalence is adjudicated in a more conventionally philosophic context by a much more coherently philosophic mind, but one that maintains a clear affiliation with a Burkean politics. This is not to suggest that Coleridge was always and entirely a Burkean—he was not. His early writings, especially, make clear their distance from the "mad sorrow, and more than funereal ululation" of the *Reflections* and its "delirious invectives."[69] This was a Coleridge who was scathingly critical of the "Dictionary of aristocratic Prejudice" in which "Illumination and Sedition are classed as *synonimes*" (p. 56), and who was willing to pronounce Muir, Margarot, Gerrald and Palmer to be true patriots (pp. 12ff.). At the same time, Coleridge was never an Enlightenment rationalist and never in sympathy with the advocates of "proud Philosophy" (p. 46) as a substitute for Christianity and for the homebred English virtues of benevolence, domesticity, and personal sincerity. His deliciously ironic anecdote, in a letter to Edwards of January 1796, is the perfect epitome of Coleridgean radicalism. Here he reports seeing *The Watchman* picked up by an "Aristocrat" who glanced at the epigraph and pronounced it to be the work of a *"seditious Dog,"* only to be told that the words came from "JESUS CHRIST."[70]

In the habitual search for a genial middle ground that characterized much of even his early work, Coleridge gave Burke credit even as he differed with him. He almost quotes Burke directly in his aspiration to show "the necessity of *bottoming* on fixed Principles," and the fixed principles to which he returned became more and more Burkean as the years went by.[71] His vocabulary of "principles" is a deliberate alternative to Paine's use of the same lexicon; and, like Burke, he takes up the task of trying to capture the vocabulary of method from its traditional and recently ratified association with a radical "left." In *The Statesman's Manual* Coleridge specifies "principles" and "ideas" as the property of the scriptures rather than of the secular-rationalist mind, and proposes the Bible as the unique source of a "Science of *Realities*" appealing to the "pure Reason."[72] The rationale for *The Friend* is the same search for *"fixed* principles" (1:1), now to be carried on in the Baconian middle ground between "speculative reasoning" and the "merely empirical" (1:4). By now, Paine is a figure of "presumptuous arrogance" and the ungodly successor of Thomas Hobbes (1:32). Painite theory is bad theory, like Jacobinism, a "lawless alternation" between disparate parts of other theories (1:178–79). There are indeed principles that are "above all expedience, all accidental consequences" (1:63), but these are moral rather than rationally epistemological.

The effort to capture the vocabulary of method from the "left" is one of the most consistent energies of *The Friend*. Coleridge first declares that the deduction of "the social Rights of Man and the sole rightful form of government from principles of Reason" does not imply any necessary commitment to "the democratic, or even the representative, constitution" (1:196). On the contrary, he says, most eighteenth-century rationalists were monarchists rather than democrats, and it is this tradition that has endorsed Bonapartism and encouraged in Napoleon himself a "predilection for a theory conducted throughout with mathematical precision" (1:197). By thus scrambling the familiar codes, Coleridge creates something of a space for a definition of his own "Principles of Method" (1:446), which do not entail any faith in a "general illumination" but depend upon the responsibilities of an enlightened clerisy to a Christian culture (1:447). The "uneducated" do *not* show any evidence of an achieved or achievable "method" (1:451). For Coleridge, there is no ready and easy way. The organicist interaction between empirical material and mental initiative, each qualifying and balancing the other in a process of evolution governed ultimately by a prefigurative idea, a "primary act positively *originating* in the mind itself" (1:453), is not open to happening in the minds of all. The *"leading Thought"* (1:455) that makes this process cohere, and ensures that self-projection will indeed produce a true account of the world, can only be the property of a few. Coleridge's argument synthesizes the workings of method with the operations of the imagination—which also brings together "things the most remote and diverse in time, place and outward circumstance" (1:455)—and with the giving of "law" (1:459). All are finally emanations of the ultimate radical, the "will," without whose integrating principle science itself can only remain "an elaborate game of shadows" that "begins in abstractions and ends in perplexity" (1:520).

The ingenuity of Coleridge's method consists in its putting together the vocabulary of Protestant election (and self-election) with a model of each-in-all that derives from the *Naturphilosophie,* in science, and from Burke's "method of nature"—and Coleridge uses the very phrase (1:499)—in politics. This "union and interpenetration of the universal and the particular" (1:457) is at once synchronic and diachronic. It explains the distribution of priorities at any one time, as well as the movement of will and imagination through time. It reconciles the operations of observation, experiment, and hypothesis in science, and of idealism and realism in philosophy. It further synthesizes science, philosophy, education, and religion into a whole culture (1:463, 493–94). The "method" is, like the English constitution according to Burke, a mixed one, supposing "a union of *several* things to a common end" (1:497) and aiming at "progressive transition without breach of continuity" (1:476), the same evolutionary sequence that Burke had projected for the body politic. While Burke's *Reflections* inevitably exposed its assumptions as in awkward relation to the unignorable events of history (most notably those of 1642 and 1688), Coleridge's more abstract schema is able to remain at the magisterial level of a "world" history as he traces the career of "method" through Hebrew, Greek, Roman and Christian eras (1:504–6). His universalism is, like Hegel's, distinctly Eurocentric. More specifically it is nationalistic, as his vocabulary wanders purposively between "race" and "nation," with the second becoming the exemplary instance of the first. Method in the "race" can be traced from the classics through to Christianity, and it is in this that the "unlettered African, or rude yet musing Indian" (1:512) are deficient, "guided by the light of no leading idea" until the "friendly missionary" arrives to teach writing and reading (1:513). This indulgence in mere particularities, unconnected by any organic principle, is what the "proud fact-hunting materialist" shares with the "imbruted African" (1:518). Within the "race," already thus exclusive, it is "trade and literature" that produce the "nation" by balancing the external-material with the internal-spiritual needs (1:506). In this way the best of the race is incarnate in some nations. And, after all that has now been said, no prizes need be offered for identifying Coleridge's candidate for most-favored-nation status. The famous attempt to reconcile Bacon and Plato as disciples of the same doctrine of ideal-realism (1:482ff.), which allows for deficiencies in Bacon exactly insofar as he was the exponent of a bourgeois-Puritan moral gloom and class partiality (1:485–87), is the closest Coleridge's exposition of method comes to any sustained internationalism. The "Essays on Method" are introduced, indeed, as the lucubrations of "a lover of Old England" (1:446), and they are imbued with a Burkean vision of the English tradition as the "true historical feeling, the feeling of being a historical people, generation linked to generation by ancestral reputation, by tradition, by heraldry" (1:447). Burke himself becomes the exemplary man of method (1:449), and his literary analogue is Shakespeare, whose characters variously show the achievement, mere facsimile, and complete lack of method (Hamlet, Polonius, Mistress Quickly), while his productions viewed as a whole demonstrate the vindication of an authorial method, revealing a sense of "the same human nature, which is everywhere present as the vegetable sap" in all the parts of the tree (1:457).

The "universal" language of method has here been firmly anchored in the expressive habits of the English nation, the best of the "race," and in the educated ranks of that nation (for both class and gender separate Hamlet from Mistress Quickly), as the essence of Englishness has been identified in Burke and Shakespeare in politics and literature respectively. It is not just the "imbruted African" and the "proud fact-hunting materialist" who are here left out, but also the ordinary and very English men and women who lack, for Coleridge, the balance of education and intuition necessary to see things steadily and see them whole. Much the same ideological work goes on in *Biographia Literaria,* where Coleridge attempts to establish the national literature as the most important cohering principle for both the individual psyche and the national culture as a whole. The famous philosophical speculations of the central chapters, again committed to the demonstration of "unity and system" as the "end and purpose of all reason," are but a part of a general modeling of the author's literary life.[73] This life is at once "introductory" to a statement of Coleridge's own "principles" in philosophy (1:5) and exemplary of a general potential in the national literature for the constitution of a national personality. Once again Burke's presence is implicit throughout the narrative, and he is mentioned as one who "referred habitually to principles" (1:191). But in the sphere of the literary his proxies are Shakespeare and the Wordsworth who is fairly aggressively reinvented by Coleridge as, at his best (and he is often not at his best, for Coleridge), the modern Shakespeare.[74] In the original edition of 1817 the conclusion to the *Biographia* was preceded by a reprint of "Satyrane's Letters" and of Coleridge's previously anonymous critique of Maturin's *Bertram*. These items have often been left out of subsequent reprints, though they are restored in the latest and best edition cited in this study (2:160–233). The critique of *Bertram* takes issue with the licentious productions of an Irish dramatist, and the letters describe Coleridge's first trip out of England, to Germany in 1798–99. They had already been reprinted in *The Friend* in 1809, and they detail the young poet's distinctly patriotic reflections on first meeting various classes of foreigners. Coleridge reports the bad reputation of the French émigrés in Germany as corrupt, unprincipled, and untrustworthy. It affords him an "honest pride" to contrast them with "the stern yet amiable characters of the English patriots, who sought refuge on the Continent at the Restoration" (2:181). In chapter 4 I will account for the image of Germany in the British imagination at this time. Now we turn to those very Frenchmen in whom, as we saw at the beginning of this chapter, Coleridge found cleverness, talent, and wit, but little of genius or sense, and a besetting predilection for theory and particularity. What were the reasons behind Arthur Young's violent dislike of "French theory"?[75] And what were the implications of its place in John Bull's image of the alien and the undesirable?

3

THE MYTH OF FRENCH
EXCESS

A Nation of Philosophers

Since at least the Restoration of 1660, and emphatically in Dryden's writings, the British national character had been defined chiefly in terms of its difference from the French. In chapter 6 I will discuss the consequences of this for a model of the national "literature" as anti-methodical, beyond containment by mere rules, and analogous to the mixed economy and political constitution in its proclivity for variety, lively disorder (even unto the sublime), and tolerance for special cases. All of these priorities were familiar by about 1700, and the anti-French articulation remained normative even as the projections of Frenchness changed somewhat with the times. France, in its specific incarnation as William of Normandy, had been blamed by the English left-liberal commonwealthman tradition as the exterminator of ancient Anglo-Saxon liberties, as Christopher Hill has famously shown.[1] Even the eighteenth-century "left," in other words, was used to articulating its democratic aspirations in a patriotic, anti-French vocabulary. Subsequently France was variously (and even simultaneously) the home of craven Catholics and bold atheists, subservient royalists and extreme anarchists, licentious libertines and cold calculators. The French were, in other words, felt to be prone to radical extremes, and thus quite devoid of the Coleridgean faculty of "sense" that, as we have seen, was taken to characterize the Englishman (if not always the Briton).

The commendable cosmopolitanism of the British sympathizers with the French Revolution was, then, almost bound to run into trouble as it countered a national habit of self-esteem even the French themselves, through such figures as Voltaire and Montesquieu, had seemed to endorse. Arthur Young, always a good source of quotable "common sense" prejudices, argued that only a political economy conducted by those capable of seeing the world both as politicians and as farmers could avoid the errors of "the love of system, and of the vain theories that are to be found in the closets of speculators alone."[2] It is the argued absence of an empirico-bourgeois middle class—a class of English "yeomen"—that accounts for the political volatility of France; only such a class, should it be allowed to prosper, could save the nation from ultimate ruin (1:609ff.) The aristocrats are doggedly conservative, while the populists are intransigently committed to an absolute democracy (1:119). Young's worst fear—and this is before the fall of the Bastille—is of "visionary or theoretic systems" (1:139). By 1798 he has had to become even more explicit about the rights and wrongs of civil government: "Modern philosophy is the scourge of human societies; religion their best support."[3] So great is the need for more churches that it is even worth raising taxes in order to build them.

Philosophers in general, and theorists in particular, were consistently held responsible for everything that went wrong with France after 1789. On the other side, the radicals were more than ready to give credit to those same theorists for everything they felt to be going right. Mackintosh, in 1791, saw the French as having the good fortune to profit from the findings of "the philosophers of Europe." They were lucky enough to "live in a period when it was only necessary to affix the stamp of laws to what had been prepared by the research of philosophy," and sensible enough to do so.[4] But after the regicide—and, more important, after the Terror—the consequences of theory were more commonly regarded in a negative than a positive light. Either there was seen to be a seamless continuity between ideas and events, the one causing the other, or some mediation was proposed whereby, in the words of the *British Mercury,* the philosophers "sowed with poisons the fields where the Revolutionists have reaped; they were the hands that led and set on the tygers and panthers against the human race."[5] With the partial (but only partial) exception of Rousseau, to whom we will come at the end of this chapter, to condemn philosophy was to condemn theory. And as the French had given us Ramus and a dangerous input into logic and pedagogy, so in the sphere of high philosophy they had given us Descartes.

Descartes was no orthodox Ramist, but Ramist components undoubtedly figured in his education, and Ramist priorities definitely reappear in his writings, as we have seen in chapter 1. He believed in a single method, and in the powers of graphic representation, even as he disputed the usefulness of the syllogism. It was Descartes, in *The Discourse on Method,* who brought some of the Ramist assumptions fully into contact with what would become the "mainstream" philosophic tradition. Like the Ramist manuals, Descartes's *Discourse* was written in

the vernacular, in order to make the maximum appeal to "natural reason" and to acknowledge the possessors of clarity and intelligibility even
among those who "can but speak the language of Lower Brittany and
have never learned Rhetoric."[6] This assertion of the claims of "natural
reason in all its purity" against those who "believe only in the writings of
the Ancients" (1:130) emerges loudly and clearly from the pages of the
Discourse, notwithstanding its habit of irony and self-protection.[7] The
case against "example and custom" (1:87) is explicit, even as the author
cautions that the attempt to "strip oneself of all opinions and beliefs formerly received" (1:90) is not an example everyone should follow. In the
Rules for the Direction of the Mind, published posthumously in 1701,
Descartes is clear about the need for "method" to correct the habit
of "unregulated inquiries and confused reflections" that "only con-
found the natural light and blind our mental powers" (1:9). This
method consists in "certain and simple rules" (1:9) reflecting the "primary rudiments of human reason" (1:11), mainly evident in but not restricted to mathematics, and themselves so "easy and simple" that they
were obscured and mystified by the ancient philosophers, who could
not afford to give up the admiration and respect that would inevitably
disappear upon their literal publication (1:12). Descartes here reiter-
ates the traditional Ramist conviction of a negative relation between
natural reason and established culture. The "learned" have a vested interest in obscuring the "light of nature" (1:57); they may even be so
pointlessly sophisticated "as to contrive to render themselves blind to
things that are in their own nature evident, and known by the simplest
peasant" (1:46).

Despite his reservations about the syllogism, and his espousal of an
inductivist, part-to-whole method at some points in his argument (e.g.,
1:92), Descartes does then resurrect the basic elements in the social-
political challenge that Ramism had presented. He too publishes a faith
in the powers of ordinary intelligence, and in their essentially methodical identity. Arithmetic and geometry are valuable as unobscured
instances of a direct relation between achieved results and "inborn principles" (1:10). We misunderstand Descartes if we conclude, as some of
his opponents did, that mathematics was being proposed as a simple
model for the description of all other kinds of knowledge. It is its procedures that give us the model for "the direct road towards truth," and it is
the "certitude" of those procedures that we should seek to emulate
(1:5). Nevertheless, the mathematical paradigm does figure prominently enough in the argument to have attracted the attention of both
supporters and disclaimers of the Cartesian method.

And supporters there appear to have been. To accept the belief in Descartes's relative unimportance for the British tradition may be to accept uncritically the myths of the nationalist ideology. Marjorie Nicolson argued long ago that Descartes was at first perceived to be compatible with Baconian and Platonist ideas, and that he was received as a "savior" by liberal philosophers and theologians in the 1640s and 1650s.[8] She dates the onset of the discrediting of Descartes to the period of the Restoration, which was, as we have seen, responsible for a general heightening of the rhetoric of British exceptionalism. But she attributes to a popular if often unavowed Cartesianism much of the initiative bringing about the English plain style with which the nationalist propaganda would later make such headway. More recently Hilda Smith has noted the importance of Descartes's method in encouraging ideas of women's equality in the seventeenth century, especially in the writings of Mary Astell.[9]

But much of the most public eighteenth-century commentary on Descartes was in fact given over to disclaiming his achievements, in France as well as in England. It has been widely and reasonably concluded that the extreme claims of Cartesian method made it vulnerable to both the Newtonian critique of hypotheses and the Baconian critique of mentalist projections.[10] Furthermore, Descartes's rationalist project committed him to maintaining the very synthesis of individual with general that was coming more and more to be questioned as philosophers began to doubt that what one person sees and thinks can be assumed to be identical with what another sees and thinks, or that what either of them sees and thinks is in inevitable correspondence with the world as it is in itself. The evolution of these doubts *about* the rationalist project surely in some way reflects the problems of a competitive culture wherein the habits, interests, and perceptions of one person were seen to be at odds with those of others, with all equally at a distance from whatever we would call the world of "things." Skepticism about the relation between words, deeds, and things thus licenses, in the ethical sphere, a relatively unhindered utilization of resources along laissez-faire principles. If things in themselves are unknowable or debatable, they cannot be definitively damaged or possessed; when we are all at an equal distance from these things, we can preserve the image of a nondestructive and nonmonopolistic liberal individualism. Hume's innovations upon and redirections of the arguments of the philosophical subculture have proved massively influential not just because they are good arguments—though they certainly are—but also because they appeal to a consensus of which philosophical inquiry is the expression rather than (or as well as) the critique.

The Cartesian paradigm, with its rationalist egalitarianism and

mathematical idealism, was seen to propound doctrines at once absolute and democratic, thus going against both the perceived successes of
experimental science and the cultural-political consensus that sustained those successes and claimed responsibility for them. There were
no strict or absolute Cartesians after Newton. At the same time, elements of the Cartesian paradigm did survive, and did reemerge in recognizably radical ways, especially in the French tradition.

The above remarks may serve as an introduction to a very complicated debate, which I cannot here decide: that concerning the relation
of Descartes to the French Enlightenment. To begin with, it is perhaps
a mistake to imagine a single "Descartes" whose various doctrines are
fixed for all time and open to reception either wholly or not at all. We
have already seen much evidence that the arguments of and about
Ramus were by no means exhausted after literal references to Ramism
disappear from the debate. The same is true for the Newtonian and
Baconian traditions in the eighteenth century and beyond, and arguably for the Cartesian method. Voltaire, as we have seen, found
Descartes guilty of ignoring experimentation, overvaluing systems, indulging in hypotheses, and inventing too much.[11] But elements of the
paradigm did persist, as one would expect them to, given the persistence of the causes and interests for which they had originally spoken. One does not have to see the Enlightenment as "fundamentally"
anything—mechanistic, rationalist, sensibilitarian, or anything else. It
is more adequate to recognize the place and function of various artic-
ulations within the writings of its major and minor figures. Among
them was certainly a Cartesian moment, implicit or even disavowed as
it often was. Along with Nicolson and Smith, Margaret Jacob has argued for a materialist-egalitarian tradition of Cartesian thought, even
though she finds this to be far from Descartes's own intentions; and
Peter Schouls, in two recent studies, has emphasized the radical potential in Descartes's "new method" as promising nothing less than "deliv-
erance from drudgery, evil, and sickness through consistent application."[12] Aram Vartanian has also proposed a "decisive role" for
Descartes in the forming of the ideology of "scientific naturalism" and,
importantly, in the broadening of the audience for philosophical
speculation by appealing to a general, polite readership, including
women—an influence that persisted despite the decline in the credibility of Cartesian (vortex) physics by the middle of the eighteenth century.[13]

Vartanian did much to disambiguate the various components of Cartesian doctrine, and thus to account for the various uses to which they
could be put. He suggested, for instance, that Descartes's physics had

an important influence on Diderot, even as the metaphysics were repudiated. As we ponder the writings of the philosophes, we find that Descartes is often smuggled back under the unlikely imprimatur of Bacon. La Mettrie, for example, scorned him as the apostle of "innate ideas" but celebrated his demonstration of the fact that animals are "pure machines" and delighted in his skill at throwing red herrings to the theologians.[14] A similarly nuanced attitude to Descartes can be found in the other philosophers. D'Alembert's *Preliminary Discourse to the Encyclopaedia* joined in the abuse of anything resembling innate ideas or "arbitrary hypotheses" and promoted Bacon as perhaps the "greatest, the most universal, and the most eloquent of the philosophers," even though he was born "in the depths of the most profound night."[15] Newton too was applauded for the restraints he had placed on the claims Descartes had made for philosophy (p. 81). But Descartes also has a place in the pantheon, and in a clearly political role:

He can be thought of as a leader of conspirators who, before anyone else, had the courage to arise against a despotic and arbitrary power and who, in preparing a resounding revolution, laid the foundations of a more just and happier government, which he himself was not able to see established. If he concluded by believing he could explain everything, he at least began by doubting everything, and the arms which we use to combat him belong to him no less because we turn them against him. (p. 80)

Descartes, of course, was a Frenchman, and even the spirit of Enlightenment internationalism does not preclude d'Alembert's giving way to a touch of patriotism, as when he seeks to show that "England is indebted to us for the origins of that philosophy which we have since received back from her" (p. 85). And, despite the homage to Bacon and Newton, d'Alembert's argument takes a notably un-English direction in its important distinction between the "systematic spirit" and the "spirit of system" or "taste for system" (pp. 94–96). Only the second of these is improper in scientific and philosophic method, as it entails a metaphysical faith in a priori principles. The true "systematic spirit" is a quite proper procedural faculty consisting of "the art of reducing, as much as that may be possible, a large number of phenomena to a single one that may be regarded as their principle" (p. 22). This has nothing to do with "arbitrary hypothesis" but is the true "spirit of method" and includes, as well as observation alone, the application of mathematical analysis to experimental data (p. 25). D'Alembert here shows himself to be neither a pure Baconian nor an extreme rationalist, but something between the two. Unlike Ramus, he believed that the search for knowledge presented us with real difficulties, involving us in disconnected inquiries tending to run parallel rather than in series (p. 47). With Ramus, he promoted the utility of the encyclopedic tree as a way of presenting the whole "in the smallest area possible," thus affording the philosopher a "vantage point, so to speak, high above this vast labyrinth, whence he can perceive the principal sciences and the arts simultaneously" (p. 47).

While it *is* the philosopher, and not the common man, who can perceive this wholeness of field, the exclusionary rhetoric of the *Encyclopaedia* is much less evident than that of Sprat's *History of the Royal Society,* not least because d'Alembert gives so much more credit to the possibility for simplification. Axioms and mathematical theorems are both reducible to a "rather small number of primary truths" (p. 28), and the process of reduction is imaginable to the point where "the universe . . . would only be one fact and one great truth for whoever knew how to embrace it from a single point of view" (p. 29). This absolutist simplification is quite at odds with the doggedly mixed economy of the Baconian tradition, and it is accompanied by a definite extension of the franchise: there is no art or science "whose propositions or rules cannot be reduced to some simple notions and arranged in such a close order that their chain of connection will nowhere be interrupted," and that cannot then be taught "to the most limited mind" (p. 31). The difference between d'Alembert and Bacon comes clear in their respective models of the encyclopedic tree. Bacon followed a historical scheme, in which imagination precedes reason. D'Alembert inverted this sequence by following the "metaphysical order of the operations of the mind" (p. 76). We can here see him restoring a Ramist as well as a Cartesian priority in his demonstrated respect for the rational essence of the unmodified human mind—a mind that for Bacon was inevitably mired in confusion and false seeing.

The great *Encyclopédie* itself has been reasonably viewed as expounding a mixture of Baconian method and liberal ideology, rather than being a rationalist manifesto.[16] But it did much more than the historian of the Royal Society had done in admitting an artisan class to the ranks of respectable intellectuals, and in providing a format in which received knowledge would be readily and easily accessible. In his own article on encyclopedias, Diderot himself specified the method of the edition as comparable to a set of geometrical theorems; as the geometer applies one problem or theorem to another, so the reader of the *Encyclopédie* can move between one article and another, and it makes no difference whether the subject be algebra or theology, since connections and continuities are at all times clearly observed.[17]

There are elements in Diderot's writings that seem passionately antimathematical, elements that rendered him the mentor of Jacobin

nature-worship and the enemy of Enlightenment reason. But the encyclopedic enterprise retains a clear affiliation with a Ramist-Cartesian
tradition, a tradition arguably critical in the formation of the encyclopedic ambition itself.[18] The article on "logic" endorses the increasingly mainstream eighteenth-century discrediting of a discipline now
associated with "dry and pointless subtleties" and "barbarous terms and
phrases" (9:637). But the respect for method in its Cartesian format re-
iterates the original Ramist priorities. Descartes is the "true restorer of
reasoning" (9:638); and the article on "method" (10:445–60), even as it
displaces any reliance on the syllogism, still looks to "the means of arriv-
ing at an end by the most convenient route" (10:446), now mathematical. (Diderot is alluding to the etymology of *method* as "path" or "route".)
When the great work of Diderot and d'Alembert was recycled and
redesigned for the next generation, under the direction of Panckoucke,
it was as the *Encyclopédie méthodique,* with an even more systematic format than the original alphabetic one.[19]

The same ambiguity about the rationalist heritage (and the even
more residual Ramist tradition) as is found in the *Encyclopédie* can be
traced in the work of the other philosophes. Here too there is a widespread acceptance of the letter and even the spirit of the "English" way
of doing things, instanced in the figures of Bacon and Newton, as well
as a commitment to the virtues of the "French" approach founded in
rational system and theory. La Mettrie, one of the most consistent of the
early Enlightenment materialists, proposed that "experience" speaks
"in behalf of reason" rather than against it, so that the two may be prof-
itably "combined."[20] Helvétius, after whom Paris named a street in
1792, had good words for Bacon but endorsed Hobbes much more ex-
tensively in his claim that pain, pleasure, and love of power accounted
for all human behavior, and in his explicit refutation of Shaftesbury's
principle of disinterest.[21] With the Baconians, Helvétius claims to as-
cend from "facts" to "causes" by a process of "experiment"; but he applies the model to ethics, which strict Baconians would not have
accepted as an appropriate use of the methods of the natural sciences.[22]

But Helvétius was no unreconstructed rationalist. A materialist nec-
essitarian, he supposed that humanity must inevitably take on "an in-
finity of different forms" because no two persons could ever share an
identical composition of experience and predisposition. He further
recognized the deviations and compositions resulting from the existence of "several classes" in society.[23] At the same time, he did prepare
the ground for a rational calculus of the passions, whose operations he
believed to govern all human action and whose principles he saw to be
"as certain as those of geometry." Disagreement is the result of differ-

ences of interests; geometrical propositions only achieve consensus because in these cases men have "no interest in taking the false for the
true." Custom and interest diversify the operations of reason, but they
are there nonetheless, and therefore open to a gradual implementation
under favorable conditions. This analysis led Helvétius to endorse enlightened despotism as the best opportunity for bringing power and
reason into line: if a monarch be truly enlightened, then his possession
of absolute power becomes a convenience. Absolutism, however, is only
the conclusion of this method, which, like Hobbes's, leaves itself open to
other applications and redirections. Helvétius's commitment to the
principles of morality and public good as geometrically "rigorous" in
their demonstration, and to the idea that "every truth is essentially com-
prehensible to every mind," identifies him as a Painite in the making.
His model of "method" is, moreover, recognizably Ramist-Cartesian in
its respect for abbreviation and speediness of execution, allowing us to
exert the "least effort of attention" and thus to suffer a "less painful sensation, by studying in that order, then any other."[24]

The other great Enlightenment Hobbesian, Holbach, was neither a
rationalist nor a populist. He saw the world as an ever-varying composition of matter in motion, and never intended his atheist philosophy to
be "for the vulgar," who are too much under the influence of custom
and superstition ever to apprehend its truth. So little is man aware of
the forces that move him that he is merely passive in relation to them.[25]
But Holbach's case against a democracy of reason only served to impli-
cate him in another negative mythology of Frenchness—that of libertine materialism. Meanwhile, there were enough methodically minded
French theorists to keep any commonsense Englishman happy in his
insular self-esteem. Bacon was commonly the declared patron of their
researches, but the rationalist paradigm reappeared nonetheless.

Condillac, for example, began by declaring himself against any worship of systematized political establishments: "If there is one genre
where one should provide against systems, it is politics." A pattern
derived from one phase of political history cannot account for its evolution into others. This conviction leads Condillac into a Montesquieu-
like recognition of special circumstances: "To design a system in such a
case, we should not search our imaginations for the most perfect government. . . . We must study the character of a people, inquire into its
habits and customs, isolate its abuses." This preference for "cir-
cumspection" over rationalist fiat made Condillac even more popular
with the French legislature after Thermidor than before.[26] This is the
Condillac who argued against Cartesian innate ideas, against the

"mania for defining" the human sciences after the model of the geome-
ters, and in favor of moving from parts to wholes, by procedures of
"analysis" and induction rather than by "definitions, axioms, and principles."[27]

But Condillac's Baconian rhetoric is directed toward the production
of a proper system rather than against the entire systematic ambition.
While obedience to "general and abstract maxims" should govern only
the disposition of our thoughts, where they are appropriate, without
leading us into "the mania for systems," it remains the case that the
proper conduct of the inductive method will produce an ordered set of
principles—in fact, a system.[28] For Condillac, something that looks like
empiricism—an observance of the priority of sensations—produces
something that looks like rationalism, an ordered account of human
knowledge and its progressive potential. Condillac's sensationalism is
unmarked by the Baconian insistence on the necessity of the corrective
functions of experiment, and experiment controlled by the fit and the
few, by the same "disinterested" minority that was privileged in Sprat's
History. Here there are no idols of the mind. The order of analysis
is exactly the "order of the generation of ideas," and it is a natural
order, one that reflects the sequence of our instinctual needs and
is as coherent as any imaginable form of things in themselves. This
coherence allows for Condillac's reinvention of the Ramist single
method:

It must be remembered that this method is unique, and that it must be absolutely the same in all our studies: for to study different sciences is not to change
the method, it is merely to apply the same method to different objects.[29]

He also restates the Ramist admiration for simplicity. Every system is
made up of various principles, but "the system is the more perfect the
fewer of them there are: it is even to be hoped that they could be reduced to one only."[30] And, again like the Ramists, Condillac is explicit
in his democratization of right reason. The capacity for "analysis" is not
restricted to a philosophical elite but is a process "known to everyone."
Indeed, there are "people with accurate minds who do not seem to
have studied anything," and it is principally the "learned" who have
trouble admitting what everyone else knows and performs instinctively.
Condillac makes his appeal to and on behalf of the ordinary reader in
terms that, however opportunistic, carry with them the charge of two
hundred years of radical methodicality:

And so I write only for those who are unlearned. Since they do not speak the
language of any science, it will be easier for them to learn mine: it is more within

their reach than any other language because I have learned it from nature, which will speak to them as it does to me.[31]

For Thomas Sprat and so many of his countrymen, it is only the subculture of liberal-minded gentlemen that can free itself from the restrictions of particular occupations and of the language of a specialized "science." For Condillac, this ideal is open to the commoner.

By 1795 Condillac's *Logic* had become a standard text in France.[32] Its displacing of geometry was accomplished only to make way for an algebraic-linguistic paradigm for the correct ordering of ideas. From this position, Condillac specifically criticized the concept of "second nature" on which Burke would place so much emphasis as a "deformed and corrupted nature" maintained only by "superstition, by governments, and by bad philosophy."[33] ("Second nature" presupposes that only a society heavily worked upon by culture can afford a civilized existence.) Radical method no longer comes brandishing the syllogism, but it is perhaps all the more radical for that very fact.

In the figure of Condorcet, more directly involved than any of the philosophes in political legislation after 1789, even the nominal concession to Baconian priorities has disappeared. Condorcet authored the (unsuccessful) Girondin constitution, and in 1795, after he himself had died in prison under the Jacobins, his *Sketch for a Historical Picture of the Progress of the Human Mind* was approved for national distribution by the Committee of Public Instruction, which had three thousand copies printed for the purpose.[34] Condorcet found even the American constitution insufficiently simplified, because of its commitment to ideas about "identity of interests" rather than to "equality of rights." He wanted France to generate a politics that would be "purer, more precise, and more profound" than this, and one beyond "every kind of prejudice." And he believed, and announced, "that the perfectibility of man is truly indefinite."[35] Progress in politics is explicitly a consequence of progress in "philosophy and metaphysics," much of the credit for which he gave Descartes, who "brought philosophy back to reason" and "gave men's minds that general impetus which is the first principle of a revolution in the destinies of the human race," and one tending toward "complete and pure social liberty." The way, again, must be the way of method, as Condorcet made clear in his 1782 speech to the French Academy:

The method of discovering truths has been reduced to an art, one could almost say to a set of formulae. Reason has finally recognized the route that it must follow and seized the thread that will prevent it from going astray. These first truths, these methods spread through all nations and carried into two worlds, can no longer perish.[36]

Method renders the "social art" a "true science," so that society has a "real duty" to promote that very "discovery of speculative truths" of which the British establishment was so suspicious. These "simple truths and infallible methods" must accelerate the progress of the species, because they are progressive and international. Admiring at least the "small number of maxims" of the American constitution, in contrast to the unwieldy complexities and contingencies recommended by Montesquieu, Condorcet, like Condillac, dreamed of a single method, a fundamental unity holding together all the sciences.[37] He argued against Montesquieu and against the suitability of the English "double principle" (king and parliament) for France, which requires "unity of principle" and "one single principle of decision."[38] He criticized the twenty-ninth book of De l'esprit des lois in precisely the terms that the British radicals would criticize Burke: "No analysis, no discussion, never a single precise principle; always one or two examples which most often prove only one thing, that there is nothing there so common as bad laws."[39] Against Montesquieu's elaborate case for a recognition of cultural relativism, Condorcet held to the conviction that "a good law must be good for all men, just as a true proposition is true for all" (p. 420). The only losers by such a simplification of political practice will be the lawgivers themselves, who "would lose the advantage of exclusive knowledge of its forms" (p. 422). Condorcet did not propose a constitution fixed for all time but one subject to "reform at fixed intervals" to allow for changing circumstances.[40] The principles governing these reforms would, however, be consistent and progressive.

This, then, is the figure whom Burke saw, in 1791, as "the most furious of the extravagant republicans," the "fanatic atheist and furious democratic republican," the bigot who "would be ready to plunge the poniard in the heart of his pupil, or to whet the axe for his neck."[41] To most historians of ideas, he is, more modestly, the philosophical mentor of the Girondins. He shared the traditional radical faith in the power of print as the means of disseminating correct method.[42] He believed in the usefulness of schematic charts to enable the less educated to master much material in a little time.[43] He was also, along with d'Alembert, the principal exponent of the mathematical method against which Burke took such an explicit stand. Algebra, for Condorcet, contained within it "the principles of a universal instrument, applicable to all combinations of ideas."[44] His own applications of mathematics to the social sciences were probabilistic rather than definitive; he accepted the impossibility of absolute certainty. But they were mathematical nonetheless, and aimed at the rational control of social behavior. And, of course, they were French.

System and Sensibility: Rousseau

We have seen that there was considerable support for the British image of French philosophy among the philosophes themselves. Even self-declared Baconians like Condillac produced models governed by the Cartesian and Ramist emphasis on clear and distinct ideas and a single method, often with a visibly mathematical foundation. With Condorcet there is hardly even lip service to the sacred cows of English methodology, Bacon and Newton. Newton's mathematical genius is indeed applauded, but there is little interest in the establishment hero of the antihypothetical method. The French philosophers were confident enough in the powers of metaphysically derived models for social and political behavior that Bonaparte could opine, with some prospect of being taken seriously, that "it is to the metaphysicians that we owe all our troubles."[45] Many conservatives in both France and Britain came to the same conclusion.

Paradoxically, in the light of this negative mythology of method, it was the Jacobin revolt *against* rational system that accompanied and sponsored the most violent phase of the Revolution in 1792 and 1793. The philosophic mentor was no longer Condorcet, who was indeed imprisoned, but Rousseau, invoked as the apologist not of rational perfectibility but of natural virtue and spontaneous emotionalism. The British nationalist presses were thus given a perfect opportunity to diversify their critique of all things French by appealing to another side of the traditional mythology. France transferred its national imagination from an excessive worship of reason to an equally excessive celebration of sensibility, and heads rolled to seal the transition. The middle ground of common sense and gradual evolution was imaged as unavailable to the French; when they were not carrying out the directives of a cold and calculating reason, they collapsed into behaving as sentimentalists, rakes, and libertines, exponents of the "Gallic frenzy" that T. J. Mathias saw as taking possession of "our *unsexed* female writers" by a momentum that was at once sexual and political.[46] The two extremes of the French national character, as imagined by the British, were easily conflated: everything became a consequence of "philosophy" or "theory" or "metaphysics." Thelwall made little headway with his intrinsically cogent argument that, far from being the incarnation of the evils of philosophy, Robespierre and his kind were incapable of "vision-ary subtilties and metaphysical abstraction," effectively legislating a sit-uation wherein "philosophy was silenced, science was proscribed, and daring speculation soared no more."[47] French philosophy, in the eyes of its antagonists, was an emanation of the French national character and thus unable to negotiate a place of rest between the two extremes of mathematical abstraction and chaotic emotionalism. Of this second ex-treme, Rousseau was the type and incarnation.

Much has been written on Rousseau's role in the French Revolution, and on the apparent oddity of *The Social Contract*'s remaining almost unread for years after its first publication, only to be rediscovered in 1790 and 1791. Joan McDonald has argued that Rousseau even had a career as a counterrevolutionary hero before he was embraced by the governing party, suggesting that "it is possible to find at every stage in the Revolution individuals in practically every faction who appealed to Rousseau's authority, and who were familiar with and admired his works."[48] Perhaps it is indeed unwise to imagine a "single" Rousseau available only in support of a simple set of narrowly defined doctrines. Mallet du Pan himself located the danger of Rousseau's writings as much in their popularity as in their actual contents. Voltaire had made no effort to reach the common people and was an avowed monarchist; Diderot, d'Alembert, and Condorcet, for Mallet du Pan the most intel-lectually disruptive writers of all, were similarly obscure. But Rousseau was read widely, having "a hundred times more readers than Voltaire in the middle and lower ranks of society."[49] It was Rousseau who pub-lished the doctrine of the sovereignty of the people and provided, in *The Social Contract*, the "*Koran*" (p. 363) of all the various factions reg-nant from 1789 through 1791:

In 1788 I heard Marat read and interpret the *Contrat social* in the public high-ways, to the applause of an enthusiastic audience. I could scarcely cite a single revolutionary who was not carried away by these enthusiastic theorems, and who did not burn with desire to put them into practice. (P. 362)

True or not, this was the view that became increasingly commonplace among the conservatives of the late 1790s.

Rousseau's "general will" was and still is a difficult concept. Rousseau accepts the position associated above all with Montesquieu, that there is no single form of government that would be best for all peoples. Nor is his model "democratical"—for democracy would be a system imagin-able only for "a nation of Gods."[50] The relation between individual in-terest and general will is problematic enough for Cassirer to read it as an analogue of the Kantian categorical imperative, as a universality dis-

covered when the individual suppresses particular interest and creates
a relation between single and general will, while some of Rousseau's
statements suggest that the general will is best described as an empirical
aggregate of the differences between the expressed interests of individuals, factions, and "partial associations," albeit most accurately recorded when such associations are either absent (the utopian extreme)
or multiplied to the extent necessary for them to balance each other
out.[51] Both individualist, conscience-based and quantitative (utilitarian) models may thus apparently be argued out from the evidence of
The Social Contract, and they indeed come together to some degree in
the emphasis on freedom as consisting in the willed acceptance of constraint. However the balance is tipped, it is always clear that Rousseau is
no man of method, in the accepted rationalist sense. He declares that
"geometrical precision is not to be expected in treating of moral quan-
tities," and he scorns Descartes for having believed that he had "constructed an universe with cubes and vortices." Human reason is not "a
common determinate standard," for it is always modified by different
circumstances and applied to different ends.[52] No more is Rousseau an
atheist, though his "natural religion" is radical enough in its emphasis
on intuitive faith, its attack on sectarian intolerance, and its awareness
of the tensions that Christianity specifically has introduced into the
functioning of the state.[53]

We might say, then, that Rousseau was against theory, and that this
accounted for his appeal to those Jacobins engaged in the discrediting
of their rationalist precursors. His expository style, as professed, is almost Burkean. In the *Reveries of the Solitary Walker,* he offers "a record of
my readings without trying to reduce them to a system," proposing to
"give free rein to my thoughts and let my ideas follow their natural
cause, unrestricted and unconfined." So little of typicality does Rousseau assume for himself that he introduces the *Confessions* with the supposition that he is "like no one in the whole world."[54] And nothing
beyond the unpredictable sequences of sensibility offers a basis for consensus. The young Émile has "little power of generalisation and "no
skill in abstraction," and, in contrast to the traditional Enlightenment
commitment to the pursuit of exact knowledge, the Kantian *sapere aude,*
the Savoyard priest advises his pupil to "learn how to be ignorant."[55] In
the third volume of *La nouvelle Héloïse* Julie judged St. Preux's moral
improvement exactly in terms of his progress beyond faith in "theories":

I find also that experience has cured him of that dogmatical and peremptory air
which men are apt to contract in their closets; . . . he is less ready to establish
general propositions. . . . In general, the love of truth has banished the spirit of

system: so that he is become less brilliant, but more rational . . . now he does not affect to be so wise.[56]

The Rousseauvian vices, in the eyes of his many critics, were sexual frankness, freely confessed erotic and moral instability, and self-obsession. His declaration that no human heart, "however pure," could fail to conceal some "odious vice" was coupled with a defiant subjectivism about the nature of truth in fiction and confession as "based more on feelings of integrity and justice than on factual reality," and least of all on "abstract notions of truth and falsehood."[57] The power of his depiction of the passions was so great that his parable of passion conquered, *La nouvelle Héloise,* was more famous for its scenes of virtue at risk than for its message of virtue triumphant. Hannah More, in her *Strictures on the Modern System of Female Education,* found this novel typical of the threats posed by novels in general: its "pernicious subtlety" first "annihilates the value of chastity" and then presents the heroine as "almost more amicable without it." The "engaging virtues" of the criminal prevent us feeling any horror at the crime. Wollstonecraft's *The Wrongs of Woman* describes Maria's "restless rotations of thought" as taking on further intensity from her regular readings of Rousseau's novel. And Mary Hays's Emma Courtney finds in that same volume, savored and then forbidden, a "pleasure" approaching the "limits of pain," a "tumult," and an irresistible awakening of "the ardour of my character."[58]

When Richard Price, in the 1789 tract that provided the occasion for Burke's *Reflections,* dissociated himself from the idea of "rakes and atheists" in office, it was probably the materialist philosophers he had in mind.[59] But, especially after the publication of the second volume of the *Confessions* in that same year, Rousseau came more and more to stand out as the very incarnation of libertinism. Although the letter of his texts was highly critical of the passions, and of the consequences of allowing them space to develop, their spirit was such as to make it easy for them to be received as instances of the very problem they claimed to redress. Priestley denounced him as a sexual profligate and a bad father, and indeed the story of Rousseau's abandoned children (true or not) became a leitmotif of the 1790s and thereafter.[60] Burke, who had had little to say about Rousseau in the *Reflections* of 1790, identified him in 1791 as "the great professor and founder of *the philosophy of vanity*" and as the patron of both the "mischief of the day" and the "debauches of the night." Burke's polemical genius picked out Rousseau as the apologist of both "metaphysical speculation" and "the coarsest sensuality," and thus the author of "a ferocious medley of pedantry and lewdness." The unnatural father unable to cherish the "spawn of his disgustful amours" could pretend benevolence only toward those to whom he was not related: "benevolence to the whole species, and want of feeling for every individual."[61]

Burke's targeting of Rousseau, just one year after the *Reflections,* was presumably as much the result of the publication of the notorious second volume of the *Confessions* (1789, translated into English in 1790) as of the course of French politics. Edward Duffy, among others, has argued that Rousseau's British reputation was in the 1790s a central motif in the general discrediting of sensibility as provocative of both political violence and sexual license.[62] There were some loyal Rousseauvians, like Capel Lofft and Brooke Boothby, but the radical rationalists, like David Williams, took issue with his failure to recommend a single and "permanent Constitution."[63] The cult of sincerity and moral self-improvement was too emotionalist for the Painite radicals and too improprietous for the dissenting Christians. The conservative press followed Burke in pronouncing Rousseau both personally immoral and politically misguided; the *Anti-Jacobin* specified him as appealing only to those who mistook "*impressions* on their hearts" for "the *conviction* of their heads," and who were thus prone to a confusion quite at odds with "the solid, strong understanding, the power, and habits of cool and profound investigation which distinguish the British philosophers."[64]

Rousseau himself was, of course, no Frenchman but a citizen of Geneva. And he stood for that side of the French character that was increasingly identified with the German: sensibility and sexual freedom. The image of Germany will be the subject of the next chapter. Let me end this one with a brief review of the debate about the relation between the violence of the Revolution and the role of the philosophers. Did philosophy "cause" the French Revolution? And did theoretical reflection impel it toward a bloody and violent evolution? Many commentators, on both sides of the political fence, answered yes to these questions, notwithstanding the efforts of Thelwall and others like him to discriminate between the doings of Robespierre and anything that could be called philosophical. Sieyès himself had expressed the hope, after all, in 1789, that the forthcoming legislation would be "the work of a philosopher," and many were content to assume that it was.[65] Some of the radicals tried to explain political violence as the inevitable legacy of the injustices of the old regime, rather than the result of the deliberate policies of the new one. But this became more and more difficult to argue as the national interest was seen more and more to conflict with that of the French in general, whose characteristic volatility (from tyranny to anarchy and back again, as it were) was increasingly seen to con-

sist in extremes themselves, rather than in any single attribute. Voltaire
and Rousseau, after all, had both gone into the Panthéon, signaling the
French tolerance of both aristocratic skepticism and bourgeois emotionalism; and these two figures were commonly and comfortably identified in the British imagination as symptoms of what was wrong with
France.[66]

In the early 1790s both radicals and reactionaries were enthusiastic
in emphasizing the power of written ideas in bringing about significant
historical change. Paine famously invoked a grammatological analogy
in specifying the American constitutions as doing for liberty what
grammar does to language: "They define its parts of speech, and practically construct them into syntax."[67] He applauded the intellectuals for
their efforts in the cause of liberty. From the other side of the fence,
Burke warned of the dangers of "the political Men of Letters" who were
working with "great method and perseverance," along with the new
"monied interest," to corrupt public opinion.[68] Subsequent historians
have gone back and forth on the question of the power of ideas in the
bringing about of the Revolution. Early endorsements of the influence
of philosophy have given way to a series of mid-twentieth-century explanations favoring social and material causes.[69] The most recent phase
of historical attention has tended to stress discourse—a Foucauldian
fusion of ideas-in-practice and ideas-as-practice—as the effective component in representation and, implicitly, in causation.[70] The very problems and ambiguities of this approach, when handled critically, seem
calculated to preserve, at least for a while, the question of causation by
ideas as an open question, and one requiring rather detailed elabora-
tion, both theoretically and empirically, as we explain such conjunctions as that whereby the aristocratic and monarchist Voltaire could be
embraced by the most populist of the radicals, le Père Duchêsne
(Hébert), as the first to attack the "monstruous edifice" of the establishment.[71]

A study of the half century or so after 1789 suggests, not surprisingly, that the responsibility of philosophy, or theory, for violent
political events was most passionately invoked when some immediate
polemical capital could be gained thereby. The association became especially common in the two or three years after 1799, in relation to the
Irish question, but by 1814 even the *Quarterly Review* minimized its importance. As early as 1807, by which time the national consensus was
solidly patriotic and anti-French, none other than the *Anti-Jacobin* felt
able to review d'Alembert's works and to find in the *Encyclopaedia* that
the "Frenchman is no more. We find the solid sense of the Englishman."[72] But the connection between theory and political disaster could

always be resurrected, as it has been so often in the twentieth-century academy and beyond. Coleridge, who had of course a professional interest in endorsing even a negative model of the power of ideas, argued that "the rise and fall of metaphysical systems" has coincided with the great events in world history, so that these events are directly related to what happens "in the closets or lonely walks of uninterested theorists."[73] Theories, for him, become both more appealing and more dangerous when the times are critical, so that in 1789 even the "remotest villages" could be heard echoing "the almost geometric abstractions of the physiocratic politicians and economists" (p. 16); thus:

It is with nations as with individuals. In tranquil moods and peaceable times we are quite *practical*. Facts only and cool common sense are then in fashion. But let the winds of passion swell, and straitway men begin to generalize; to connect by remotest analogies; to express the most universal positions of reason in the most glowing figures of fancy; in short, to feel particular truths and mere facts, as poor, cold, narrow, and incommensurate with their feelings. (P. 15)

What the French have done, the British might also do, unless they are able to preserve the common sense that has so far remained the major element in their national character.

The association of France with excessive faith in theory along with an excess of sensibility thus became a fixed idea in the British national imagination, as indeed it still is. On-the-spot observers like Mary Wollstonecraft and Helen Maria Williams did their best to disambiguate the various phases of French politics after 1789 and tried to encourage attention to more complex transitions than could be described by attributions of mere Frenchness. Mackintosh, in the same spirit, criticized Burke for his vague use of the term "revolution," identifying at least three moments that might deserve the name, none of them associated with public violence.[74] But such attempts at scrupulous definition were predictably lost in the general outpouring of statements for and against Burke, for and against theory and method, for and against privilege and democracy. It was relatively unapparent, or unpublicized, that the events of 1789 did not totally transform the social order.[75] The rhetoric, of course, suggested otherwise; and what the historians have rather condescendingly called a merely bourgeois revolution did touch on political possibilities that were quite definitely radical. Sieyès's definition of the "third estate," for example, included everyone outside the nobility and clergy; but precisely by not distinguishing between the bourgeoisie and the working class he created a space for contestation and interpretation, and thus for the articulation of rights the legislators themselves never clearly intended to recognize (for instance, those of women and the lower orders). Similarly the French constitution of September 1791, however limited its actual or intended effects, proposed to abolish "nobility, peerage, hereditary distinctions," the "feudal regime," and everything based on "distinctions of birth."[76] If "no individual" had any rights beyond those of other individuals, then political rights could be argued to extend to all people, even if the legislature intended a restricted electorate, as indeed it did.

If there was no simple causal sequence connecting the ideas of the philosophes with the events of the Revolution, then it is equally clear that there was no absolute disconnection. Even ·· l ·n the available theories were exploited by the ruling interests for short-term advantages, they remained open for debate and reinterpretation in ways that threatened those interests. But this process of contestation was less vigorous outside France, especially for those Britons who were used to acquiescing in the terms of the myths of national characters. These myths have remained as critical components in the constitution of our subsequent political languages. In 1919, in the aftermath of another terrible international crisis, Irving Babbitt felt the need to take issue with the "Rousseauistic philosophy of life" and its "naturalisms."[77] Many less significant crises in the Anglo-American self-image have subsequently resorted to the same rhetoric.

4

THE IMAGE OF GERMANY

Conspirators and Freemasons

As a rhetoric of compromise and judicious mediation, the paradigm of British common sense required both a Scylla and a Charybdis between which it could inscribe its own way of modest moderation. As we have seen, one extreme was imaged as "French theory," which Arthur Young so detested, and the other was associated first with Rousseau, the citizen of Geneva, and then increasingly with the German national character as evidenced in its literature, drama, and philosophy. This particular mythologizing of late eighteenth-century "Germany" (and there was of course no such national entity at the time) will perhaps be surprising to modern anglophone readers who have been accustomed to a different though equally parodic image of the German as an efficient, rule-governed, and indeed methodical personality. Kant was among the first to publicize these traits. He granted the Germans a cosmopolitan adaptability (and this alone would render them suspicious in the eyes of those countries aggressively modeling themselves as "nations") but pronounced them also obedient and conservative, so that "in keeping with their penchant for order and rule, they will rather submit to despotism than venture on innovations." They evince "a certain mania for method" and a consequent inclination to uphold a detailed social taxonomy based on "degrees of precedence and hierarchy." This interest in tiny degrees of rank and status produces the appearance of "pedantry."[1]

Kant here lays out most of the personality traits of the stage German, as he appears today. But this figure did not achieve general popularity in Britain until the Bismarck years, by which time the German had been conscripted to serve in the role previously assigned to the French, as the blinkered devotee of method and abstract theory. There are hints in the Romantic period of this later image, in alliance with the more common one of excessive sensibility and social instability: the Rousseauvian personality. An account of the image of Germany thus adds an important

to our study of the Romantic composition of the British na-
acter.

end of *Biographia Literaria,* as we have seen in chapter 2,
saw fit to reprint the text of "Satyrane's Letters," describing
journ out of England, in north Germany. The nationalist
1798 is here recycled and obviously felt relevant to the read-
817. Coleridge misses no opportunity to beat the drum for
He trades words with Klopstock over the relative merits of En-
German for translating the Greek, and declares the German
ses" less comfortable and elegant than "an English dust-
mere portrait of Lessing, whom Coleridge has neither read
enough to judge him, on physiognomic grounds, a "man of
voluptuous feelings; of an active but light fancy; acute; yet
observation of actual life, but in the arrangement and man-
f the ideal world": in short, a stage German. Coleridge also
arsh words for the "pantomimic tragedies and weeping com-
otzebue and his imitators" and for a national drama that
"moral and intellectual *Jacobinism* of the most dangerous
he more dangerous because British audiences find it appeal-
cause of its origins in the older English theater.[3]

re pointedly judgmental variations on the German national
as Coleridge defines it in *The Friend:* "cosmopolitanism . . .
sympathy . . . enthusiasm, visionariness." There he specifies
ns as preoccupied with past and future at the expense of the
allows them genius and imagination but also sees mere tal-
cy, the latter exhibited in "wild combinations and in pomp
nt"; and, prophetically, in noting their proclivity for the
intends reference to the inclination to "speculation, system,
Their urge toward "TOTALITY" is evidenced in their "en-
c learning, exhaustion of the subjects treated of, and the pas-
mpletion and the love of the complete."[4] Here are both sides
sh image of the German—the wild, emotional visionary, and
ng man of method. Several years before, in *The Watchman,*
had set forth yet another component of the myth of Ger-
of a culture originating in the warlike, primitive democracy
bed by Tacitus, a culture that defeated the Romans, knew
luxury or decadence, and treated its women as "equals and
as."[5] This notorious sexual and political democracy was to
nservative British critics with numerous opportunities for
ation of late eighteenth-century German culture.

ge presents a complex and compound image of Germany
rman national character: visionary but methodical, imagina-

tive and fanciful, systematic but also wildly emotional, sexually egalitarian and libidinally unembarrassed. All of these elements find their way
into Romantic writing, and they allow for a wide range of comparisons
between the British and German national characters. Germany seemed
to stand for both sides of the French disposition—toward theory *and*
profligacy—at the same time as it incorporated traits that brought it
into closer and perhaps threatening proximity to the ideal of Englishness: genius and imagination (and, for Kant, domestic virtue). For this
reason, among others, the image of Germany was perhaps even more
urgently contested in the late 1790s than was that of France, already
firmly enough established as a negative paradigm.

Indeed, much of the British anxiety about the German character
may be attributed to an imperfect ideological differentiation between
the two countries, of the sort that would inevitably cause problems for a
reductively nationalistic rhetoric. England, after all, had imported a
Hanoverian king in 1714, along with a court that conversed in German
rather than in English. England's was an officially Protestant culture
having both ethnic and linguistic affiliations with the German states. In
his *History of the Royal Society* Sprat had celebrated the Germans as near-
kinsmen, noting

their peculiar dexterity in all sorts of manual Arts, and also in regard of the
plain, and unaffected sincerity of their *manners:* wherein they so much resemble
the *English,* that we seem to have deriv'd from them the composition of our
minds, as well as to have descended from their *Race.*[6]

Reciprocally, many eighteenth-century Germans were diligent wor-
shipers of English culture and the English constitution. Their writers
and critics expounded the superiority of Shakespeare over Racine and
the French tragedy, and of Gothic imagination over neoclassical restraint. Fretting under the pressures of French cultural hegemony,
they looked to England as to a companionate society.

British attitudes to Germany had been, nonetheless, traditionally
uneasy, not least because of the visibility there of the more radical Protestant subcultures. Donald Kelley has noted that as early as the 1520s
"Lutheranism" became "a catch-all term for any heresy short of ana-
baptism" and contributed to the reputation of Germany as the source of
all threats to orthodoxy.[7] Ong's account of the dissemination of Ramism, moreover, shows that the vast majority of texts and adaptations of
the *Rhetoric* and the *Dialectic* before 1630 or so were published in German cities: no fewer than twenty-nine cities figure in the list of imprints,
as compared to four in Britain and five in France.[8] It was to Herrnhut,
in Germany, that John Wesley journeyed in search of Zinzendorf and

spiritual guidance, in the spirit of a piety that Byron would come to ridicule as peculiar to the "nations of the moral North," where "all is virtue," not least thanks to the climate.[9] And Wesley too, as we have seen, was tarred with the brush of the "German" national character: methodical and disciplined, enthusiastic and visionary, and sexually licentious.

Radical Protestantism, then, was at best, and for obvious reasons, an uneasy linkage between Germany and England. In the immediate aftermath of 1789 the British press worked hard at vilifying the French, this being a time when the German states were, for the most part, military allies. As late as 1793 the first issue of the *British Critic,* which openly declared itself for the conservative cause, was able to review a goodly number of German books without demonstrating any animus against them on national grounds. The same journal maintained a fairly measured response to German publications for most of the decade, but by 1799 it was taking issue with the "sickly sentiment" of German drama and its "profanation" of the name of God.[10]

The main reason for this new sensitivity was undoubtedly the "Illuminati" controversy, which obsessed the English conservative press in 1798, in the wake of the Irish rebellion. Burke, prophetic as he so often was, had written as early as 1791 of the secret influence of the "*Illuminatenorden* and *Freemasons*" in Saxony, as part of his analysis of the dangerous imminence of a general European revolution. He reported that "a system of French conspiracy" was "gaining ground in every country," with Germany being in a particularly "critical situation," one most likely to produce "a great revolution."[11] But it was only in the last years of the century, at the time of the Irish crisis, that this view became widely marketed and popularly received.

The Illuminati were a small society of rationalists who had gathered around Adam "Spartacus" Weishaupt, a professor at Ingoldstadt. They lasted only about ten years and were dissolved by the Bavarian government in 1785. But they had connections with the freemasons, who were widely thought by all sorts of people to be up to all sorts of mischief: not for nothing did Mary Shelley describe Victor Frankenstein as learning his science at Ingoldstadt. Recent historians have generally discounted the idea of the freemasons being responsible for any sustained political organization or conspiracy in eighteenth-century Europe. Diderot, Voltaire, and Helvétius were all masons, but then so was Sir Robert Walpole. Freemasonry was a nationally differentiated rather than an internationalist movement, and in England especially it appears to have been quite conformist.[12] At the same time, it was secret, it was composed of male citizens of various classes (if mostly middles and uppers), and it did have libertine associations. Margaret Jacob has thus argued that freemasonry provided at least a "social nexus" for the discussion and publication of the "radical Enlightenment," even if no deliberate conspiracies were set going.[13] The established interests, after all, could always argue that such conspiracies were in existence.

The most popular exponent of this view was the Abbé Barruel, who had already found favor with the conservatives for his *History of the Clergy during the French Revolution* (1795), a book dedicated "to the English nation" and reciting, in the words of one reviewer, "the bloody triumphs of French philosophers and assassins over a body of virtuous, patient, unresisting fellow-citizens."[14] Two years later, in 1797, his *Memoirs Illustrating the History of Jacobinism* provided the major publicity and the apparent evidence for associating the Illuminati, and thus Germany in general, with an ongoing European conspiracy against established governments. Barruel defined a threefold "conspiracy": first, the "philosophers" attacked religion; then those same philosophers, in alliance with "the Occult Lodges of the Freemasons," attacked monarchy; and then the freemasons "coalesced" with the "Illuminés, who generated the Jacobins."[15] Barruel's rhetoric carries on from Burke's: "In the name of their equality and disorganizing liberty, they trampled under foot the altar and the throne; they stimulated all nations to rebellion, and aimed at plunging them ultimately into the horrors of anarchy" (1:ix). The chief demons among the philosophers were Voltaire, d'Alembert, Diderot, and Frederick II of Prussia, who corresponded with one another in "secret language" (1:37). Condorcet was another "fiend" (1:289). The last two of Barruel's four volumes are largely about the Illuminati, who from the "narrow compass of the town of Ingoldstadt" created first Jacobinism and then an international revolutionary conspiracy (4:1).

In the spirit of Barruel, John Robison's *Proofs of a Conspiracy* (1797) was widely accepted as the confession of a former freemason who knew the lodges of France and Germany. The first edition (Edinburgh, 1797) sold out in a few days. Robison identified the Germans as "in the foremost ranks" of those susceptible to the "gross absurdities" of all sorts of superstitions, including political ones. His special contribution was to play up the rhetoric of sexual revolution. The Illuminati, he argued, proposed to "enlist the women in this shocking warfare," allowing him to recall (so to speak) those women in the French Revolution who "threw away the character of their sex, and bit the amputated limbs of their murdered countrymen."[16]

The enormous success of Barruel's and Robison's books sponsored a whole series of paraphrases, reprints, and analogues. Seth Payson's *Proofs of the Real Existence of Illuminism* opened with the rather winning

confession that there were no "solid proofs" but went ahead anyway
with a tirade against "this theorizing generation" for its attacks on "patriotism and private affections" and on "marriage," attacks he found to
be popular in "the German universities" and now spreading all over
Europe. Payson, like many others, was especially keen to reproduce
Barruel's scurrilous anecdote about Weishaupt's aborting of the child
he had fathered in an incestuous relationship with his sister-in-law.[17]
Thomas Atkinson and William Hamilton Reid also published in the
Barruel tradition, emphasizing the particular threats that the European conspiracy posed to England, most evident in the spread of infidelity among the lower orders. Robert Clifford, Barruel's translator,
published, at 1s.6d, the *Application of Barruel's Memoirs* (1798), focusing
on England and Ireland and again stressing the German connection.[18]
In 1799 Mallet du Pan identified Hamburg as the center of a European
network of revolutionaries, communicating with one another through
the disguises of commercial transactions and newspaper articles. And
he found in the United Societies, originating in Ireland but now spead-
ing into England, "an art, a connected organization, and a refinement
of theory of which the French Jacobins never had need."[19]

Not everyone believed these arguments, of course. The *European
Magazine* impishly found Barruel's case to be "judiciously methodized,"
while the *Analytical Review* saw only the dreams of an "irritated fancy."[20]
The *Anti-Jacobin* of course gave Barruel and his followers plenty of
favorable space, while Mounier attempted a reasoned refutation of the
entire conspiracy-theory industry—an industry that must surely have
contributed to the patriotic vigilance that brought a government spy
to Stowey and Alfoxden to report on Coleridge and Wordsworth.
Mounier tried to turn the tables on du Pan, finding that the philosophers did not produce the Revolution but that the Revolution "produced their influence." But his own belief that the love of liberty was no
"invention of modern times" but "a natural instinct of the human
heart" made him vulnerable to the criticisms the *Anti-Jacobin* was not
slow to register.[21]

Scandal on the Stage

At the turn of the nineteenth century, then, "Germany" was clearly established as the new evil empire in Europe, even more urgently
demonized than France. The French had had their Jacobins, but the
Germans, it seems, had invented and organized them. Perhaps by this
time the French were so thoroughly discredited, thanks largely to the
invasion of Switzerland and the beginnings of Bonapartism, that there

was less need than before to excoriate them at the expense of other imaginary enemies. By 1800 the British national consensus stood fairly solidly against the French. Now it could afford to turn its critique elsewhere, and for other if related reasons.

For Germany was no national-political threat; it was was not even a nation-state, let alone a powerful one. There had been some proto-revolutionary initiatives in the German states, along the lines Burke had predicted, but these alone could hardly have justified the strong anti-German (especially central and south German) sentiments of the conservative press.[22] The most visible contributory cause of this new object of patriotic outrage was the increasing popularity of German literature, and especially of German drama. Even at the height of the British radical movement in the early 1790s there had been little sustained enthusiasm for French literature, against which the British readership had become inured by at least a century of steady propaganda. German literature appeared a more insidiously appealing medium. It was, as Coleridge observed, often based upon English prototypes, and it invoked English aesthetic criteria. If *The Sorrows of Young Werther* and Bürger's ballads were found threatening enough, it was above all in dramatic criticism and in the theater that the campaign against Germany was fought out.

Writing in the *Anti-Jacobin* in 1801, one correspondent proposed that upon "literature" depended "the very salvation of this country," and suggested that salvation was very much in doubt at a time when the theaters were full of "German errors, German inconsistencies, German politics, and German blasphemies."[23] And full indeed they were. Versions of Kotzebue's *Rollas Tod*, usually translated as *Pizarro*, were all over the London stages. One signing himself "A Lover of Variety" complained in 1799 of being "*Pizarroed* out of my memory and recollection, in every company I enter, and every society I frequent,"[24] Samuel Bardsley commented that, "like Aaron's Rod, the Tragedy of Pizarro swallowed up every other Competitor. It not only took sole possession of the Theatre, but also intruded itself into every private Society."[25] Fifteen of Kotzebue's plays were translated into English in 1799 alone, some of them by more than one hand. At least ten of these adaptations were actually performed.[26] Benjamin Thompson's six-volume *The German Theatre* (1801) was dominated by translations of Kotzebue and contained only a few plays by Lessing, Schiller, Goethe, and others.

The rage for Kotzebue had hit the French theaters somewhat earlier, around 1790, and this may well have negatively influenced his reception in England.[27] And who was Kotzebue, this object of so much critical attention? John Britton noted that "it has been his ill-fortune to be considered by the Jacobins as an aristocrat; and, by the aristocrats, as a violent republican." For Britton, and for other enthusiasts, Kotzebue was the voice of "nature" and the exhibitor of "the passions and the feelings of the human heart."[28] Willich, the translator of Kant, described him as a thoroughly Wordsworthian genius:

His knowledge of the human heart and its secret meanders is unquestionably great: he has not only made the prevailing manners, oddities, and vices of the age, but also man himself, as influenced by a variety of ardent passions, the subject of his minutest research.[29]

Willich's rendering of Kotzebue's claim to attention makes clear both the context and the anxiety of Wordsworth's irritation, in the 1800 preface to *Lyrical Ballads*, at the popularity of "sickly and stupid German tragedies." For Wordsworth too proposed to follow "the fluxes and refluxes of the mind when agitated by the great and simple affections of our nature," to render "flesh and blood," and to find a common human identity in the experiences of "low and rustic life."[30] All these claims were made for Kotzebue in the months preceding the publication of Wordsworth's preface, and made so loudly and so often that it is hard not to read that preface as itself a document in the "Kotzebue debate." To examine this debate is to learn much about the appeal Wordsworth was hoping to make, as well as about the accusations he was seeking to avoid.

The most frequent accusation was that of sexual indiscretion. Bardsley complained of Elvira, the heroine of *Pizarro*, that her "departure from the strict rules of female chastity and refined delicacy, is too gross to be palliated by a shew of half-stifled repentence, lofty sentiment, and energy of character."[31] But it was *Lover's Vows*, the play most familiar to English readers by way of the improprietous theatricals in Austen's *Mansfield Park*, that raised the most vigorous objections of this kind. *Lover's Vows* did have some defenders who were not sexual and political radicals. The *British Critic* approved Inchbald's translation, and the *European Magazine* commended its "exquisite sensibility" and "moral and satisfactory object and termination."[32] But these mild affirmations were more than balanced by the negative judgments of the play's sexual and political frankness. The *Anti-Jacobin* had from the first observed a tendency in the German drama "to excite discontent among the lower classes of society, by representing *obscurity* and *virtue, rank* and *vice,* as close and inseparable associates," and Kotzebue in particular was said to have written plays "calculated to encourage immorality and insubordination." Reviewing two different translations of *Lover's Vows* in 1801, the same journal pronounced it "time to put a stop to this

degenerate and polluting species of literature." Although Inchbald had
omitted much of the "offensive matter," what was left was still too
strong for British stomachs.[33] Anna Plumptre, a rival translator, had
already judged Inchbald to have overplayed the role of the heroine,
Amelia, as an independent woman:

The Amelia in LOVER'S VOWS, so far from being the innocent, artless Child of
Nature, drawn by Kotzebue, appears a forward Country Hoyden, who deviates,
in many Instances, from the established Usages of Society, and the Decorums of
her *Sex,* in a Manner wholly unwarranted by the Original. The most amiable
Traits in her Character are distorted and disguised, by a Pertness which greatly
detracts from the Esteem which her benevolent Conduct would inspire.[34]

Inchbald herself had declared Kotzebue's rendering of Amelia's love to
be "indelicately blunt"; and even Plumptre renders the marriage pro-
posal as explicitly made by the woman: Amelia says, simply and directly,
"I love you."[35] In Kotzebue's play, women take the initiative in romantic
relations: no wonder Fanny Price was horrified. Furthermore, the
careers of Agatha and Frederick posited a clear contrast between the
virtuous poor and the corrupted rich. The enlightened aristocrat
Wildenheim wants his daughter to marry only for love, and when she
finds her man it is indeed a social inferior she selects—her tutor, and an
employee of the family. The same frisson arose over this as had arisen
over *La nouvelle Héloise* (and it would be written into Keats's "Isabella");
here again was a woman breaking ranks for love. Inchbald may have
softened Amelia's forwardness, but she did not rewrite the plot, and in
playing up the indirectness of her longings she may well have made the
scene even more titillating.

Kotzebue's political charge was largely carried through his representation of the power of sentiment to dissolve or bypass class boundaries,
rather than in any forthright propositional enunciation of democratic
ideals. But the Jacobins too had been accused of exploiting both reason
and sentiment, so that Kotzebue not unpredictably became the embodiment of Jacobinism in the theater. As late as 1805, by which time much
of the heat had gone out of the debate, the *Anti-Jacobin* picked him out
as the publicist of "that infamous, revolutionary, atheistical and licentious doctrine" so popular in Europe: "Kotzebue, by his simple appeals
to the passions and prejudices of the lower orders, and particularly of
the female sex, has been, we fear, too successful in corrupting their
moral principles."[36] With his reputation as a corrupter of female virtue,
and as an apologist of the virtues of the lowly, Kotzebue became a kind
of theatrical Methodist. What the Wesleyans were doing on the streets,
and the readers of Rousseau in the closets, Kotzebue was doing in the

theater, a place dedicated for several generations to the performance of the titan of the English national literature, Shakespeare. So significant was the dramatic experience felt to be that it was in the process of being "privatized" by a Romantic aesthetics arguing that a properly dramatic effect could only be expected to be produced in the mind of the educated reader, rather than in the unpredictable public space of the commercial theater.[37]

Wordsworth was thus not alone in his fears about the corruption of the public taste by the theater, which he expressed even as he sought to capture for his own poetry some of the popular appeal of Kotzebue and his kind. Rousseau too had feared the stage, and in saying so had reactivated a rhetoric going back to Plato. The dramatic spectacle raised the passions of numbers of people at the same time and in the same place. At best this might be a virtuously consolidating social experience, a display of the principles of social and national unity, as the production of Shakespeare was sometimes meant to be. Schiller's "Essay on the Effects of a Well-Regulated Theatre," translated in the *German Museum* in May 1800, described how the stage at best "opens a spacious field to a mind eager for exertion, affords nourishment to all the faculties of the soul, without overstraining any one of them, and unites the refinement of the understanding and the heart with the most innocent kind of amusement." Schiller also tells us what can go wrong. Partly quoting Sulzer, he gives an opinion that could well have contributed to the preface to *Lyrical Ballads* on which Wordsworth would be working a few months later, as he explains the negative determination of the appeal of the theater:

Being exhausted by a too strenuous exertion of the mental faculties, enfeebled by the sameness and pressure of his professional occupations, and satiated by sensuality, man could not but feel a vacancy in his soul totally repugnant to the unremitting impulse to activity inherent in human nature.[38]

So, he goes to the theater and watches whatever is put before him. The critics of the time complained of the theater in very much the terms we now see associated with watching television. William Preston, one of the most emphatically negative critics of the fashion for German drama, attributed its popularity to the "excessive luxury'" that had eroded civic virtue to "a sort of supercilious apathy, the moral foe of literature and genius," and that could only be gratified by the false productions of the German national character. Commerce and luxury themselves produced social instability, so that for Preston the conditions for "revolution" were already there and could only be exacerbated by a "revolution in taste." The eruption of "*Gothic* barbarism" creates an appetite for a literature "founded on the loves and the heroic acts of beggars and bunters, of thieves and cutpurses, of tailors and seamstresses"; a literature whose "heroes and heroines are bedlamites," and whose aim is "unsettling all our notions of decorum."[39]

These are exactly the terms in which the negative criticism of *Lyrical Ballads,* and especially of its preface, would be phrased, and they suggest that consciously or otherwise Wordsworth's poetic doctrines were clearly allied with the "Kotzebue" faction, even as he sought to tone down the more extreme sexual and political freedoms associated with it and to transfer its energies from the public space of the theater to the private reading of poetry. Perhaps, indeed, Wordsworth's strong claim for the therapeutic urgency of a proper poetic experience can be read as a domesticated alternative to the same potential whose negative instance others had found in the theater, and in far more dangerous ways. Hannah More, among others, identified the German drama as the most powerful contemporary literary medium, inviting "female infidelity" and encouraging its readers and hearers to "the most unbounded gratifications, with all the saturnine coolness of a geometrical calculation."[40] Preston accused the Germans of a lack of method rather than an excess of it in remarking a "wilful or even studied departure from symmetry, consistency, and regularity." At the same time, this very style was associated with "the crude innovations of the new philosophy, the pernicious reveries of the anarchists."[41] Thanks to Methodism, Rousseau, Kotzebue, Sterne, and the philosophy of sentimentality, even the emotional sublime was now seen to have a plot and a purpose—to be, in short, within the orbit of a pernicious "theory."

The Derangements of Theory

The climate of nationalist opinion fostered in Britain by the Illuminati scandals and the debate over the German drama does much to explain why the inordinately complex meditations of the great German philosophers were received as they were. If Germans are constitutionally afflicted with a "wayward sickliness of spirit," so that "what would be with us extravagance, is with them but nature," then even the most restrained and exacting speculations, published in an obscure language that very few Englishmen can read, may be dismissed as the products of deranged imaginations.[42] Even the benign universalist Joseph Priestley had found the German language "but little removed from its ancient barbarity," and the reputation of German writers for spasmodic and disjointed prose only added to this reputation.[43]

The pressure of the nationalist mythology was such that very few

among those who first commented on Kant, for example, were prepared to admit that they might not understand him, or that they might
be judging by inadequate translations. Kant's incomprehensibility was
Kant's own doing, the natural result of being a German. The *Analytical
Review* found in him (by way of Nitsch's adaptation) "an entanglement
of understanding, a defect of penetration, and a confusion of intellect,"
although the very same journal had been, since 1789, translating without comment many more patient German reviews of Kant's work.[44] In
the late 1790s it was fashionable to be anti-German, a fact that makes
Coleridge's and Wordsworth's decision to sojourn there seem almost
courageous. The *British Critic* reacted to Nitsch's volume as a threat to
Christianity and hoped that "the sterling sense of Britons will reject any
such airy theories, and adhere to solid fact, where fact can be ascertained, for the basis of true faith."[45] Willich, another of Kant's "transla-
tors," engaged in a public correspondence with Barruel on the matter
of the philosopher's reputation, drawing forth the following response
from the hero of the royalist establishment:

Though all Germany were to rise in judgment against me, I will unmask its
decrepit *Autocrate,* this self-created authority; and I hope to prove, in spite of his
pretensions to philosophy, that nothing but impiety can have raised the altar,
while wickedness alone can have veiled the ignorance and incapacity of the
newly-created idol.[46]

The *German Museum,* in the same year, tried to point out the inadequacy
of any judgment based on the authority of a mutilated French translation by an anonymous writer, and it observed that the same doctrines
pronounced atheistic in Germany were found by the Dutch to be themselves the best remedy for "the rapid progress of unbelief."[47] Three
years earlier the *Analytical Review* had translated a German review that
explained Kant's politics as those of a reformist republican rather than
a revolutionary, and even the *Anti-Jacobin* admitted to finding them "*tol-
erably*" moderate," albeit marked by "too great confidence in an un-
limited perfectibility of the human mind." But a correspondent in the
same journal found Kant's doctrines "extremely dangerous" as paving
the way for "the sublimest flights of *the newly deified intellect of man.*"[48]

   Casual inspection of the prefaces to the first and second editions of
The Critique of Pure Reason (1781 and 1787) might certainly have provided enough buzzwords and familiar concepts to convey to a con-
servatively minded reader the whiff of radical thought. Gerrard
Winstanley, we may recall, had spoken of a "pure reason" as the authority for his radically remade world, and, even if his texts were not in circulation in the eighteenth century, the ideas he and others like him

expressed had, as we have suggested in chapter 1, a continued existence in the radical tradition.[49] Although Kant insisted that his mediations were never intended for a popular readership, and that they were intended to discourage rather than to support "materialism, fatalism, atheism, free-thinking, fanaticism, and superstition," there were enough elements of the rhetoric of rational method to suggest an affiliation with a radical politics.[50] In some ways the first *Critique* is an exercise in strenuous limitation, showing what cannot be supposed or demonstrated in order to establish firm grounds for what can be—relatively little, in the light of the traditional claims of philosophy. At the same time, Kant's introductory language is the language of achievement and completeness. The disavowal of "illusory knowledge" (*Scheinwissen*) and the celebration of "free and open examination" in the spirit of an "age of criticism" has the ring of Enlightenment radicalism; and the claim to deduce a complete and systematic metaphysics from sources in one's "own self" has the ring of radical Protestantism, equally threatening to the British establishment's preference for a hierarchical church.

Kant's criteria of "*certainty* and *clearness*" surely recall Descartes.[51] In the preface to the second edition Kant further articulated his faith in the necessity of a stringent self-consciousness about the grounds for a metaphysical method: anything less would be "dogmatism." He made even clearer than before his concern with the a priori component of knowledge in language that is rhetorically (if not in all its implications) anti-Baconian. Thus the great scientists have learned

> that reason has insight only into that which it produces after a plan of its own, and that it must not allow itself to be kept, as it were, in nature's leading-strings, but must itself show the way with principles of judgment based upon fixed laws, constraining nature to give answer to questions of reason's own determining.

Instead of trying to have our knowledge follow objects, as Bacon had insisted that we must, Kant proposed that in the realm of metaphysics we would do better to suppose "that objects must conform to our knowledge."[52] He is writing about metaphysics and not about natural science, so that these "objects" are strictly speaking already mental and subjective—not things as they are, but things as they appear or must be thought to be. Nonetheless, the language is clearly antagonistic to the rhetoric of British common sense, justified on simplified Baconian principles. The *Critique* is a "treatise on the method, not a system of the science itself," and there is no assumption of a simple and unmediated Ramist correspondence between mind and world. But something of that tradition survives in Kant's claim for the ubiquity and sufficiency of phenomenal rather than noumenal knowledge in the realm of ordinary experience. It is the phenomenal world of things as they appear to be, and as they are represented, that corresponds with (and is given by) the concepts of the understanding. This absolves Kant of any claim to be offering a rationally complete account of the world as it is in itself. But the claim to completeness of another kind is there as "pure speculative reason" governs the prefigurative conceptual apparatus of the mind: it is not simply able but "bound" to "trace the complete outline of a system of metaphysics." The system is organic in the sense that any incorrect part "must inevitably betray itself in use," so that if the system be once correct, it will also be fixed and unchangeable: "Any attempt to change even the smallest part gives rise to contradictions, not merely in the system, but in human reason in general." With this kind of language Kant is exemplifying what he himself respectfully called the German "spirit of thoroughness" and constructing a method that, even if it does not claim to apply simply to a description of the world, has all the trademarks of rationalist completion and coherence: "orderly establishment of principles, clear determination of concepts, insistence upon strictness of proof, and avoidance of venturesome, non-consecutive steps in our inferences."[53]

Most of those who passed judgment on Kant in the 1790s and early 1800s did not, however, base their opinions on any extensive acquaintance with the original texts. They consulted the reviews, and the early adaptations and epitomes published by Nitsch and Willich in 1796 and 1798 respectively. Nitsch's *General and Introductory View* set out to emphasize Kant's religious orthodoxy, though it did preserve the priority of the moral law in its explanation of the necessity of a rational belief in God. Nitsch also stressed the importance of Kant's claim for a "universally evident" answer to the question of "what is knowable," albeit with the qualification that this did not mean that everyone in the "lower classes of a nation" could or should understand such truths.[54] Willich's *Elements of the Critical Philosophy* was less technical but more ideologically melodramatic in declaring Kant's debt to none other than Adam "Spartacus" Weishaupt. But once again his religious orthodoxy is emphasized, and his commitment to republicanism is distinguished from anything that could be taken for democracy.[55] Perhaps neither of these accounts, taken alone, could have produced the image of a radical Kant or a radical German philosophy. If anything, they underplay the rhetoric of method in Kant's own argument. But, in the context of the reputation of German drama and of the "Illuminati" scandal, they did allow for the association of the Kantian philosophy with all that was threatening to British self-esteem.

Ironically, the adverse reputation of German philosophy at the turn of the nineteenth century was considerably exacerbated by one element in it that had evolved as a reaction against Kant, in Schiller's 1793 essay "On Grace and Dignity." In the second of his major works, the *Critique of Practical Reason*, Kant had proposed an ethics that reserved the name of a moral law only for that which could be pronounced in despite of instinct and self-interest—somewhat akin to Rousseau's model of the social contract, but here more thoroughly restricted to an individual act of conscience quite uncontaminated by any utilitarian purpose. Many of Kant's followers found this to be an uncomfortably disciplinarian and denatured ethics. Responding thus, Schiller looked back beyond Christian culture to the Greeks, who (he argued) never sought to separate out soul and body, will and instinct, as good and bad. Kant, he thought, had made it seem "that the inclination can never be for the moral sense otherwise than a very suspicious companion, and pleasure a dangerous auxiliary for moral determinations." Schiller proposed that moral perfection might be better identified in the accord of duty with pleasure and inclination, in a harmony that is both spiritual and physical. In Kant's model "ascetic and monastic" overtones are too apparent. True moral perfection is to be looked for in the "beautiful soul" (*schöne Seele*), in the person who can abandon himself to inclination or desire (*Trieb*) without "having to fear being led astray by her." Here the "entire character" is moral, through and through; it produces by instinct all that duty can require, and does so unselfconsciously.[56]

Schiller's essay was significant not least for its rearticulation of a tendency in eighteenth-century philosophy that had been popular before Kant and had taken on a new lease of life with the cult of natural virtue associated with Rousseau and thence with his Jacobin "disciples." Hume's *Enquiry Concerning the Principles of Morals* had confessed the difficultly of devising any ethics based merely in "austerity and rigour" and had decided that "humanity and benevolence" must derive from a "direct tendency or instinct" not describable by "any scheme or system." Like Schiller, Hume argued the probability that "*reason* and *sentiment* concur in almost all moral determinations and conclusions."[57] In a more popular and differently weighted formulation, Rousseau defended an ethics decided "by the voice of conscience rather than the light of reason," proposing that "the service of the heart is our first moral duty." Reason may deceive, but "conscience" never does; "it is to the soul what instinct is to the body." Conscience is available for intuitive consultation: "I need only consult myself with regard to what I wish to do; what I feel to be right is right, what I feel to be wrong is wrong."[58]

This instinct for giving the law to oneself is more closely akin to Kant's than Schiller's paradigm, since Rousseau means to distinguish "conscience" from passion, desire, or mere inclination. And even though we may know the superiority of conscience, we do not always obey it, so that we are not always in harmony with ourselves, and thus not "beautiful souls." Such disharmony is wittily described by Rousseau in a passage recording the relation between immediate and recollected experience:

My moral instinct has never deceived me. It has always remained sufficiently pure within me for me to put my trust in it, and if in my conduct it is sometimes swayed by my passions, it has no difficulty in regaining its authority in my recollections. Then it is that I judge myself as severely perhaps as I shall be judged after death by the Supreme Judge.

This is an anxious rather than a beautiful soul, made so by the power of the passions to subvert even the innate sense of what is right and wrong. To follow one's "natural disposition" need not, then, be to do the right thing, when that disposition is formed by desire as well as by conscience. Rousseau suggests that this condition produces acute schizophrenia rather than harmonious balance; duty brings no pleasure, and pleasure itself can turn to "aversion" if it happens to be coincident with duty.[59] Rousseau's life, as he reports or invents it, is exemplary of an immanent tension between duty and desire, a tension resolved neither by Schillerian harmony nor by Kantian repression.

The paradigm of the "beautiful soul" appeared to offer a path to moral self-esteem by way of the experience rather than the repression of pleasure, and it was this that made it at once so popular and so threatening. The reliance on intuitive sentiment seemed to promise a ready and easy way to virtue, a pagan synthesis of things centuries of Christian doctrine had kept apart. It promised a bypassing of the prudent procedures of bourgeois self-discipline that marked so much of the popular and philosophic rhetoric of moral behavior. Werther, the hero of Goethe's extraordinarily popular novel, perfectly expresses the desire for a revolution against the constraints of predictable and accountable behavior: "There is something coldly uniform about the human race. Most of them have to work for the greatest part of their lives in order to live and the little freedom they have left frightens them to such an extent that they will stop at nothing to rid themselves of it."[60] Werther's own "wildly fluctuating" heart knows no such limits. Prudence promises us a safe life, but a dreary one: "Rules and regulations ruin our true appreciation of nature and our powers to express it." In both personality and literary style Werther is the fictional embodiment of the spasmodical sublime, "a whole litany of antitheses" with no patience for those who do things methodically, "step by step," and those who insist that "one sentence follow the next in the same sing-song rhythm."[61]

Rousseau's *La nouvelle Héloise* had raised similar subversive possibilities, only to appear or at least pretend to sublimate them into a mature domestic harmony with eros tamed into affection and class conflict turned to patriarchal idyll. But Werther's war against "rules and regulations" does not evolve into domestic peace. Schiller's "beautiful soul," coming later, may be seen as an attempt to move the pendulum back to the middle, away from the extremes of wild enthusiasm (*Schwärmerei*) and a suspiciously inert quotidian routine. But it was received as recommending merely impulsive behavior. In 1808 Leigh Hunt's *Examiner* deplored the "simple enthusiasts who affect a great deal of what is called German sensibility" and respond only to "pure nature, or what is called *the heart,* that is . . . something abstracted from reason and therefore from common sense." For him this "desperate sensibility" was the behavioral norm of the "madmen of the French Revolution."[62] It appears again, only a little softened, in Austen's characterization of Marianne Dashwood (published in 1811) as a woman whose sorrows and joys "could have no moderation" and who believes, with Rousseau, that "we always know when we are acting wrong" and, with Schiller, that when we do know that we can feel "no pleasure."[63]

By about 1800, then, the image of Germany was sufficiently manifold to include the traditionally French proclivities toward both system and theory and libertine self-indulgence. Both the rationalist idealism (and atheism) of the philosophes and the enthusiastic sensibility and nature-worship associated with Rousseau and the Jacobins were combined in a German national character whose deviations were the more threatening because emanating from a generally Protestant culture. The encyclopedic spirit—"of systematic books there is no lack amongst us Germans," wrote Lessing—went along with a tendency to wild and visionary as well as logical speculation.[64] This was precisely the paradoxical personality of which Burke accused the Jacobins (and most French politicians after 1789), and it was as "Jacobins" that the Barruels and the Robisons characterized the German writers and philosophers. Fichte, in the wake of the notorious *Atheismusstreit* (atheism controversy) that drove him from his professorship, was renominated, aptly enough albeit out of ignorance, as the fearsome "*Furchte,* professor of philosophy, or, rather of *philosophism.*"[65] For the *Anti-Jacobin,* theoretical, political, and sexual liberation came together:

In short, such a scene of corruption as Germany now exhibits, the English mind shudders to contemplate. The young women, even of rank, uncontrolled by that natural diffidence, unchecked by that innate modesty, which at once heighten the allurements of, and serve as a protection to, beauty, but which there have been destroyed by the fatal infusion of philosophical principles, consider the age of puberty as the period of exemption from every social restraint, and sacrifice their virtue to the first candidate for their favour, who has the means either of captivating their fancy, or gratifying their avarice; while the dreadful number of abortions serves to proclaim the frequency and extent of their crimes.

When, in the next issue, this image of female sexual abandon was queried, the editor responded piously that "we have advanced nothing, but from the best authority." Now it was sex as well as systems that threatened English common sense and social life, for "to *immoralize* a Nation is the surest way to *revolutionize* it."[66] Wordsworth and Coleridge, whose *Lyrical Ballads* received a favorable review in this same journal in 1800, were tainted by association with one of their friends (probably Crabb Robinson) who went to Göttingen to become "an adept in the mysteries of philosophism" in order to achieve "the eradication of British *prejudices*."[67] Germany above all had been seduced by the "dashing systems of France" into a "metaphysics, by which the mind is totally bewildered" and the passions simply let loose. German philosophy defended what German drama performed: "immorality and licentiousness, particularly in respect to marriage."[68] As early as 1793 the *European Magazine* had reported on a German analogue of the carmagnole, "the indecent *Allemain* dance" that allowed men to whirl women about "in the most wanton manner" and so violently as to produce a rash of miscarriages.[69]

By 1803 and 1804, with the resumption of the European war against France and Napoleon, the anti-German propaganda died down somewhat, though it was by no means entirely antiquarian when *Mansfield Park,* with its notorious resurrection of the Kotzebue debate, was published in 1814. By 1825, in Hazlitt's *The Spirit of the Age*, Coleridge's German predilections were deemed responsible for obscurity rather than for any incendiary sexual or political imaginings.[70] The opposition to things German increasingly took the form of complaints against confusion and difficulty, not against radical content. In 1816 William Roberts took issue with Coleridge's embracing "the cant and gibberish of the German school . . . profound nonsense, unintelligible refinement, metaphysical morals, and mental distortion."[71] To indulge in German philosophers was still to offend "common sense and common nature," but the charge was now one of obscurity rather than of political treason.

Marilyn Butler has noted that, for "about a decade from 1802, no translations from German were published in England," partly a result of the
continental blockade and the diminished supply of books, but also a
symptom of waning critical interest. She identifies the existence after
1815 of a "post-war right-wing cult of the Germanic" evolving in opposition to a "left-wing cult of the classical" and thus representative of a
near-complete turnaround in the political image of Germany from that
prevalent around 1800.[72]

In *Nightmare Abbey* (1818) Peacock is still able to allude to Werther-
ism, but now largely as an object of ridicule. His satire on German metaphysics stresses its inconclusive inertia rather than any political or
methodological radicalism, as he makes fun of Coleridge in the figure
of Mr. Flosky:

> Now the enthusiasm for abstract truth is an exceedingly fine thing, as long as
> the truth, which is the object of the enthusiasm, is so completely abstract as to be
> out of the reach of the human faculties; and, in that sense, I have myself an
> enthusiasm for truth, but in no other, for the pleasure of metaphysical inves-
> tigation lies in the means, not in the end; and if the end could be found, the
> pleasure of the means would cease. The mind, to be kept in health, must be kept
> in exercise, so that you are perfectly sure of losing your way, and keeping your
> mind in perfect health, by the perpetual exercise of an interminable quest.[73]

Peacock's satirical narrative parodies that Romantic irony whose emphasis is on means over end, process over product, self-conscious reflection over practical engagement. Its emphasis on the self-vindication or
self-creation of values and perceptions may have had radical Protestant
associations and might have registered as some kind of methodological
incarnation of the spirit of 1789, but Peacock here represents it as safely
accommodated to the conservative cause; and Coleridge was indeed
one of the chief agents of the conversion.[74]

Seamus Deane has described Mme de Staël as another such agent,
seeing in her *Germany* (translated in 1813, and one of the first extensive
guides to the affairs of a largely unfamiliar culture) an invocation of the
German idealists as a political alternative to the French materialists.[75]
De Staël did indeed set out to distinguish France and Germany as "two
extremes of the moral chain," the French being mere sensationalists,
the Germans imagining "all impressions as proceeding from preconceived ideas." These preconceived ideas are now quite free from
any Cartesian associations, and indeed from any practical implementation. For de Staël, the Germans are speculative and theoretical precisely
because they are politically without identity and vocationally unful-
filled. Schiller can now be domesticated and received as "the best of

friends, the best of fathers, the best of husbands."[76] Even the dreaded Kotzebue can be partly redeemed: he failed, indeed, to respect "strict virtue," but not out of any "adherence to system." Kant is now interpreted as having sought above all to "raise the human species from its degradation, under the philosophy of materialism," and as having achieved exactly what Schiller thought he had failed in: connecting "the evidence of the heart with that of the understanding," and making "abstract theory" support rather than negate "sentiments at once the most simple and the most powerful." Both duty and beauty become "innate" dispositions, harmonized along with every other faculty in the "one focus" that is the "soul."[77] De Staël does still register the troubling degree to which "love is a religion in Germany," leading to a high divorce rate and a slackening of the female virtues. But otherwise all is organic, intuitive, and harmonious—a popular rendering of what would become the more technically refined Coleridgean image of Germany after *Biographia Literaria*. De Staël too stresses the power of "leading ideas," of "inward conviction and spontaneous feeling," and regrets also that philosophy alone cannot perform the socially and nationally cohering function that belongs to "political and religious institutions" in the formation of "public spirit."[78] But Germany is still a positive model, since the dominance of "religious sentiments" puts it in the vanguard of opposition to those who would "extend the dominion of algebra over the universe."

De Staël's Germany is now the source of idealism and of a depoliticized criticality open to being applied "whatever may be our situation upon earth"; it is the expression of "essential" human attributes, which function in despite of any wordly constraints.[79] In this image of Germany the critical philosophy has been thoroughly made over into a friend to the established order. But the Germans have not quite hit the happy medium. They put too much emphasis on a rigorously self-conscious individuality and thus run the risk of diminishing or disguising the "national interest." They have "not enough of national prejudices"; they are too cosmopolitan and too unappreciative of the benefits of political liberty.[80] The unmentioned ideal is, of course, England—now an England that can accept German philosophy as an ally against the postwar threats of utilitarianism and popular democracy. After Coleridge and de Staël, the ghost of Ramus no longer spoke in German.

5

ENGENDERING METHOD

The Case for Female Reason

Throughout this study so far the subject of sex, for want of a better word, has appeared time and time again in the description of the various establishment reactions to the threats posed by method, system, and theory. Abraham Fraunce's Aristotelian spoke of a logic now "profaned" and "prostitute," "robbed of her honour" and "made common to all."[1] Levellers, Ranters, and Diggers spoke (and were even more often accused of speaking) of equal sexual rights and something resembling free love. John Wesley's "love-feasts" were the subject of similar scandals. French philosophers were imaged as libertines, and German dramatists were accused of putting their filthy theories on the English stage. In the seventeenth century it was "method" and occasionally "reason" that threatened or accompanied a perceived dissolution of the hierarchies of gender; by the end of the eighteenth century it was more often "theory" that was the object of analogous attention among social and political conservatives. The connection between these generally (though not inevitably) democratic initiatives of method and theory and the liberation of women is perhaps not surprising given the generally patriarchal conventions of early modern society. By the Romantic period, motifs of sexual and political liberation were visibly reinforced and perhaps confirmed by a degree of economic liberation: the literary marketplace was more and more recognized as inhibited and even dominated by women writers, who played a major part in establishing the readership for which the Wordsworths and the Coleridges were obliged to compete.[2]

There are both long-term and short-term explanations for the urgency of feminist initiatives in the late eighteenth and early nineteenth centuries. Christopher Hill, for instance, has argued for the culture of Puritanism as most immediately masculinist while maintaining tendencies toward the equality of the sexes, tendencies that may have been further fostered by Methodism.[3] Certainly the Puritan revolution brought forward the question of the rights of women in dramatic and visible ways—in the writings of Ranters and Diggers, and in the explicitly repressive response of the 1650 act punishing adultery by death.[4] In the middle (but still arguably radical) ground, John Milton was arguing for divorce on grounds of incompatibility.[5]

Perhaps in reaction to these and other related tendencies, the institution of science reemphasized its masculine status. In the preface to *The Advancement of Learning* Bacon contrasted James's fecundity with Elizabeth's failure to produce an heir to the throne, and he announced his preference for a style "active and masculine, without digressing or dilating," and for a method marked by "prudence and soundness of direction" and by a "straight and ready way" (though not, of course, that of the Ramists).[6] Cowley's prefatory poem to Sprat's *History of the Royal Society* makes Bacon the hero of modern science and specifies the gendered properties of true philosophy in its very first stanza:

> Philosophy, I say, and call it *He*,
> For whatsoe're the Painters Fancy be,
> It a Male Virtu seems to me.

And Sprat himself sought to give a "good, sound, masculine colour, to the whole masse of knowledge."[7]

Bacon and Sprat, as we have seen, defined themselves in opposition to the rational method, but it too declared its faith in a masculinist rhetoric, most melodramatically in Thomas Fuller's image of the "clunch-fist of logic" that could "knock down a man at a blow," and more persistently in the long tradition of radical references to the male propriety of reason.[8] John Thelwall never tired of recommending "the manly energies of reason," "manly firmness," and "the powerful energies of manhood."[9] Mackintosh saw the new political theory as the emergence of an "original masculine thought" and scorned those who expressed reservations about the violence of the French Revolution as giving way to a "womanish and complexional sensibility" at the expense of a "manly and expanded humanity."[10] Thomas Paine too regarded the new republic as having "breeched itself in manhood," outgrowing both infancy and femininity in the achievement of a "gigantic maturity" and "gigantic manliness."[11] Even Mary Wollstonecraft found herself contrasting the "effeminate court" of old-regime France with the "enlightened sentiments of masculine and improved philosophy" that now prevailed.[12] In her early response to Burke, *A Vindication of the Rights of Men*, it is Burke himself who is feminized as a slavish sentimentalist and participant in an aristocratic-effeminate culture: "All your pretty flights arise from your pampered sensibility; . . . vain of this fancied pre-eminence of organs, you foster every emotion till the fumes, mounting to your brain, dispel the sober suggestions of reason."[13] Two years later, in *A Vindication of the Rights of Woman*, Wollstonecraft is much more careful with this gendered rhetoric (though it reappears in her history of the Revolution). Burke's love of prejudices is now described as an instance of "what is vulgarly termed a woman's reason": critical distance is established. She refrains from attributing a "masculine understanding" to the admired Catherine Macaulay, "because I admit not of such an arrogant assumption of reason."[14] This landmark feminist text in fact offers a sophisticated explanation of the origins of gendered behavior as it equates kings, aristocrats, soldiers, and women as uniformly feminized by cultural experiences. Wollstonecraft's insistence on "reason" as a faculty common to men and women, and only monopolized by men as a result of interest and habit, is perhaps the summary expression in this period of the tendency in the radical method toward equality of the sexes. Even Godwin—or perhaps especially Godwin—found this hard to take, as he complained of her "rather masculine" sentiments and her "rigid, and somewhat Amazonian temper" at the same time as he dismissed her as a "female Werter," a creature of "intuition" who "reasoned little," and one "eminently deficient in method and arrangement."[15] Like the Jacobins and the Germans, Wollstonecraft is here imaged as at once overrational and quite irrational, hypermasculine and hyperfeminine, and doubly damned.

Even sympathetic modern readers have had some difficulty in recovering the radical integrity of Wollstonecraft's feminism, and for some of the same reasons. Her claim to reason has been felt as a concession to masculinist priorities and as a denial of femininity, at the same time as her often spasmodic and digressive expository style has been received as an instance of an unreconstructed feminine manner. Mary Poovey's extended and influential account of Wollstonecraft's career— the first extended modern analysis—still tends to suggest a failure to recognize and adapt to the claims of "sexuality," as if there were an available subject-position from which to express such a thing.[16] But Wollstonecraft inherited from Rousseau a discourse, and from her own life an experience, that nominated passion as the principal agent of the repression of women. The models of plain living provided by the Dissenting tradition were all she had available for the expression of alternatives. Her failure to pursue her case to its "logical, radical extreme," as Poovey puts it (p. 48), may indeed indicate a psyche in considerable conflict with the given terms of self-expression and self-experience, but this has been the fate of many such psyches caught up in antithetical and contradictory ideological determinations. Wollstonecraft's texts do

seem to display a range of attitudes that are not always mutually adjusted and appear to be beyond such adjustment; but it is hard not to
suspect at least an element of dramatic irony in her flights of passion,
which are often transcribed in prose that can be taken to indicate a very
conscious awareness of the expectations of a female reader in the
middle ranks of society, or of a male reader reading the productions of
such a person. In *The Female Reader* of 1789, Wollstonecraft proposes
that those whose "passions have never led them to reason" cannot be
affected by abstract, theoretical arguments but require "amusing tales"
and "allegories": philosophers, she writers (quoting Barbauld), "dwell
too much in generals." But some progress can be made, and women
readers may yet respond to "a methodical order in the arrangement of
pieces" calculated to develop "habits of order" and not yet attempted by
the editors of anthologies.[17]

Women, in other words, have potentially methodical minds even if
they are currently unlikely to understand conventional philosophical
argument. In the second *Vindication* Wollstonecraft thus observes that

to do every thing in an orderly manner, is a most important precept, which
women, who, generally speaking, receive only a disorderly kind of education,
seldom attend to with that degree of exactness that men, who from their infancy are broken into method, observe.

Here she has found the perfect mediation between the discipline of
domestic life, approved for women in countless Puritan conduct books,
and the "higher" powers of rational inquiry, which have conventionally
been limited to men: "the power of gaining general or abstract ideas."
The one can lead to the other, and Wollstonecraft can thus seem to observe the rules while exploring their potential for radical extension.
Rousseau, among others, had denied the power of abstraction to
women, but for her this is "the only acquirement, for an immortal
being, that really deserves the name of knowledge."[18] Wollstonecraft's
genius here is that she has managed to situate the condition of women
exactly in the inherited vocabulary criticizing the decline of civic virtue
within commercial economies, one of the major ethical discourses of
the eighteenth century.[19] This removes the "woman question" from
any potentially single-issue status and embeds it within a general analysis of the negative effects of a surplus (luxury) economy. Women are
classified with monarchs, the rich, and soldiers in suffering the psychological and intellectual enfeeblement consequent upon worship of social distinction and the urge to novelty. By implication it is only when
the institutions maintaining these inequities are removed that women,
along with the others, will break free from their oppression—an op-

pression that is not just instrumental and crudely coercive but also internal and self-imposed. This, I think, is the essence of Wollstonecraft's radicalism, that it looks to a time when the "gloom of despotism" will subside and the natural reason of *all* human beings can develop unhindered. Kings as much as women suffer personally from a system that has placed "women on thrones" and corrupts even those who think they profit from it. It affects the family as it affects the state, for "every family might also be called a state." The original "poisoned fountain" determining most present evils is "property": it is for this that "one class presses on another." Hereditary property is the greatest evil of all, for it has not even the limited virtue of exercising the faculties that acquire it.[20]

This general analysis, surrounding and explaining as it does what might otherwise seem a gentle plea for the recognition of the rational potential of the female mind, makes the second *Vindication* a complex and visibly radical document. It is partly a Puritan self-help manual, and partly protocommunist (in the manner of Wollstonecraft's radical contemporary Thomas Spence) in its remarks on property and on the effects of rank and privilege. For Wollstonecraft, the seeds of rational thought can only flower in a world where old corruption has disappeared; reflexively, the best hope for the removal of that order comes with the fostering of that same rational method wherever it can be found. She does not think that women of the middle ranks can make a revolution, but she does seek to persuade them to respond and contribute to any revolutionary tendencies that might be apparent. There is more going on here than the reliance on "individual effort" and "the values of individualism" that Mary Poovey finds in Wollstonecraft's argument.[21] If the *Vindication* does not articulate a modern revolutionary manifesto, it does complicate and extend the rhetoric of bourgeois self-help that its author inherits from the literature of Dissent. And it does so in the context of the radical debates in political economy that were part of the discursive landscape of the late eighteenth century.

The tentative and dispersed quality of Wollstonecraft's argument does, however, make it obscure. She does not reproduce the propositional mode associated with the Painites and subsequently recognized as the signature of radical method in the 1790s. Her principal propositions have to be tracked across various pages and chapters, emerging out of digressions and illustrations and requiring the construction rather than the mere acceptance of the terms of her general analysis. One could identify this as a "feminine" style, as perhaps it partly is. But one could also understand it as the dramatization or exploitation of a rhetoric designed at once to appeal to female readers and to disguise the undoubtedly radical implications of its argument when baldly stated. Thus we find her directions through her indirections. Godwin himself, after all, relied upon volume and digression to understate the threat presented by his *Enquiry Concerning Political Justice.* The expense of his book, and its tendency to bury some of its most challenging arguments in obscure chapters, taking refuge in sheer variety, certainly helped its author to avoid prosecution.

I do not mean to suggest that Wollstonecraft's second *Vindication* is to be received as completely and exclusively the product of a rationally controlled anticipation of audience effects; but I would contend that there is more deliberate artifice than can be allowed by the supposition of her imprisonment within a feminine style. The mixing of plain language with ironic and parodic apostrophe suggests an artful intelligence as well as a tortured psyche, and one well aware of its need to appeal to a readership composed of women of the "middle class," neither hopelessly lost to "false refinement" nor so brutalized by work and the scarcity of leisure as to be unable to pick up a book at all.[22] She wrote for and about women of the middle ranks—exactly those unstable, bourgeois mentalities whose fluid social-psychological condition might well have been expected to predispose them to respond to the appeals of an unstable style.[23]

Wollstonecraft's personal communications, posthumously published, also bespeak an intelligence that well understands the public determinations affecting private lives. She expresses a dislike of Imlay's "commercial face" and of a "commerce" that "debases the mind, and roots out affection from the heart," and here she reproduces a classic concern among eighteenth-century social critics.[24] Imlay, indeed, has here been feminized, in the conventional eighteenth-century way: he has been made subservient to outward appeal and external values, as women were thought to be, and thus rendered incapable of achieving any attachment to person or principle—in other words, to method. The commercial psyche disturbs the balance of reason and passion (or "imagination") that alone constitutes the developed personality, one able to "convert appetite into love, cemented by according reason."[25] For Wollstonecraft, the same imbalance marked the course of the French Revolution, whose positive initiatives—method, reason, democracy, and sincerity—had to do battle with the inherited customs of "the most sensual people in the world," rendering them "cold and artificial."[26] It is not passion itself she deplores, but passion in a personality whose other faculties are relatively undeveloped. As Maria opines in the fragmentary novel bearing her name, the passions appear "strong and disproportioned" when the judgment is "weak and unexercised";

they gain "strength by the decay of reason, as the shadows lengthen during the sun's decline."[27]

The balance between the rational and the emotional is an ideal stressed by Wollstonecraft even at those moments when she is deploring the vulnerability created by the passions. The same desire to mediate extremes informs her account of the French Revolution, even as it is posited within the accepted gender codes. She approved the early phases of the Revolution as "the enlightened sentiments of masculine and improved philosophy" working to arouse "the sleeping manhood of the French," hitherto lulled by an aristocratic effeminacy.[28] It was the failure of any synthesis, and the continuing strife between manly method and feminized enthusiasm, that provided for Wollstonecraft the clue to the failure of the new political order. Her critique of the French National Assembly, which she saw as entertaining "ingenious theorists" without any attention to "practical knowledge," appears to be in the mainstream of British conservative rhetoric, as is her complaint about the effects of an "unbounded licentiousness." But she does not denigrate method and theory in themselves, as always and inevitably disastrous: again, it is the balance that is missing in France. Wollstonecraft's version of the middle way is not merely that of the nationalist myth of common sense; it attempts a genuine synthesis of theory and practice. Burke and his kind denied any value to the rationalist project, producing practice as a stick with which to beat theory. Wollstonecraft admits enough of the virtues of "practical knowledge" and "experience" to preserve a credible place for system and method. After the Terror she realized that reason, like woman, is not born into an innocent world but must come into conflict with established interests and habits. And because of this, she proposed, only a gradual revolution could hope to achieve a genuine and lasting change for the better.[29]

Wollstonecraft's rhetorical and analytical career may thus be read as an attempt not only to make the case for woman's ability and right to reason and to methodize, but also to argue the need for an incorporation of the rational faculties into a whole and complete personality, of the sort that could only occur within a whole and complete culture. Godwin's scornful and defensive allusions to the "Amazonian" temperament perhaps register how little this attempt was understood. Wollstonecraft faced enormous difficulties in reaching a suitable readership. While the conservatives despised all method and reason, the male radicals who approved it for themselves were seldom deeply committed to the emancipation of women.

The problem is particularly clear in the debates about the popularization of scientific knowledge. As soon as its treasures threatened to become available to women (and ordinary readers), throne and altar as well as home and family were seen to tremble. The general availability of "method" had been one of the major results of Ramism, even though one does not find there any specific invitations to female readers. But after the printing of Descartes's works at least one observer noticed that "ladies reasoned much more sensibly in metaphysics than three-fourths of the nation's theologians."[30] Later, the Declaration of the Rights of Man inevitably gave rise to reflection on the degree to which women might share them. And, at the same time as Wollstonecraft and others were arguing for female participation in a "reason" that had been traditionally claimed by men, science itself was taking on a feminized form and language. The philosophy of sensibility, with its roots in a materialist-atomist epistemology, made no clear distinctions of gender; all beings were seen to tremble under the same pressures. The benign rationalization of sexual attraction that Erasmus Darwin most famously poeticized was threatening not only because it offered no ethical sanction against the expression of sexual desire *in* women but also because, as embodied in the conventions of poetry, it was so readily available *to* women. Darwin proposed that women should be offered a general scientific education in chemistry, mathematics, and "experimental philosophy" in order that they might become fit companions for the new generations of male inventors and industrialists.[31] And his own doctrines, for all their poetical aspirations, were also intended to observe a methodical taxonomy. Samuel Latham Mitchill, in his preface to the American edition of the *Zoonomia*, compared Darwin's ambitions to those of the "*Methodic* sect" of classical physicians in his search for a single, mechanistic explanation for the entire "animal economy." In his own words, Darwin hoped to "reduce the facts belonging to ANIMAL LIFE into classes, orders, genera, and species" as a clue to a "theory of diseases." And in the ideal simplicity of such a theory he imagined some of the same social consequences that had so alarmed the opponents of the Ramists: henceforth men of "moderate abilities" could "practise the art of healing with real advantage to the public." He went on to echo, for the sphere of medicine, the terms of Sieyès's defense of reason quoted in the opening pages of this study:

There are some modern practitioners who declaim against medical theory in general, not considering that to think is to theorize; and that no one can direct a method of cure to a person labouring under a disease without thinking, that is, without theorizing; and happy therefore is the patient, whose physician possesses the best theory.[32]

Much more notoriously, Darwin's "The Botanic Garden" chronicled in poetry all the details whereby "Love and Beauty rule the willing world."[33] Here he not only accords these traditionally feminized attributes the essential role in the organization of the universe, and in an openly sexual manner; he also blurs the distinctions between the sexes themselves. He enthusiastically describes the unpredictable distributions of sex among plants, and in "The Temple of Nature" he goes on to propose that "mankind and quadrupeds were formerly in an hermaphroditic state."[34] In Darwin's world distinctions of sex are fundamentally unstable and materialistically secular. Similarly, social hierarchy is a mere superstructure set insecurely atop the indiscriminate processes of animated nature: the same cycle of death and regeneration obtains whether "a Monarch or a mushroom dies." Sexual attraction is the principle that binds society in "golden chains" and rivets "mind to mind."[35]

The first *Anti-Jacobin*'s parody of Darwin, "The Loves of the Triangles," made an astute connection in linking sex and geometry, and not just by thus putting together the two major components that the conservatives perceived in the radical tradition.[36] For it was rational and scientific knowledge that Darwin threatened to make available to the female reader through the pleasurable devices of poetry, along with knowledge about the female condition itself, now no longer absolutely differentiated from the male. Richard Polwhele spoke out against "the female Quixotes of the new philosophy," linked in his mind with the "Gallic freaks" of a fashion that allowed women to wear minimal clothing, to "sport, in full view, the meretricious breast," and to acquire, thanks to Darwin, the habit of studying "the sexual systems of plants." Women were formerly content to inhabit the discourse of inert, consolatory sentiment:

> Ah! once the female Muse, to NATURE true,
> The unvalued store from FANCY, FEELING drew;
> Won, from the grasp of woe, the roseate hours,
> Cheer'd life's dim vale, and strewed the grave with flowers.

Now it only draws "each precept cold from sceptic Reason's vase."[37] As women gained access to reason, so sentiment, as we have seen, ceased to be merely the property of women, and became indeed something far more dynamic and disturbing than Polwhele remembers it to have been.[38] William Preston, responding to the threat of German plays on British stages, made the point perfectly in 1802:

These writings sap and unnerve the soundness of the intellect. They feed and diffuse a prevailing malady of the times, which has taken too full possession of the female world, and, indeed, of many men, under the name of *sentiment;* a malady which deifies a certain unmeaning, indescribable quickness of feeling; and exalts a morbid and absurd sensibility, into the perfection of human nature.[39]

It was as if, in the sphere of cultural identity, men were becoming women and women men, just as Darwin said that they originally were. As men became vehicles of sentiment, so women claimed access to reason and method. This too was perceived as one of the ways in which the French Revolution had turned the world upside down. Cobbett, who heavily exploited sexual anxieties in his antidemocratic propaganda against that Revolution, introduced Polwhele's poem with a derogatory reference to "the impious Amazons of republican France."[40]

A Revolution among Women

It is hard to defend any exclusive definition of what the libertine tradition meant to the eighteenth century; but it seems to have been dominantly a male tradition, closely identified with theories of phallus worship and habits of phallic fantasy.[41] Richard Payne Knight, or "*Priapus* Knight," as Mathias called him, saw the Roman liberty cap, soon to be adopted by the French republicans, as a symbol of fire-worship and an image of "the active or male powers of Creation and Generation," evident in sublimated forms in the iconography of Christian architecture.[42] But Knight's treatise was published as a luxurious folio for gentlemen readers. And *The Progress of Civil Society* (1796), his hymn to the harmonizing powers of "sensual joy," also holds the argument within the sphere of class and gender control. He has nothing good to say of "Gaul's dire hydra," finding there only a scene where "rapes and murders grow the rights of men." His social prescription is, indeed, completely Burkean:

> Then let not legislators think to find,
> Or render perfect, the still varying mind:—
> Still, as he is, let them consider man,
> Not for more perfect beings form their plan.
> Let Britain's laws abuses still correct,
> And from corruption's fangs her state protect;
> But let not wild reforms or systems vain,
> The legal influence of command restrain.[43]

Here, in the Hobbesian tradition, the atomistic incoherence of human experience is used to argue the necessity of firm legislative control. Neither women nor the lower orders of men are allowed to exercise their

114   CHAPTER FIVE

volatile desires in any sphere beyond the bedroom. Not for nothing was
Knight interested in the phallus as much as—indeed at the expense
of—the penis. John Wilkes, who was at least a demogogue and in some
respects a democrat, similarly devoted much of his *Essay on Woman* to
the admiration of men: women look upon man's "instrument of joy"
and fix their "longing eyes to view its pride." Admiration precedes and
perhaps precludes pleasure.[44] The same phallocentrism informs *Fanny
Hill* and other libertine tracts.

Libertinism, then, was dominantly the product of male and masculinist imaginations. But it was a volatile rhetoric nonetheless, and one
tinged from the first, as we have seen in chapter 1, with political and
theological as well as sexual radicalism. Studies by Iain McCalman and
David Erdman, among others, have described the power of obscenity in
the hands of political countercultures; and the association of pornography and radical politics was strong in France before 1789.[45] The materialist philosophy that was its chief support certainly demanded no
distinctions of gender. Helvétius, who was fond of shocking anecdotes,
reported one concerning the women of the Gelons, who did all the
physical labor in their society and were given in return the privilege of
choosing their sexual partners. What is miscalled women's "falsity," after all, is only the result of an opposition between nature and culture,
between the "desires of nature" and the "law of decency."[46]

As we have seen, to account for the threat that sensibilitarian theories
were to present to the social and sexual establishment is not in fact to
digress from a focus on the political charge of method and theory. The
conservative rhetoric of the late eighteenth century consistently identified these apparently different tendencies as mutually implicated, most
visibly in the "Jacobin" personality. Thus Holbach (as "Mirabaud") was
at pains to point out that "atheist" was not synonymous with "profligate
debauchee," nor did it signify the "hoary despoilers of connubial happiness"; Volney affirmed that the "law of nature" prescribed continence
rather than libertinism; and Richard Price felt obliged to insist that the
repeal of the Test Acts did not entail permission for "rakes and atheists"
to occupy political offices.[47] After 1789, as we have seen in the imaging
of France and Germany by the British nationalist press, the association
of radical method with sexual emancipation became even more inevitable. Pigott's *Political Dictionary* argued in its entry on "wedlock" that
debt and economic instability in the contemporary social system encouraged delayed marriage and even celibacy by creating a psychology
of insecurity: this drove women to prostitution, men to concubinage,
and both to diseases and an early grave. Here he was repeating a familiar eighteenth-century argument, for which sexual happiness and so-

cial stability could only be conjoined outside the luxury economy. After 1789 such a position implied nothing less than revolution, which Pigott indeed declared to be itself nothing more than "a re-assumption by the People of their long lost rights."[48] This is what appeared to have happened in France, and along with it came a higher degree of sexual freedom for both men and women.

There was some basis for this association. Sieyès wrote of "pleasure" (*jouissance*) as well as of justice as the proper goal of political reform, even though he himself counted women, along with servants, tramps, and beggars, among those to whom "political confidence" could not be extended.[49] The debate about political rights was commonly carried out in the rhetoric of radical universalism, so that women, along with the other social identities who were implicitly or explicitly left out of the "third estate," were able to employ the same rhetoric in making their own claims for rights and recognition. Arthur Young, traveling in France in the early months of the Revolution, thought that the political upheaval had actually reduced the influence of women, who had formerly involved themselves in everything but now had to attach themselves to some "celebrated leader" if they were to play a role. Young approved of this as a restoration of women to their proper place, the inferior status "nature intended them for."[50] But, before the suppression of the women's clubs by the Jacobins, there had been a high level of political activity by women and an active public discussion of women's rights. In 1790 Condorcet argued for women's admission to citizenship; and three years later, in hiding, he declared that domestic and national happiness could only come with the disappearance of prejudice against women.[51] Women had always been prominent in the bread riots and in the campaigns for price fixing before the Revolution.[52] Similarly, they were notoriously evident in the march on Versailles, even though Mary Wollstonecraft and others responding to Burkean propaganda claimed that the march included many men disguised as women and was created not by a spontaneous outburst of female energy but by the machinations of the Duc d'Orléans.[53]

Joan Landes has persuasively documented the brief period after 1789 during which gender roles were most actively contested, and before they were once again consolidated in the interests of bourgeois men; additionally the materials gathered together by Levy, Applewhite, and Johnson make clear the degree and variety of women's efforts at participating in the definition of the new French society.[54] For a short time women like Pauline Léon, Olympe de Gouges, Etta Palm d'Aelders, Claire Lacombe, and Théroigne de Méricourt threatened to earn acceptance as architects of the Revolution. Masculinist ironies

abound, of course. De Méricourt was not even known under her own
name (her surname was Terwagne), and she never acknowledged the
imposition of the one by which she is known to history, with its gestures
toward gentility.[55] Mythologized by the royalist press as a licentious
Amazon, she was declared mad in 1794 and lived out the rest of her life
in an asylum.

De Gouges's *Les droits de la femme* (1791), addressed to the queen, set
forth, in the very methodical format that Mary Wollstonecraft would
avoid, the consequences of recognizing that "women is born free and
lives equal to men in her rights."[56] A butcher's daughter and a play-
wright, Olympe de Gouges (real name Marie Gouze) was, predictably,
an ideological mixture: a royalist who may have invented the women's
societies, and who manifested in her writings a global consciousness
that identified, for instance, the rights of women with those of conquered peoples. She proposed that property should belong to both
sexes.[57] But in 1793 the Society for Revolutionary Republican Women
was suppressed, and de Gouges went to the guillotine. J. B. Amar pronounced that women were "scarcely capable of high speculation and
serious meditation"; so convincingly, it seems, that de Gouges and others like her have disappeared from the mainstream histories of the Revolution. De Gouges herself does not even earn an entry in the name
index of the massive and pseudo-exhaustive *Critical Dictionary of the
French Revolution* (a publication that also devotes a mere 5 of its 1032
pages to the "Enragés," and 6 more to the "Sans-Culottes").[58]

Even if the revolutionary women's movements were generally defeated, there were gradual gains for women. The constitution of 1791,
which was not favorable to women's political rights, did make marriage
a civil contract. Even though the Thermidorean constitution of 1795
made clear that no one could be a good citizen who was not a good "son,
father, brother, friend, and husband," the cult of domestic virtue seems
not to have entirely stemmed the liberal consequences of the 1792 divorce law.[59] Lynn Hunt has found that there were some thirty thousand
divorces in France between 1792 and 1803, under a law that was not
fully abolished until 1816. It is not credible to make liberal divorce laws
identical with women's needs or rights, but Hunt has discovered that
two-thirds of the divorces in Lyons and Rouen were initiated by women,
though she does not specify the time span or the size of the sample.[60]

However we decide these questions and others like them, there is no
doubt that the British counterrevolution seized on these signals of
female emancipation and initiative as evidence of a comprehensive assault on civilized life. The French, as we have seen, had already been
cast as at once effeminate and prone to fantasies of rational perfec-

tability through the application of method. With this in mind Pigott's *Political Dictionary* sought to save the radical case by defining "effeminacy" as prevalent in France only before 1789, since when it had come to characterize the descendants of the "British patriots."[61] But he was arguing against a deeply embedded nationalist stereotype, and Burke, as ever, exploited it fully. The rhetoric of chivalry was one of the guiding motifs of the *Reflections*, which ingeniously appealed to gendered norms and anxieties about gender. The notorious image of aristocratic chastity under threat in the molested and "almost naked" Marie Antoinette was accompanied by accounts of lower-class women liberated into brutality and sexual self-indulgence. France, for Burke, had lost the little hold it had had on an "austere and masculine morality," while British radicalism offered only "provocatives of cantharides to our love of liberty."[62] In 1791 he wrote of Rousseau as inculcating a blend of "pedantry and lewdness" tending to encourage women of the "first families" toward the ultimate "levelling" of marrying their servants.[63] By the time of the "Letters on a Regicide Peace" (1796), France is depicted as in a state of complete sexual mayhem: prostitutes revered as goddesses, marriage reduced to the "vilest concubinage," the whole spiced with the sauce of parricide and cannibalism.[64]

Excessive as this rhetoric might seem, it is mild when compared with that of such texts as Cobbett's *The Bloody Buoy* (1797), which is full of such salacious "facts" as those of a man eating a woman's heart "reeking hot," two naked women tied to the guillotine on which their husbands were being executed, Carrier raping his victims on the scaffold, unborn children ripped from the womb and impaled on pikes, gang rape of white women by emancipated black slaves, and a whole catalogue of right-wing pornography published under the name of one who still subsists in English literary history as some sort of populist hero.[65] Thomas Taylor's parodic but vicious *Vindication of the Rights of Brutes* took the case yet further by suggesting that the doctrine of equality should extend to animals, beginning with the elephant, "a beast by nature very amorous; and from his prodigious size, very well calculated to become the darling of our modern virgins, who having wisely laid aside the foolish veils of antiquity, and having assumed greater boldness, are seldom intimidated by anything uncommonly large."[66] The first (weekly) *Anti-Jacobin* poeticized Louvet as fond of having sex in public; T. J. Mathias saw in France the reign of a "lawless lustihood"; while John Courtenay parodied the conservative concerns over the new constitution by complaining that adultery would now be subject to law instead of discretion.[67] On the other side of the fence, Pigott tried to present the sexual revolution as a positive event by arguing that aristo-

cratic women would now be freed from inhibitions and allowed to enjoy
the "delirious trance of ecstatic joy" that had always been the lot of the
peasant's daughter; Thomas Spence's *Rights of Infants* looked forward
to women taking over parish administration as an alternative to the mis-
erable failures of men; and in *The Restorer of Society* the same author
argued for a divorce law that would refigure marriage itself into a "con-
tinual courtship" ruled by Cupid instead of by the "chains of
Hymen."[68]

The war of words was not, as it seldom is, waged on equal terms. The
conservatives definitely seem to have held the high ground in the
1790s, as they projected the total disintegration that would follow from
women being granted sexual and political rights. As we have seen, even
Godwin felt threatened by a radical feminist spouse, and the dangerous
Rousseau himself transcribed mostly his confusions in the titillating
pages of *Julie* and the *Confessions*. In his political doctrines he was a
masculinist civic republican, highly critical of the temptations of passion and luxury and all the things conventionally associated with the
feminine. Helen Maria Williams's account of the Revolution emphasized female heroism rather than sexual independence: at the storming
of the Bastille, women showed a "spirit worthy of Roman matrons."[69]
So the Revolution came to Britain heavily informed by the vocabulary
of sex: in the language of public debate, and in the private life of the
young William Wordsworth, as well as in his declared poetic affiliation
with that same Helen Maria Williams.[70]

Some of the intensity of the conservative (and other) representations
must surely be attributed to the degree to which women writers and intellectuals had already made their way into the literary marketplace.[71]
Such women were by no means all political radicals; and some, like
Hannah More and Jane Austen, were clearly political conservatives in
the general sense. But even an Austen could be outspoken in defense of
a middle-class woman's moral and intellectual integrity, the recognition
of which she indeed often presents as the last hope of an ailing upperclass patriarchy. And Hannah More, who had no love for "female war-
riors" or "female politicians" and was a leading defender of conventional female "propriety," could still take to task those who allowed
women only a "defective education" and then blamed them for imperfect behavior, at the same time as she distanced herself from Burke and
his kind, those who wished only to restore "the frantic reign of chivalry"
by romanticizing "the rubbish of the Gothic ages."[72] Even female political conservatives, in other words, could retain some radical affiliations
on matters of women's rights.

Few went as far as Mary Wollstonecraft in putting the case for a methodical, theoretical capacity in the female mind. Many in fact denied just this, and Wollstonecraft herself refrained from the Painite, propositional format that might have been seen as its natural medium. Maria Edgeworth announced herself "more intent on their [women's] happiness than ambitious to enter into a metaphysical discussion of their rights."[73] Christian pacificism informs much of Anna Laetitia Barbauld's writing, which is suspicious of the "deep philosophy" and "maze of metaphysic lore" into which she thought Coleridge had strayed.[74] But Barbauld was a friend and admirer of Priestley, a feminist Dissenter, and a sympathizer with the world's less fortunate beings; and these allegiances placed her firmly on the radical side of the fence at a time when mediated positions were not much entertained or recognized. Amelia Opie's *Adeline Mowbray* offers an explicit feminist critique of male hegemony and male misconception but is equally explicit about the dangers of women meddling in theory without a corresponding attention to practice. Mrs. Mowbray, who forms her daughter's principles, is fully involved in "imagining systems for the good of society" while indulging in "the culpable neglect of positive duties." The novel's narrative is built upon the disconnection between theory and practice: while the mother is cynically able to defend "common custom" at the same time she is amusing herself with "new theories and systems," the daughter disastrously attempts to unite the two. Only Adeline's tragic life and death fully convert the mother from a "romantic, indolent theorist, and inactive speculator," to an honest philanthopist. Even here, the Baconian heritage makes its claim.[75]

These discursive and ideological ambivalences both within and beyond the "feminist" aspiration in the 1790s indicate that there was something afoot that seemed to call for fictional prophylaxis, as indeed there was. Mary Wollstonecraft, Priscilla Wakefield, and others represented a different femininity than the "bluestockings" who were their immediate precursors. Pigott could reasonably poke fun at Mrs. Thrale and Mrs. Montagu as respectively royalist and plutocrat, and prudes both, while the conservative Polwhele could still produce them and their peers as examples of ideal womanhood.[76] But the female tradition could also produce, as well as Wollstonecraft herself, such figures as Catherine Macaulay and Mary Hays. Wollstonecraft cited Macaulay's career as evidence that "a woman can acquire judgment, in the full extent of the word," and as a person whose "argumentative closeness" was not achieved at the expense of "sympathy and benevolence."[77] Macaulay was one of the earliest critics of Burke's *Reflections*, which she found deficient in "close reasoning," methodical only in its support of the *"methodized sentimental barbarism"* of dueling, and hostile to any at-

120   CHAPTER FIVE

tempt to *"convince"* rather than to *"captivate."*[78] Her own career by this
time was almost over. In 1767 she had published a critique of Hobbes in
which she disputed both "the innate quality of selfishness" and the ideal
of monarchism, while mounting an argument against the "aristocrati-
cal accumulation of property."[79] She went on to defend the American
Revolution and to attack, in 1770, an earlier version of Burke's defense
of the aristocatic interest, his "Thoughts on the Cause of the Present
Discontents." Between 1763 and 1783 she published an eight-volume
history of the seventeenth century that was outspoken in its criticism of
Hume, Clarendon, and the 1688 settlement and pronounced the Levellers to be the "truest friends to Liberty" that the period had to show.
Lilbourn (*sic*) was guilty only of attacking the same abuses under which
England suffers "to this very day"; and in saying so Macaulay declared
herself well aware that no history favorable to "republican principles
and notions" could hope to be popular among readers habituated to
the "royal sway" of a monarchist culture.[80] In her *Letters on Education* of
1790 she bravely announced herself a philosopher, an admirer of asso-
ciationism's "modern metaphysicians," and an exponent of "metaphysical observations."[81] Before 1789 Macaulay's kind of femininity proved
acceptable among at least some of the parliamentary Whigs: they called
for a public celebration of her birthday on April 2, 1777, which even the
eventually conservative Richard Polwhele attended as a promising
youth of seventeen.

    After 1789 republican women had a harder time, especially if they
were not well-connected. English republicanism was now inextricably
involved with French paradigms. In her *Memoirs of Emma Courtney*
(1796) Mary Hays was indiscreet or brave enough to quote Helvétius,
among others, four times, and to portray a woman capable of creating
rather than passively responding to a sexual initiative, just like
Kotzebue's heroine.[82] Emma also delights in exercising her methodiz-
ing talents: "I love to class and methodize," she says, on the way to pronouncing that "there is no subject, in fact, that may not be subjected to
the laws of investigation and reasoning."[83] Hays's *Appeal to the Men of
Great Britain* (1798) introduced its author not as a "fury flinging the
torch of discord and revenge" but as a "friend and companion bearing a
little taper to lead them to the paths of truth, of virtue, and of liberty."
But it was "rational liberty" that Hays sought for women, along with an
education that, if not strictly "scientific and philosophical," would proceed at least "by methods rational and interesting." In her claim that
"mind . . . is of no sex," and in her wish to "write for all classes," Hays's
challenge was as radical as Wollstonecraft's, and like Wollstonecraft she

did not forswear an appeal to the hearts and imaginations as well as to the reason of her female readers.[84] In her pathbreaking *Female Biography* she accepted that women might require "pleasure to be mingled with instruction." Like Wollstonecraft in her *Female Reader,* she imagined women's understandings to be "principally accessible through their affections," which must be appeased if women are to advance "in the grand scale of rational and social existence."[85]

Any moderation in Hays's positions was not, it seems, enough to avoid Coleridge's condemnation. In a letter to Southey of January 1800, he describes himself thinking "not *contemptuously,* but certainly very *despectively*" of her intellect, and as much offended by hearing "a Thing, ugly & petticoated, ex-syllogize a God with cold-blooded Precision, & attempt to run Religion thro' the body with an Icicle."[86] Women, it seems, could be the coldest (and most phallic) of cold metaphysicians when they dabbled in rational philosophy. Hays was cruelly satirized as "Bridgetina Botherim" in Elizabeth Hamilton's *Memoirs of Modern Philosophers* (1800), and again the mixture of "homely plainness" with the desire to "generalize" was pointed out, as if womanhood were betrayed on both counts.[87] While the merest hint of an interest in theory and system was enough to cast any writer as a Jacobin, the threat was all the greater if the writer or heroine happened to be a woman. In Helen Maria William's *Julia* (1790) it is the male character, Frederick Seymour, who is the admirer of Werther and the one unable to align his passions with his reason, while it is the women, Julia and Charlotte, who set the highest standards of self-control and generosity toward others.

Though a republican, Williams wrote an account of the events of the Revolution that was favorable to Marie Antoinette as well as to Mme Roland, the heroine of the Gironde and an early victim of the Terror. Williams herself went to prison during the Terror, and she identified Jacobinism as especially hostile to women as well as to intellectuals.[88] But it was, as we have seen, the smear of Jacobinism that was used by Burke and others against those same women and intellectuals. Williams's published reports of French events are detailed and complex, perhaps too much so for the heady and extreme distinctions that were being made in England at the time. In 1801 she concluded that women had remained relatively neutral in the major political debates, not least owing to their gendered reluctance to reasoning "from abstract principles to remote consequences" at the expense of "sentiment." By this time it was also clear that women were not much better off after the Revolution than they had been before: noting the "justice which has been withheld from the female part of the State," Williams remarks that "the women of France have nothing at present to do with the Constitution but to obey it." Such was the cruel reward for the sublime "heroism" of women in the early phases of the Revolution.[89]

In these mature meditations Williams was trying to preserve a difficult and complex balance in her assessment of the aftermath of 1789. Political liberty was afoot and would not cease, despite the appalling events of the Terror. Women had suffered and experienced setbacks, but that liberty must, like "axioms in mathematics," eventually extend to them. Skepticism and atheism would disappear, but religion would emerge purified by having had to encounter them. Literature and eloquence would prosper, as the true heroism would be that of peace, displacing the "shielded metaphysical gowns-man who prates of war."[90] But the British national consensus was not receptive to any vindication of France, however qualified; and, at the same time, Williams's attempt at that vindication involved a sad recognition of the demise of women and a strong dissociation of women from the habits of method and reason that Hays and Wollstonecraft had sought to make available to them. By 1800, and perhaps before, theory and method had been both demonized and remasculinized; that is, their latent masculinist associations had been reaffirmed by the vilification of those women who did seek a rational identity for their sex. Godwin, the pious egalitarian of the *Enquiry* and the apologist of liberal divorce laws, pronounced his spouse a "female Werther." And Coleridge, with his genius for compression, here encapsulates the whole ideological package in a sentence from *The Statesman's Manual* of 1816:

The rational instinct, therefore, taken abstractly and unbalanced, did *in itself* ("ye shall be as gods!" *Gen.* iii 5) and in its consequences, (the lusts of the flesh, the eye, and the understanding, as in verse the sixth,) form the original temptation, through which man fell: and in all ages has continued to originate the same, even from Adam, in whom we all fell, to the atheists who deified the human reason in the person of a harlot during the earlier period of the French revolution.[91]

Man fell, of course, thanks to woman: Eve was the original philosopher, believing in some relation between her senses and her reason instead of in her "faith." Man becomes demonic, so to speak, in repeating this feminized error. While all women are threatening because they evoke this foundational moment, women with rationalist aspirations are especially so. Reason is always dangerous to the social-theological hierarchy; it is even more dangerous in the reborn Eve who is both sensuous and smart.

The argument of chapters 2, 3, and 4 of this book has been that Romantic nationalism contributed mightily to the demonization of theory that was and remains such a feature of the British and (if less hyperbolically) the American national characters. We can now suggest that theory and method were just as energetically removed from women as they were from Englishness in general. But if theory was thus remasculinized, it was as a Satanic masculinity: the English are not supposed to practice its rites, but those who do had better be men, and thus licensed transgressors, albeit still transgressors. Theory thus becomes the province of alienated male rationalists like Victor Frankenstein, who learned his lore at Ingoldstadt, Adam Weishaupt's university. The negation of female rationality was in this way doubly determined: no one should embrace it, but the licensed opposition had best be male.

The question then arises: what was the discursive opportunity for literature and the aesthetic within this nationalist, and gendered, paradigm? Generally, the literary was feminized exactly to the degree that it was nationalized. That is, as literature came to be more and more defined and redefined as a nontheoretical and immethodical genre, glorying in its imprecisions, so it was increasingly assimilated to a feminized identity, women traditionally being those least prone to the exercise and understanding of clear and distinct ideas. This situation, I suggest, produced a series of tensions rather than neatly defined subject-positions for writers and for the "literary," tensions that were especially urgent for male writers seeking a place in a social subculture that was, both symbolically and actually, more and more the domain of women. The profession of poetry and letters was not easily imaged in terms of the utilitarian work ethic that was becoming more and more the emergent nineteenth-century incarnation of the ideology of British common sense. And this inevitable insecurity generated visible anxieties in such writers as Wordsworth and Coleridge, who are often to be found reflecting on what kind of "job" they are doing and what "worth" it might have.[92] A. L. Barbauld, in her preface to an edition of Collins's poems, makes the point perfectly:

A real Poet must always appear indolent to the man of the world. The alacrity and method of business is not to be expected in his occupation. His mind works in silence, and exhausts itself with the various emotions which it cherishes, while to a common eye it appears fixed in stupid apathy. The Poet requires long intervals of ease and leisure; his imagination should be fed with novelty, and his ear soothed by praise.[93]

As the recipient of novelty and praise, and with the appearance of "stupid apathy," the poet here closely images the posture of the society lady, examples of which populate the pages of Jane Austen's novels and

negate the model of active femininity, which even the politically conservative Austen, within limits, endorsed. Poor Collins, Barbauld reminds
us, did not make it: he "fell into that malady most humiliating to a being
possessed of rational powers" (p. viii), he went mad. But it he were not
allowed or supposed to exercise those *rational* powers in the production
of poetry, his madness is perhaps unsurprising.

In her preface to *The Female Reader* Wollstonecraft had quoted the
same Mrs. Barbauld to the effect that philosophers, in their attempt to
"grasp the whole order of the universe" and to "reduce every thing
to the operation of general laws," were seldom able to "leave room
for those particular and personal mercies which are the food of grati-
tude."[94] More and more, these particular and personal moments became the food of literature, of a genre predisposed against general laws
and universal truths, aspiring instead to chronicle the minutiae of everyday life and the intricate, asystematic complexities of social and psychological identities. More and more, what did not invite these tasks
would be dismissed as unliterary, whether in the form of the overheated
Gothic, a genre that remains the hallmark of a too popular culture, or in
the chilling propositions of a philosophical rigor. The business of a specifically *literary* criticism would become, more and more, the delineation
and celebration of the ordinary, or at least of an ideology of enhanced
ordinariness, in the construction of which it would be much assisted by
the institutionalization of psychoanalysis.

At the same time, the discursive space that here opens up for the
specification of the "literary" is inevitably unstable, not least since the
category of the ordinary is hopelessly imprecise as soon as one moves
beyond criteria of self-evidence. As the ideological signature of a bourgeois identity, moreover, the category of the literary had to reflect the
same instabilities that went into the social experience from which it em-
anated and which it sought, in some sense, to stabilize. The experience
of being "middle class" has never taken on the fixity that it may appear
to have in some versions of sociological theory; one could in fact propose that that experience is one of constant insecurity and anxious vigilance, so that apparent stability may be best described as the result of
two mutually canceling vectors, fear of falling and efforts at rising. This
balance is perhaps as often disturbed as preserved by a subculture of
writers whose very obligation to some appearance of originality has
persuaded them to present the ordinary, with its attendant worship of
common sense, as turned inside out: one thinks of Lawrence, Woolf,
and Joyce, among others.

The radical contestations of the ideology of the ordinary have not,
however, generally resorted to theory and system as the medium of

challenge; these models have remained, almost without exception, un-literary, so that the forms of criticism that have sought to reanimate them have also tended to be received as beyond the pale. At various moments claims have been made for the capacity of literature to absorb, dramatize, and even anticipate science, as Wordsworth and Shelley thought it might. The early defenders of *The Waste Land* saw in Eliot's sensibility a new synthesis of the two cultures (and also, I think, a desired remasculinization of the literary itself). But the tensions have not disappeared. The coexistence of a gendered antithesis (men do science and theory, women do literature) with a nationalist mythology (the French and Germans do theory, the British stick to the facts) has exerted strong pressure on the debates about theory and literature in the Anglo-American academy, many of whose reflections may be read as attempts at making virtue of these prefigured necessities. In the next chapter I turn to an account of the relations between system and literature as they were perceived and negotiated by the Romantics themselves.

6

SYSTEM AND LITERATURE

The Sublime: A Masculine Confusion

In a recent essay in the widely read academic journal *Critical Inquiry*, Frank Lentricchia disputed what he took to be the claims made by some feminist critics for a uniquely unprivileged status shared by women writers.[1] Taking Wallace Stevens as his example, he argued that many creative writers, especially poets, in the modern American tradition have been subject to feminization and to the assumption that literature is simply not man's work. While there is no doubt that some women writers may have had to endure a double marginalization, as both women and writers, Lentricchia's point seems right: the literary is a generally feminized category, notwithstanding the efforts of the Hemingways and the Mailers to render it otherwise. Poets, as Mrs. Barbauld's remarks on Collins made clear, are basically dreamers.

This generically gendered categorization was certainly not the invention of Romanticism. It seems unwise to pronounce at all on the matter of absolute origins; but if we were to set about the reconstruction of a history for this syndrome, we would have to admit the importance of the transference of the notion of "literature" from the classical languages (generally unavailable to women readers and, with a few exceptions, not written by women) to the vernacular, and of the extension of the readership to a middle class that has been deemed to be rising ever since it came into being, whenever that was. Both of these formative determinations, at any rate, considerably precede the late eighteenth century. Furthermore, the socially indeterminate and vulnerable identity of the literary career has been described at least as far back as the early Renaissance, suggesting that some measure of insecurity (and thus of feminization) may be a long-term feature of the relation of the nonnoble person of letters to the modern state, as well as to the ideology of nationalism that was used to publicize it.[2]

Leaving aside the question of ultimate origins, then, we may reasonably propose that the aftermath of the French Revolution saw in Britain both a reemphasis on the feminized identity of the literary and the aesthetic (of which the poetry of Keats would become a prime example) and a corresponding remasculinization of the vocabulary of theory and method. Both the perception of the feminized character of the literary and the anxiety about it must have been to some degree the result of the dramatically increasing number of women professional writers. And it might have seemed plausible that women, given their traditionally marginal social-economic role, would be the most likely inheritors of the condition of disinterest that had previously been the property of upperclass males. Women too, although for quite different reasons, understood the creative potential of leisure and the privileges coming from being beyond the reach of worldly pressures, and these attributes had been frequently prescribed as the very prerequisites for adequate aesthetic or philosophic reflection.

All of this, not surprisingly, placed considerable pressure on the male writer, who found himself obliged to compete in a marketplace already predisposed to recognize and reward visibly feminized virtues. The nationalist ideology could here be turned to his assistance provided that a distinction could be drawn between that aspect of Britishness that was simply imprecise and antisystematic, and hence incipiently feminine, and that other and sturdier "common sense" that imaged its middling preferences in practical, energetic, and hence masculine terms.

In the eighteenth century the aesthetics of the sublime seems to have offered male writers a way of having things both ways. On the one hand they could celebrate the principle of confusion and a decidedly antirationalist expressive convention; on the other, and precisely as exponents of the sublime, they could inscribe themselves into a posture of control and thus of gendered superiority. The sublime, as has been widely recognized, was a masculine mode, dealing out darkness and terror in the Miltonic manner. Burke made this clear, and subsequent critics have pointed out his gendered priorities.[3] But Burke sidles into this posture behind the screen of a Baconian mock-modest inductivism, a "timorous method of proceeding" that can never produce anything as simple as a "certain determinate role to go by."[4] This scrupulous miniaturism is soon abandoned, however, as he heats up the argument by way of a distinction between clarity and passion. The less we understand, the more we are impressed, and the more impressionable we become. "Clearness" (which was, we recall, Descartes's first value) is an enemy to "enthusiasm"; a "clear idea" is the same as a "little idea" whose appearance is "highly contrary to our idea of magnificence," while "dark, confused, uncertain images have a greater power on the fancy to form the grander passions than those have which are more clear and determinate."[5] The God of Job and Milton displaces Descartes. Ideas of pain and terror create the strongest human emotions, and these are the effective ingredient of sublimity.[6] Militant masculinity in control of absolute power is thus the natural possessor of sublimity. Pleasure, love, and harmony, the attributes of the beautiful, are reciprocally feminized. Beauty is kept away from any identification with a merely mathematical symmetry—for "method and exactness, the soul of proportion, are found rather prejudicial than serviceable to the cause of beauty"—but it remains a quieter and less disturbing play of incommensurables than that at work in the sublime.[7]

This gendered distinction between beauty and sublimity very much suggests a distinction between two kinds of literature, the bourgeois novel of pastoral and the epic, the one appealing to and representing a familiar, comfortable world, and the other overpowering us with natural or world-historical eruptions. In its weakest and most accommodating forms, the sublime could simply be cast as a welcome relief from the boredom of the quotidian, as it had been by Addison: "We are indeed so often conversant with one Sett of Objects, and tired out with so many repeated Shows of the same Things, that whatever is *new* or *uncommon* contributes a little to vary human Life, and to divert our Minds, for a while, with the Strangeness of its Appearance."[8] Burke, however, was interested in a more intense function for the sublime. As men make war, so men deploy the sublime. While his famous observation that words alone can be more powerfully sublime than any experience of nature might seem to open the field to women writers, his examples all presuppose a male writer or narrator in whom the power of words and worldly power are closely identified. At the still center of chaos, there is a masculine principle. At the end of *Paradise Lost,* as the earth's poles shift, the climate becomes more exigent, and the landscape of paradise gives way to one requiring hard labor, it is God who calls the shots; the natural and psychological sublime comes into being as part of the male God's punishment for the fall, and thus for humanity's preference for sex over soul.

Burke's account of the aesthetics of the sublime thus allows him to preserve a place for the male author, and specifically for the *English* male author, who can indulge his disdain for neoclassical rules and regulations, the trappings of a methodized mind, precisely as the signature of manliness. Against a general disempowering of the literary as a feminized medium, Burke shores up a position for masculine imprecision. As Paine and the other radical critics later sought to demystify the element of the sublime in Burke's own rhetoric, they resorted to accusations of effeminacy, and thus invoked a more general critique of the literary itself and of the fictional license that gave it its defining credibility. As early as 1757, knowingly or otherwise, Burke had laid down the defense against these criticisms, and his task would always be that of claiming for the masculine imagination the very tropes and techniques that were otherwise becoming more and more feminized. In the political sublime that is so often the subject of the *Reflections*, he finds it quite appropriate that our "passions" should "instruct our reason" and that literature should give the rule to public life. The Athenian audience would not, he says, have tolerated even as a spectacle the "real tragedy" of the present; the theater here functions as an index of the "natural sense of wrong and right" that requires no "elaborate process of reasoning" to reach its decisions.[9]

Burke's vindication of the intuitive, literary judgment as at once proper and masculine is a direct if implicit attack on the radical Protestant equation of fiction with mystery, and hence of literature with deceit. Much of Hobbes's philosophical polemic, for instance, depends upon the opposition between "philosophy" and "the paint and false colours of language" and the "ornaments and graces of the same." The final book of *Leviathan*, "Of the Kingdom of Darkness," is nothing less than a critique of the Christian sublime, of the machinery of hell and devils that has grown up to terrify mankind into obedience to worldly power. Ostensibly an attack on Catholicism, the analysis of "spiritual darkness" leads to much broader questions about the relations between civil and religious power: for "it is not the Roman clergy only, that pretends the kingdom of God to be of this world."[10]

What we have here is a competition for the masculinist high ground. Burke wants to feminize Enlightenment reason as generating only "little" ideas, while the philosophes and rationalists who are the heirs to radical method want to claim that femininity is properly to be attributed to the aristocratic ideology of mystery and confusion, hence to the sublime. At the same time, the faction behind this sublime function was clearly the possessor of power, and sometimes knew itself as such. Clement Walker, in a passage already cited, had proposed to head off any repeat of the turmoil of the 1640s by ensuring that "proper mysteries" be used to inculcate "civil devotion and obedience."[11] Coleridge can be found arguing much the same thing. This allowed the radicals to make the association between power and femininity, and hence between power and luxury and moral decline, but their failure to obtain anything we might call hegemony by way of this conjunction is a good instance of the degree to which historical solutions are the result of more than merely rhetorical determinations; despite the disadvantages of a feminized identity, the ruling interests did not tumble before the power of the radical critique. That critique is one flooded with the language of light—light dispelling darkness, day supplanting night, the sun chasing away the clouds, truth displacing mystery.[12] The account of the genesis of the priesthood by the manipulation of mysteries and hieroglyphics in Blake's *The Marriage of Heaven and Hell* was a standard item in the radical polemic.[13] The empire of radical reason meant the end of the sublime.

Unruffled masculinity was, then, the discursive goal of both Burke and his critics, although Burke, by his very commitment to the natural language of the heart, appealed to a more complex model of what masculinity might encompass. While his own affection for the Gothic and its attendant imagery was held to be compatible with masculine power—indeed, it was its very manifestation—for his critics it was merely the symptom of a feminine disorder. For Joel Barlow, Burke's was "the great Sublime of weakness and of force"; for Joseph Towers, it was the signature of "an historical romance"; and for Mackintosh, Burke was the possessor of a "prolific imagination, goaded by the agonies of ardent and deluded sensibility."[14] Mackintosh, at the same time, well realized that to feminize Burke would not serve as an adequate critique. He saw that Burke's contempt for the "laws of vulgar method" was working in the service of an established order that projected disorder onto others, and was publicizing a confusion aimed at inhibiting the leveling functions of "analysis and method," which, "like the discipline and armour of modern nations, correct in some measure the inequalities of controversial dexterity, and level on the intellectual field the giant and the dwarf."[15] Burke's own psychic incoherence thus accommodated a darker purpose; he reproduced in his own style enough of the confusion that he claimed to see around him to play upon the reader's passions, but never put at risk the still point of patriarchal control. The world, like woman, needs to be kept under tight control, so much so that even Burke himself is incipiently vulnerable to its instabilities. Mary Hays analyzed the male image of woman as "chaos" precisely as an instance of the projected sublime, one designed to keep women in a state of "PERPETUAL BABYISM" behind a "mysterious veil." The critique of Burke thus reasonably included an argument for the liberation of women.[16]

The sublime, then, occupied a somewhat unstable place in the relations among literature, system, and gender after the French Revolution: for Burke, it signified the need for male dominance, albeit decked in the trappings of chivalry, and for his critics it could appear as the symptom of an improper and feminized view of the world. Each faction tried to have the debate on its own terms. In the *Vindication of the Rights of Men* Wollstonecraft even tried to argue for the true sublime as that of principle and rational morality, while casting Burke's rhetoric as a false sublime.[17] The very reliance of the language of the sublime upon the tropes of excess always threatened the collapse of its (Burke's) claim to authority into a merely femininized disorder. Even some among the conservatives felt that Burke might have gone too far in his portraits of revolutionary excess, thus contaminating historical analysis with personal pathology. Radical critics correspondingly opined that the *Reflections* had done far more for their cause than had any of their own writings. In the nineteenth and twentieth centuries the hyperbolic image of sublimity would either be taken inside the individual mind and reproduced as psychological symptom, or marginalized as the signature of popular or lesser literature, as it implicitly had been by Wordsworth in his references to the "gaudiness and inane phraseology of many modern writers" and to "sickly and stupid German tragedies."[18] Jane Austen and other "common sense" critics of the Gothic similarly despised the excitations of sublime excess, and latterday commentators have weighed in against the temptations of cinema and paperback in the same spirit. It was to prove increasingly difficult to pretend to be Milton or Job, authentic exponents of the sublime, in a bourgeois world increasingly dominated by secular ideologies. Even the Gothic novels that Austen and others attacked often cast the horrors of the full sublime as typical of other, usually Catholic, nations, and thus inscribed the superiority of English common sense into the very pleasures of reading about the alternatives.

The Place of English Literature

English literature has most commonly defined itself as consisting in the avoidance of excess of any sort: political, sexual, or stylistic. As Raymond Williams aptly remarked: "When in doubt, the English imagine a pendulum."[19] The rhetoric of the English politician and aesthetician is familiarly that of even-handedness: "on the one hand . . . on the other hand." Thus the absolute sublime, once detached from its place in absolutist theology or political science, is almost as uncomfortable within the English idiom as is the rationalist embrace of theory and system. But the limited sublime could always find a home as the proper emanation of primitive energy, Gothic and English, so that it was never as thoroughly alienated from the national character as were the aspirations toward methodized literary forms and conclusions. After the reconstitution of the image of the English national character that followed the revolutionary and Napoleonic period, literature and its criticism were rendered even more forcefully antirationalist than they had previously been. And they had already been so identified. Claims for the logical basis of literary intelligence, conversely, had also been made before, and once again the Ramist debates may provide a significant precedent. Perry Miller has argued that the Ramist assumption of a total description of natural human reason included the sphere of literature, so that Abraham Fraunce could reasonably direct us to read Homer, Tasso, Virgil, and Sidney as exponents of natural logic.[20] Others have suggested that this inclusiveness was taken as a denigration of the literary, now subsumed by logic and rhetoric and indeed preparatory to their purer forms (Hegel would threaten the same subsumption).[21]

Wordsworth's famous dissent from what he saw as a contemporary tendency to murder to dissect thus closely echoes Bacon's complaint about the Ramists' compulsion to "torture things with their laws of method," thus producing only "dry and empty husks" in place of the "seeds and kernels of science."[22] Similarly the Ramist tradition of graphic representation by dichotomies may be one latent target of Blake's critique of Urizenic "dividing." While there is hardly any exact reference to Ramist doctrine in Romantic writing, the long rationalist tradition there addressed obviously includes the Ramist legacy. Again, the Romantic reaction against method employs a model of the national character and its literature that goes back at least to Dryden, and probably beyond. In the cause of vindicating "the honour of our English writers from the censure of those who unjustly prefer the French before them," Dryden had made a place for the disorderly and unregulated expression of "humour and passions" and the aesthetic of "variety and copiousness" that they upheld. He related this explicitly to the political culture of the Restoration, which made possible a "masculine fancy" and "spirit" now redeemed from the clutches of a "barbarous race of men."[23]

This increasingly standard definition of Englishness took shape in reaction to both French neoclassicism and Puritan intensity (itself, as we have seen, a mixture of the visionary-irrational with a methodized, disciplinary regime in personal and military matters). The Miltonic sublime is allowed into the nationalist aesthetic under construction in the eighteenth century, but only as an affective category, by way of a listing of the exemplary passages that are supposed to move us. *Paradise Lost* is denarrativized and decontextualized, stripped of its theological and political referentiality and made fit for a "modern" reader educated in little more than the national language and the national sensibility. Even more than Milton, it was Shakespeare who provided the model for the English literary self-image, as the author of a drama that was, in the words of Richard Flecknoe, "like a well contriv'd Garden, cast into its Walks and Counterwalks, betwixt an Alley and a Wilderness, neither too plain nor too confused." For Addison, in the same spirit, Shakespeare was the primary instance of the "great national Geniuses that were never disciplined and broken by Rules of Art." The poor French, to cite Thomas Purney, were in contrast limited to "the common known mechanick Rules of Poetry."[24]

These rehabilitations of Shakespeare and Milton were not uncontested. Some critics (and even the same critics) did see the need to re-edit *Paradise Lost*, to deplore the barbarities of style and substance in Shakespeare, and to lament the loss of both classical literature and the civilization that produced it. But such voices became less and less audible as the eighteenth century progressed. A century of wars and rebellions, numerous even before 1789, did little to discourage the constitution of a national character founded in measured disorder. Pope reproduced Homer as a Greek Shakespeare, a Nilus among poets whose "wild paradise" might be deemed too luxuriant only because of the "richness of the soil."[25] Shaftesbury's liberal image of effortless poetic creation in nature—"They [poems] move chiefly as she moves in them, without thought of disguising her free motions and genuine operations, for the sake of any scheme or hypothesis which they have formed at leisure and in particular narrow views"—began as the expression of an aristocratic revulsion against the bourgeois culture of specialization and professionalization.[26] But, as it passed down to the middling orders themselves, it came to function defensively, and in the realm of the aesthetic, as an avowed triumph over the very conditions of specialization and professionalization that made bourgeois culture itself possible. The famous quarrel between the "ancients" and the "moderns," in which context Shaftesbury's preference for the virtuoso over the scholar is a quintessential defense of antiquity, may be read as an ideological fantasy of choice: as if the men of letters in the middle ranks of society could really elect to demonstrate the freedom from interest and the spontaneity of intuitive tact that had always been theorized as the privilege of the gentleman.[27]

The legacy for subsequent literary critics is evident: they too have felt the need to defend the notion that Shakespeare and Milton and their kind do not need exegesis (the mark of professionalization) but can be apprehended in spirit or in essence by a lively mind unencumbered by pedantic concerns. (The extreme instances of this syndrome rely heavily upon statements about human nature.) A modest disorder becomes the analogue of right reading, wherein one is free from the restraints of reason while still being defended from the instabilities of the full sublime by the guardianship of common sense. Charles Lamb's Lear, who demonstrates that the "aberrations of reason" themselves reveal a "mighty, irregular power of reasoning, immethodised from the ordinary purposes of life," typifies at once the orderly disorder that signifies great literature, and the passage of that literature into the theater of the reading mind, where it may more easily be contained and measured against a private rather than a public verification.[28]

The immethodical spirit of the domesticated and nationalized sublime—a sublime kept from its own excesses—prescribed for literature and criticism an irrationalist and even at times anti-intellectual identity. That this was a *national* rather than a merely disciplinary tendency is instanced by the appearance of the same priority across different discursive conventions. In philosophy the "common sense" movement was doing similar work in the eighteenth century to that performed by the emergent vocabulary of literary criticism. James Beattie, one of its most visible popularizers, prefigures and parallels Burke in his determination to present his findings in no "systemic order" but in "the order in which they first occurred to me." While the "art of reasoning, or rather of wrangling," can easily be taught, true "common sense" cannot be mechanically acquired. Beattie in fact turns to literature as the proper vehicle for an exact understanding of human nature, and as an alternative to the delusions of philosophy. Literature can only be written or properly read by one who is untouched by the "metaphysical spirit." For

the metaphysician is cold, wavering, distrustful, and perpetually ruminates on words, distinctions, arguments, and systems. He attends to the events of life with a view chiefly to the system that happens for the time to predominate in his imagination. . . . He contemplates nature through the medium of his favourite theory, which is always false; so that experience, which enlarges, ascertains, and methodises, the knowledge of other men, serves only to aggravate the natural darkness and confusion of his.

Such a person is blind to the "endless varieties of human character" it is the principal business of literature to represent.[29] For Beattie, as for many of his Romantic successors, a degree of methodicality is allowable as long as it does not claim incarnation in an achieved system, of the sort that might offer others a ready and easy way to a knowledge they have not themselves worked for. He affirms the same discipline of criticism that Shaftesbury had specified as being the necessary complement to natural talent and costing "antecedent labour and pains."[30] The same prequalification would inform Burke's idea of statesmanship:

only those who have already done it are fit to do it. The "method" that Coleridge would approve would be similarly limited to educated minds and unavailable to a merely natural intelligence, which could only reproduce the unrelated and unorganized immediacies of sense impressions.[31]

Literature, then, comes to be imaged as either immethodical and tending toward the sublime, in which case it can be contained by a cultivated aesthetic (for the sublime was always that), or the product of a method that never appears as such and cannot be understood or mastered by all and sundry (as the Ramist method, for instance, had promised to be). In both cases, literature does not lend itself to the upholding of systems or the devising of theories. The centrality of drama, and especially of the Shakespearean drama, to the English literary self-image further enhanced the cult of immediacy that originated along with the declared commitment of the literary mode to the replication of "life" in all its varieties and complexities, in a gesture that was at once the expression of the diversified social economy that typified the bourgeois experience and a compensatory alternative to the forms of discipline that its inhabitants felt incumbent upon them. The primary status of the dramatic form tended to relegate the written word to secondary significance, behind the spoken. Precisely as social subcultures became more dispersed, and more than ever required the mediation of print to perform their communicative tasks, so the immediacy of spoken exchange was emphasized as the standard of exact and proper human intercourse.[32] Seventy-four-year-old William Godwin opined that

it is in the reciprocation of answer and rejoinder that the power of conversion specially lies. A book is an abstraction. It is but imperfectly that we feel, that a real man addresses us in it, and that what he delivers is the entire and deep-wrought sentiment of a being of flesh and blood like ourselves, a being who claims our attention, and is entitled to our deference. The living human voice, with a countenance and manner corresponding, constrains us to weight what is said, shoots through us like a stroke of electricity, will not away from our memory, and haunts our very dreams.[33]

The Romantic proclivity for the oral is well known, and it produced, among other things, a tradition respecting the talkers as well as the writers of literature, Coleridge, Henry James, and Conrad's Marlow among them. These intimate inscriptions give us the illusion that modernity may retain a human voice, if not a face, and that we may read, from the timeless medium of print, the timeliness of full presence. Alternatively the belief of the radicals of the 1790s in the powers of print to carry us beyond the immediate, which for them was the repository of

superstition and worldly charm, was a potentially anti-literary ideal,
perhaps to be read as an acceptance or a making virtue of the social dis-
persal that defines modernity.

The preference for the dramatic vocabulary in describing the proper
or essential literary experience had, of course, nothing to do with a
preference for the performative genres of literature, or for any actu-
alized human interactions made possible by textual occasions. In fact
there is much evidence that we are here dealing with a phenomenon of
displacement or substitution, whereby the image of dramatic experience goes along with a denigration of the theater itself.[34] As public
spaces allowing for the assemblies of numbers of people, the theaters
aroused some concern after 1789. And more and more, in the criticism
of Lamb, Coleridge, Wordsworth, and others, the ideal intensity of the
dramatic comes to be relocated in the adverting mind of the individual
reader. It passes into the reading experience, and thus becomes subject
to the disciplines and restraints of the Protestant imagination. In this
way the vocabulary of the dramatic mode has been far more central in
British literary criticism than has the theater itself, whose performances
are largely and unignorably determined by contingent factors that cannot be explained or predicted by an aesthetic of ideal responsiveness.
(One recalls the recent unfortunate collapse of the scenery, and the in-
juries sustained by the leading lady, during a rehearsal of *The Ring* at
the Metropolitan Opera in New York.) Thus in those same writings of
Lamb, Coleridge, and Wordsworth both the contemporary theater and
the general restraints of performance are vilified as somehow less than
literary, less than responsive to the genius of great writers or to the
capacities of good critics and adequate readers. Meanwhile, the trained
mind is invited to commune with a "living" text.

Some of the reasons for the disapproval of the spectacle by literary
aestheticians after 1789 have been brilliantly documented by Peter
Brooks in his account of the revolutionary associations of melodrama.
In *The Melodramatic Imagination* Brooks explains the importance of melodrama to the governors of revolutionary France, who saw in a simplified theatrical language a means for publicizing the doctrines of the
new society. As melodrama sought to make itself clear to everyone by
employing the language and imagery of absolutes, so it implied that the
essential moral identity is describable in similarly absolute terms: good
or bad, for or against, virtue or treason. The emblematic extravagance
of the pageant-masters who organized the fêtes of the early 1790s was
thus received as analogous to that of the German dramatists, who, as we
have seen, were also held to be preaching social revolution. Not only
was the melodrama the most popular dramatic form in England in the

1790s; it could also be reasonably seen as the extreme to which all the-atrical experience tended. How, if not by simplifying, could one hope to present the "richness" of great drama, which in the theater must al-ways be consumed at the actors' speed of delivery rather than in the indefinitely extendable measure of the reading experience? Burke himself loved the melodramatic, and precisely—in the eyes of his radi-cal critics—for its privileging of the passing impression, immune to the deconstructions of sober reason. The notorious "dagger scene" he per-formed in the House of Commons was brilliantly reported in one of Daniel Isaac Eaton's shilling pamphlets:

> He has not, to be sure, absolutely produced the match, the phosphorus, and the dark lanthern; but he has produced what will ever redound to the honour and credit of his intellect—he has produced to the Commons of Great Britain, in parliament assembled—a *naked* DAGGER! And I hope that no one will be hardy enough to affirm, that a *dagger* is not sufficient evidence of a scheme to undermine our glorious constitution.[35]

It was as melodrama, and as a manipulation of the excesses of the politi-cal sublime, that radicals like Wollstonecraft and Macaulay criticized Burke's *Reflections* and defined it as a book intending principally to deceive. Both radicals and conservatives, then, shared a disdain for the theatrical mode; no radical alternative to the prevailing consensus about the national (literary) character could hope to succeed by defin-ing itself along those lines.

   While this national character is founded in its occupation of the middle ground between reason and imagination, it yet inclines some-what away from the middle, toward the intuitive-imaginative pole. As such it represents a (re)feminization of the literary and the aesthetic—already feminized media—while it tries hard to project a hearty mas-culine common sense in the spheres of philosophy and natural science. The reaction to the French Revolution only further determined a Brit-ish predisposition against method and theory, and one already and pre-viously defined *against* the perceived habits of the French. The career of Sir James Mackintosh is hardly typical in the extremity of its shift from radical rationalism to Burkean particularity, but it does serve as an instance—perhaps a melodramatic instance—of the tide of events. The *Vindiciae Gallicae* was one of the most read and respected of radical pub-lications in the early 1790s. But in the later *Dissertation on the Progress of Ethical Philosophy* Mackintosh approvingly quotes Bacon's case against the "shew of total and perfect knowledge" that "Method" projects, and warns against the beguiling claims of the "system-maker." Hobbes is brought to trial as an English philosophe and found guilty of preferring the "intellectual" part of our nature over that other part "which feels, and desires, and loves, and hopes, and wills"; he is also convicted of producing a "philosophical palace of ice."[36]

More and more, it would be the literary that would claim to express and encourage this sphere of feeling, desiring, loving, hoping, and willing, in an extended hymn to the virtues of imprecision. In his *Discourse on the Law of Nature and Nations,* the text of a series of lectures given at Lincoln's Inn in 1799, Mackintosh upbraids even Montesquieu, a founding father of liberal relativism, for an overinvestment in "the imposing but fallacious geometrical regularity of system." There is a ringing endorsement of Burke, the old enemy, in the argument that "simple governments are mere creatures in the imagination of theorists," while true freedom is to be looked for in complexity. The proper politician is one able to consider causes that are "multiplied, mutable, minute, subtile, and, if I may so speak, evanescent—perpetually changing their form, and varying their combinations." In this respect, though Mackintosh himself does not make the connection, the politician is like the poet, one who should address himself to the "general feelings and sympathies of mankind" and is "neither warped by system, nor perverted by sophistry."[37]

A definite connection between the language of legislation and that of literary creation and criticism can be adduced between Coleridge's famous description of the imagination as showing itself in the attempted "balance or reconciliation of opposite or discordant qualities" and Burke's profile of the ideal patrician class: "We see, that the parts of the system do not clash. . . . We compensate, we reconcile, we balance. We are able to unite into a consistent whole the various anomalies and contending principles that are found in the minds and the affairs of men."[38] The right sort of poet or politician may possess a methodical mind, but never a method or a system. Coleridge elsewhere argues for poetry as having "a logic of its own, as severe as that of science," but yet "more difficult, because more subtle, more complex, and dependent on more, and more fugitive causes"—so much more complex, indeed, as scarcely to be apparent as a logic at all. Wordsworth's espousal of a "mere theory," albeit of "his own workmanship," is deemed to relate hardly at all with his "genuine imagination" and true "poetic genius."[39]

These claims for a strong but inapparent element of method, discipline, and severe logic in literature, and especially in poetry, may be read as gestures toward a partial remasculinization of the aesthetic faculty, and as an effort to upgrade it out of the merely bourgeois and into the abstract-intellectual sphere, into a realm of methodic classlessness. In his edition of Pope, Warburton had stressed the poet's mastery of "method," evinced to a degree rarely to be met with "even in the most formal treatises of Philosophy" and far beyond what "some were aware of." Warburton's Pope was indeed the perfect hybrid of art and philosophy, avoiding the excesses of each and maximizing the advantages of both:

> But when the writer joins his *speculation* to the *experience* of the observer, his *notions* are rectified into *principles:* and when the observer regulates his *experience* on the *general principles* of the writer, his *conjectures* advance into *science.*[40]

These were large claims indeed, especially when made on behalf of one of the leading apologists of instinct and of great literature's immediate perspicuity. And the problem was indeed to rescue something of a manly method for a genre that otherwise tended all too readily toward simple impressionism and facile immediacy, a tendency very much accelerated, for some, by according the title of literature to a vernacular rather than or as well as to a classical language. In *The Moralists* Shaftesbury's Philocles regrets the degree to which the polite and quite proper disdain for "mere scholastics" has resulted in such an overreaction on the part of our "modern conversations"

> that by such a scrupulous nicety they lose those masculine helps of learning and sound reason. Even the fair sex, in whose favour we pretend to make this condescension, may with reason despise us for it, and laugh at us for aiming at their peculiar softeness. 'Tis no compliment to them to effect their manners and be effeminate. Our sense, language, and style, as well as our voice and person, should have something of that male-feature and natural roughness by which our sex is distinguished. And whatever politeness we may pretend to, 'tis more a disfigurement than any real refinement of discourse to render it thus delicate.[41]

Conversation must, then, remasculinize itself, but not by the attribution of so much "male-feature" as to turn it into methodical or propositional formats.

Various and variously ingenious Romantic efforts to align literature with the practices from which it was coming to be more and more distinct—science and philosophy—may be read as attempts to hold off the incumbent institutionalization of the "two cultures" mentality and of the gendered dichotomy underlying that mentality: science for men, literature for women. Wordsworth, apologizing for his famous preface while also parading the claim that it is not a "systematic defence" of any "theory" governing the poems, advances the notion that poetry is the "breath and finer spirit of all knowledge"; poetry will "follow the steps of the Man of science" or even walk "at his side," familiarizing and making pleasurable his findings for a wider readership.[42] Shelley goes further, making "poetry" the radically creative principle in all human thought and culture: "that which comprehends all science, and that to which all science must be referred." As the agent of change disturbing the reified forms of history and habit, poetry is the seed of all new thoughts and social formations. This extended definition of poetry, of which language is at once instance and origin, allows Shelley to propose a glorious future for the new age at the same time as he admits that the disproportionate cultivation of the "mechanical arts" has so far divided rather than benefited the human species.[43] Plato and Bacon may be poets, and Milton and Dante philosophers, but the synthesis of science, philosophy, and poetry that Shelley imagines also admits the disposition whereby the "grosser sciences" and the "analytical reason" may govern at least temporarily the minds and the affairs of men. His attempt to argue for poetry and the imagination as the turbulent originators of reason itself, and thus indirectly of technology (the "mechanical arts"), taps a vein that has proven of enduring interest to some humanists and philosophers, but his admission of the poets' legislation as "unacknowledged" accords them the status of an always obscure first cause, never apparent in itself. Poetry, by becoming everything, risks being received as nothing.[44]

The positive agendas of Wordsworth and Shelley were by no means uncontested. Peacock, Hazlitt, and Carlyle, among others, saw a definite decline in the status and quality of poetry. The Romantic "self" about which the traditional literary histories have been so eloquent, and which has sometimes been made over into an icon of triumphant individual expressivity, was always a highly unstable and insecure construct (and never more so than in Wordsworth, the source of so many myths of consolation). The increasing production of biography and autobiography suggests that the cultural space given over to literature was more and more characterized by an awareness of the problem of personality.[45] Rousseau's *Confessions* may have attracted attention not just for its sexual frankness (for this was hardly new in eighteenth-century French literature) but also for its determined implication of the discourse of selfhood in what Foucault would call the "analytic of finitude" and propose as the very origin of "man"—the awareness that no description can ever locate the describer in a closed analytical system available as if for third-person inspection, but must always commit him or her to a perpetual and regressive motion through biological, psychological, and historical time.[46] Rousseau's admissions of faulty memory, lying, and utter disregard for literal notions of truth are very much virtues made of perceived necessity, expositions of the attitudes to and consequences of an *un*reconstructable self, which then undermines the Protestant imperative to the construction of exactly such a self. The "unparalleled . . . truthfulness" of the *Confessions* is thus a declaration of untruth, to a degree that has reasonably made Rousseau's writings the paradigm for so much deconstructive exegesis. Nothing can be "really a lie" when there is not place from which to judge it so, not least because "memory" itself is hopelessly fallible. Add to this a compulsion to self-deprecation and an appetite for sentimental opportunities, and all hope of documentary stability disappears.[47]

In more muted and occasionally even displaced forms, Wordsworth's autobiographies make similar confessions. In the Tintern Abbey poem he admits that he "cannot paint/What then I was": he cannot *represent* what he was (an epistemological failing), and he cannot *disguise* what he was (intimating a lack of moral worth). The narrator of *The Prelude* interpolates a qualification that could and should apply to any part of the poem:

> Of these and other kindred notices
> I cannot say what portion is in truth
> The naked recollection of that time,
> And what may rather have been called to life
> By after-recollection.[48]

Imprecision and uncertainty, the spoilers of any aspiration to rational system, are written into Romantic literature as elements of the instability that "literature" itself invokes. Jane Austen's savagely hyperfeminized portrayal of Lady Bertram (in *Mansfield Park*) as one who can never remember what happened or where she put things is differently evaluated, in negative comic terms, but it has something in common with the writerly subject seeking to describe itself, both to itself and to a potential readership.

Some authors tried to steer clear of the extreme implications of the autobiographical hermeneutics displayed in Rousseau and Wordsworth, and thus to dodge or at least offset the dilemmas posed by residence within the "analytic of finitude." There were efforts at more confirmatory kinds of self-fashioning. Hegel's emphasis on the labor of the negative, on the coming-to-be of subjectivity in and through the empirical sphere experienced in time, is also a denial of the rationalist discourse for which immediate and total intelligibility might be possible, and his *Encyclopaedia* is a deliberate alternative to that famous Enlightenment project in which the constitutive role of subjectivity was obscured, ignored, or denied. His *Phenomenology of Mind* is not a conventional autobiography, but it may be read as the symptomatic career of a selfhood, Hegel's or anyone else's, that is so completely embedded in an intersubjective history that there is no ultimate anxiety of alienation. There is alienation along the way: individuals cannot *know* the degree to which they both recapitulate and advance the general course of history. And yet the hindsight of achieved philosophy assures us that nothing has been wasted in the progress toward absolute knowledge.

A more conventional and familiar confirmatory autobiography is the project of Coleridge's *Biographia Literaria*. Here the author's essential (publishable) subjectivity is declared as the product of definite educational and reading experiences nurturing an original instinct. These are reproduced as successful in the task of self-constitution, not only redeeming Coleridge's famously fragmented life from its already deconstructed parts but vindicating the genre of autobiography itself as culturally respectable, prone neither to Rousseauvian nor Wordsworthian indiscretions and articulate as the bearer of orthodox values. These are apparent, indeed, precisely in the criticism of Wordsworth and in the trenchant assessment of what is good and bad. What is bad necessarily includes the poet's refusal of an organic style and his dramatization of the problematics of subjectivity. The *Biographia* at once foregrounds a national literature, through the successive instances of William Lisle Bowles, Milton, Shakespeare, and Wordsworth, and makes that literature the analogue of a proper education (one preferring the art of memory to the Ramist tendency to "dispute and decide") and of a properly ordered personality: "I labored at a solid foundation, on which permanently to ground my opinions, in the component faculties of the human mind itself, and their comparative dignity and importance."[49] The self, as it were, is here made safe for philosophy, church, and state.

A Theory of Imprecision: Utilitarianism

We have seen the terms of a conjunction between the literary and the imprecise (or the precisely unsystematic) characterizing the image of the national literature. Utilitarian thought introduced a new item on the discursive landscape, for it concerned itself with the systematization of imprecision. As such it found itself on a site quite different from the already occupied formations, and at odds with them all. It was systematic but not rationalist, or rationalist only in the most mediated way, and it accepted indeterminacy while remaining hostile to the extreme particularizations of literature.

The origins and full implications of the utilitarian philosophy and of the social movements founded upon it require extensive study.[50] To track even Bentham's sources and influences is a major task for scholarship and interpretation, not least because of the consistently internationalist identity of his writings. For our purposes here the critical feature of Benthamism is its acceptance of the principle of imprecision. But it is handled very differently from the analogous principle that is written into the image of the national literature. Bentham neither admits epistemological despair nor celebrates indeterminacy as some kind of very English virtue, but looks to counter its destabilizing energies by a refinement of method and system: probability theory. He thus offended those who had an interest in using indeterminacy as an argument against social planning or exact speculation, whether in government or in literature. Shaftesbury had described a "sort of amicable collision" as the means by which a measure of polite tolerance might spread through society: our differences are to be accepted and respected rather than plotted or predicted. And Hume, who did discover a standard of "public utility" and "usefulness" in questions of "equity and justice," was uninterested in any redistribution of social benefits as well as in the mathematical models that might be devised to promote it.[51]

Much of the philosophical basis of utilitarianism may be found in the theories of the Enlightenment necessitarians; it is here that the inevitable differences between one person and another are most ingeniously justified and explained. The priority of self-love, of the pleasure principle, and of public utility is emphatic in the writings of Helvétius and Condillac, where it is related to an account of the potential disunity of human society as the result of the first two of these forces. Since no two persons can ever be in precisely the same circumstances, given the different predispositions and biological personalities they bring to those circumstances, then apparently similar determinations cannot be expected to produce similar results.[52] Everything is as it must be, but no two things or persons are ever alike. The atomistic chaos that Hobbes had resolved by language and monarchy (language under monarchial control) is for later thinkers subjected to a calculus of probability. Since no one circumstance can exactly predict another, however apparently similar the conditions of comparison, one limits oneself to probabilistic claims based on a computation of previous outcomes. Relatively constant conjunction replaces cause and effect; rational probability replaces rational certainty.[53]

There is something inevitably democratic about this procedure, since it appears to incorporate a majoritarian analysis of past and present into any supposition about likely futures. At the same time, its positivist refusal to query the constitution of majorities (by ideology or interest) rendered it more compatible with the status quo, whose existence it took for granted, than any straightforwardly rationalist method could ever be. Bentham was radical enough in the eyes of many, but he was almost as far out of step with the rationalists of the 1790s as he was with their conservative antagonists. Nonetheless it was as a radical that he was most commonly identified. John Stuart Mill found him "the great *subversive*, or, in the language of continental philosophers, the great *critical*, thinker of his age and country," admitting also the burden of the metaphysician that we have seen to feature so largely in the myth of the radical: "that cold, mechanical and ungenial air which characterizes the popular idea of a Benthamite."[54] So dominant has that mythology remained, not least thanks to its recirculation in so much nineteenth-century literature (for instance in Keats's "Lamia," where it is proposed that philosophy will clip an angel's wings), that it can be hard to recover the terms of the challenge that Bentham presented to his own generation. We in our turn have become so interested in the psychological-ideological discipline of the panopticon paradigm that we tend to ignore the reformist materialism of so much of Benthamism.

Bentham's critique of Blackstone, published in 1776 as *A Fragment on Government*, was a searing attack on the "blind and intractable nomenclature" of the legal sublime as deployed in the service of "the Aristocrat in all his shapes, including the fee-fed lawyer, and the tax-fed or rent-fed priest, all prostrate at the foot of the throne," and was as such an explicit anticipation of the radical attack on Burke's *Reflections* in the 1790s. Bentham too set out to "emancipate" his reader "from the shackles of authority" and to exercise "the hands of reason and of law."[55] Like Ramus he defended the vernacular as a democratizing energy, endorsing Cromwell's translation of the law from Latin into English. Without proposing any simple universalism of the sort that could be educed from Godwin's or Paine's writings, he yet believed that, when all cultural and geographic factors had been considered and when one was "possessed fully of the facts," a universal legislation could still be deduced: despite all the mediations of culture and interest a workable and systematic social schema, with general predictive efficiency, could be devised.[56] He criticized the 1791 French constitution for being too hasty in formulating "fundamental laws" without the required and preparatory "experiment and observation," but at the same time he believed that the proper precautions could produce such laws. Positioning himself somewhere between Burke and Paine he denied a purely propositional politics—"the origination of governments from a contract is a pure fiction"—while preserving a scathing contempt for the worship of custom for custom's sake. French chemistry should be gratefully received, but French politics (which he also significantly mentored) declined.[57]

Bentham argued against any redistribution of wealth and property, or any disturbance of the hierarchy of the sexes. The "chance-medley of the British Constitution" remains preferable to the false symmetries of the French. At the same time, he favored making divorce easier and encouraged republican France to emancipate its colonies.[58] He manifested a mathematical-propositional style, with numbered paragraphs and tables, giving the appearance that everything followed from or was connected to everything else, in the Ramist tradition. He practiced the sort of radical semantics that Hobbes had rendered forever threatening and that Coleridge, for one, would try to turn to conservative uses. Above all, he was a man of method and theory, so much so that Hazlitt could mock him for imagining that "tyrants had taken a sudden fancy to the abstract principles of sound legislation."[59] He believed that political and moral truths were subject to procedures "as severe as mathematical ones," albeit more complex, and in *The Book of Fallacies* he analyzed the national contempt directed at such terms as "speculative" and "theoretical" in a way very reminiscent of Sieyès in 1789. All knowledge is embedded in theory, and the misuse of theories argues for better ones and not for the negation of all theory:

Can a man disclaim speculation, can he disclaim theory, without disclaiming thought? If they do not mean thought, they mean nothing; for, unless it be a little more thought than ordinary, theory, speculation, mean nothing.

Under the name of "theory" the apologists of "custom" and of the "same sinister interests" dismiss all reference to "the end pursued . . . the greatest happiness of the greatest number." And "that quality in discourse which goes by the name of good method, or simply, *method*," is abused for the same reasons.[60]

In these ways, among others, Bentham outraged the terms of the mythology of the national character even as he upheld certain key principles in the national establishment. He was systematic enough to suffer from the same prejudices that had been directed at the French philosophers and legislators, and in this spirit he showed evidence of the radical's habit of casting the language of the opposition as merely literary and fictional. For him Blackstone was in the business of "giving to Reality the air of Fable," while his own intention was to put an end to "the season of *Fiction*" and to establish a critical distinction between "shewy language and sound sense."[61] There was thus no possible alliance between Bentham's interest in indeterminacy as a philosophical beginning and literature's commitment to the same principle as its own reason for being. Most writers felt utilitarianism to be deeply hostile to the creative imagination and its products, enough so that Mill could reasonably cast Bentham and Coleridge as the antithetical components of the national culture, even as he tried to synthesize their energies. In his important study of the relations between probability theory and Augustan literary forms, Douglas Lane Patey proposes some analogues to that theory in the plots of eighteenth-century novels but finds in the early Romantic culture of sensibility a definite alternative to and a reaction against any nonintuitive mode of verification.[62] The primacy of sensibility is at odds with any attempt at methodical classification, and may as such be read as an imaginary reaction against the very processes of modernization that gave the new reading class its economic security and social visibility. These were the processes that Benthamism came more and more to embody rather than to challenge.[63]

The tensions between accepted notions of literary production and the utilitarian project were clearly set forth in the first issue of the *Westminster Review* in 1824. The very first article, which was not so much the review it claimed to be as a movement manifesto, began by celebrating the new power of the people as the arbiters of all important knowledge, including the literary. From now on, writers must plead their cases "at the bar of the public, and not at that of the legislature or the aristocracy." This enthusiasm for populist adjudication could only have offended a subculture of literary professionals still very much at odds with the terms and implications of a mass readership. Similarly, the perceived incidence of "a dash of politics in almost every production" would not have pleased a literary establishment whose very identity was premised on the distinction between the aesthetic and the didactic. And, perhaps most tellingly of all, the fetish of originality that was at once the demand imposed upon writers and their most precious badge of self-worth was roundly undercut in the *Westminster*'s proclamation that the business of contemporary literature must be largely that of "varying the forms of our forefathers' thoughts" rather than of inventing anything new. The age requires that the "hoarded treasures" of the past be "made available for common use," so that the writer is expected to engage in popularization rather than in original thought. The by now traditional insignia of literary failure—"a good deal of resurrection, or direct and avowed republication"—are here proposed as the very desiderata of the task at hand.[64]

The manifesto introducing the *Westminster Review* suggested nothing less than the entire subsumption of the old debate between literature and metaphysics by a new discursive order whose single criterion of value would be that of use. As it demystifies the role of literature from a primary to a purely reproductive function, so it also edges out the traditional antagonists of the literary: the "geometrical purists" and the metaphysicians whose interests are equally remote from "public interest and public utility." Even the "strict geometrical demonstration" that had for Hobbes and Descartes been the very paradigm of rational intellectual economy is now seen as a "circuitous route" that has been superseded by a new "short cut of analysis" based entirely on the "expeditious and business-like way."[65]

Utilitarianism in many ways takes on the mantle of antiacademicism that Ramism had assumed two hundred years before. But literature at the turn of the nineteenth century was competing for the same space, and on rather different principles. If Benthamism was taken to rationalize the requirements of modern society, literature was more often employed to obfuscate its very operations. As long as the British were at one with nature and human nature, they did not have to contemplate the distinctions of class and kind that made the nation-state work. Literature could perpetuate this happy innocence, whereas utilitarian method took social divisions as its very reason for being, and said so. Thus Benthamism became, in its various reincarnations, the ally of liberal reform, but never of the literary imagination. Mme de Staël approved of probability theory because it preserved the interest in "general ideas" without risking any fanatical attachment to the "dogmas" of "metaphysical systems."[66] As such it found its way into the new national consensus of the reform period after 1815. Literature, however, could not make any peace with the language of method and calculation, even when it did not appear in the extreme form of a rationalist idealism. Precisely to the degree that utilitarian thought functioned as the conscious articulation of middle-class self-interest, literature and the aesthetic preserved a space for imaginary or unconscious freedom and for the experience, by proxy, of an aristocratic spontaneity in the lap of an unprofessionalized leisure. If anything, it moved further from any proximity to method and system, the signatures of science and social science, than it had been before. Carlyle complained sarcastically that we must "have our little *theory* on all human and divine things," thanks to the culture of "codification" and the "domain of Mechanism" that has "now struck its roots down into man's most intimate, primary sources of conviction."[67] Here, we are on our way to the recurring invocation of *1984*, whose images continue to appeal to those critics and intellectuals in search of a shorthand account of all that is wrong with the modern world. If literature can save us, it will only be because, *as* literature, it is thoroughly removed from the demands of the mechanical imagination. What, then, might a radical literature hope to be, when the very conditions of its reception would seem to suggest that anything popular enough to be effective would by definition have to conform to the world as it was? How could a radical literature negotiate its inherited associations with feminized attributes—intuition, particularity, sensibility, uncertainty—and still mount some sort of challenge to the world as it was?

7

A RADICAL LITERATURE?

Plotting the Middle Ground

In the 1790s, for a brief period, the language of radical reform was a propositional language, tending toward the systematic format that had, at least since Ramus, argued complex conclusions from simple beginnings and arrayed itself in a mode that all might read. After about 1815 reform became somewhat less radical and more liberal, advancing very much under the mantle of utilitarian rhetoric. Both the rationalist and the utilitarian paradigms were, as we have seen, in various kinds of tension with the signatures of "literature." And literature itself, insofar as it had any aspiration toward radical social effect, found itself caught between a rock and a soft place, the rock of masculinist theory and the soft place of feminized intuition and sensibility. Like the young Tom Jones caught between his rival tutors, Square and Thwackum, the purveyor of literature found him or herself well advised to plot a cautious route between two rather unbending and antagonistic principles, and punishable for any untoward favoring of the one over the other. In retreat from all doctrinal fixities, young Tom pronounced that "no Rule in the World" could explain his "father" Allworthy's virtues. Readers of literature would find themselves persuaded to similar judgments in describing the effects of their favorite books. With Fielding, they would commonly come to recognize, and through literature, that there is a "Sort of Knowledge beyond the Power of Learning to bestow."[1]

Some among the radical writers had thought that the cause of literature would be dramatically assisted by the phenomenon of the French Revolution. Helen Maria Williams, for one, applauded the perceived interdependence of knowledge and liberty, finding encouragement in the renaming of Parisian streets after writers and philosophers.[2] Rationalists like Condorcet and the early Mackintosh shared the same faith.[3] But the marriage of reason and imagination was never a comfortable one, as Blake realized in giving over a large part of his prophetic writings to their mythical reconciliation. Erasmus Darwin's attempt to "inlist Imagination under the banner of Science" could not avoid interpolating a hierarchy whereby the "looser analogies" of poetry would give place to the "stricter ones" of philosophy (and Hegel would say the same thing in more abstract language), just as the mythographic representations of Jove's lightnings paved the way for Benjamin Franklin. And, as Darwin's wind-nymphs shook a "tinkling rime" from the frozen oaks of England, many saw not only a subversive sexual-scientific doctrine but an inelegant *literature*.[4]

Latterday critics and readers inside and outside the academy have echoed the disapproval of didacticism in literature. In her prefatory essay to a reprint of Akenside's *Pleasures of the Imagination*, Anna Laetitia Barbauld declared that poetry should never "descend to teach the elements of any art or science" or "confine itself" to "regular arrangement and clear brevity." It is a bad poem that makes us "follow a system step by step."[5] According to this formulation poetry must eschew both the mechanical associations of artisan labor and the appearance of methodical speculation, avoiding the respectively masculinist attributions of worker and philosopher. Addison similarly opined that the pleasures of the imagination are to be exercised in a sphere between the "Bent of Thought" that is required for "serious Employments" and the "Sloth and Idleness" of complete passivity. The "understanding," or active, masculinized faculty, demands too much "Labour or Difficulty" and leads to too many "knotty and subtle Disquisitions" to provide pleasure.[6] Literature, again, must neither display nor demand too much visibly intellectual rigor.

At the other end of the spectrum, the task of criticism was to restrain literature from too complete an indulgence in the Gothic and in the stimulation of sensibility. The radicals sought to accuse Burke of just this failure; and the Gothic mode, with its romantic histories and psychological extremities, remained an important limit case against which the "best" literature could be measured. More and more in the twentieth century, as the guardians of the literary felt themselves threatened by what has often come to be called "mass culture," the symptoms of the Gothic would be located in popular forms such as paperback and cinema. At the same time, it seems fair to say that some measure of the Gothic would continue to prove rather more acceptable than any measure of the philosophic or scientific in the constitution of a proper literature. Coleridge smuggled a methodical component into his synthetic conception of the poet as one who should bring "the whole soul of man into activity," but only by insisting that the methodical element would always be unnoticed as such and, as in the case of Shakespeare, made so "habitual and intuitive" as to be inseparable from "feelings." Reciprocally the "subordination" that method always requires should be "gentle and unnoticed," as befits the conservative model of social organization that Coleridge prefers.[7] But even these self-protective tactics were inefficient in preserving Coleridge from accusations of misty and musty metaphysics lodged by readers who were so little inclined to rationalize the literary experience that they failed to recognize the thoroughly conformist ethic at the heart of Coleridge's aesthetics. Literature could have nothing of the philosophical or social-scientific about it as long as it was required, as it was by Mme de Staël, to operate as the antithesis to "the greedy calculation of selfishness or of vanity."[8]

Just as literature was proffered as an experience that could save us from the masculinized calculus of self-interest, so women were more and more coming to be regarded as the domestic counterweights to a public sphere that was just as morally corrupted as it was economically efficient. As I have already suggested, the conjunction between literature and the feminine prescribed a difficult tightrope act for writers and critics of both sexes. Mary Wollstonecraft walked it in trying to demystify the feminization of women by a luxury economy and in seeking to publicize a female rationality that was not to be identified with mere heartlessness. Among males the elitist mode of acceptably masculine disorder, which Shaftesbury paraded and William Hayley, for instance, described as the "fine play of mental powers" that could dispose of "systematic pride," became harder to maintain as the image of the reader and producer of literature became more and more middle-class and more and more identified with women—thus doubly feminized.[9] Associations between literature and corruption were as old as Plato, but they seem to have been especially urgent for those generations negotiating the new definitions of economic opportunity that are so characteristic of the eighteenth century. The taste for literature, wrote Rousseau, could only prevail in a population motivated by "idleness, and a desire of distinction," and one that was therefore hostile to a "sense of true glory" in both moral and military terms.[10] Both literature and women, as they encourage experiences of passion and imagination, are in their excessive modes a threat to civic virtue, albeit necessary in moderation to the healthy functioning of a complex human society and human psychology.

Once again we see here the unstable middle ground that literature and literary criticism would continue to occupy throughout the period of their incorporation into the universities, and on into the present. On the one hand, theory and the analytic method were discredited as scientific and, sometimes, as dangerously democratic; on the other, a too complete complicity in the language of sensibility must render literature (and criticism) hyperfeminized, and thus culturally impotent and emotionally disabling. Writers have sought both to observe and to exploit these constraints, and sometimes to flout them, while critics have set themselves up mostly to patrol the perimeters of proprietous expression, but sometimes to champion the escaped prisoners. At times literature's very miscegenated identity has been made the stuff of our salvation, as if, in a culture more and more defining itself through extremes, the composite mode of literary response can be a saving mixture.

The Wordsworth Question

The first and second generations of writers who came after the French Revolution, and hence after the reemphasized demonization of both theory and sensibility (the alliance of the two being for the British counterrevolutionary press the very trademark of Jacobinism), faced the problem of literary identity in very obvious as well as implicit ways. Wordsworth's famous modeling of an *emotion* recollected in *tranquility* involved him in a litany of oxymorons as he sought to weld together concepts that had been so visibly polarized by the rhetoric of the 1790s. Blake's and to some extent Shelley's ambiguous genderings looked to find positive possibilities in the inherited confusions that had been imposed upon literature. Models of a merely conservative Romanticism do not address these attempted mediations, even if they roughly describe their eventual outcome for the kinds of literary criticism that were built upon the ruins of Romantic writing.[11]

Wordsworth's early writings, at least, represent one of the most thoroughgoing of all attempts to redefine the disadvantages of poetry into strengths, and to create possible victories where others had seen only defeats, or nonnegotiable contradictions. In the preface to *Lyrical Ballads,* a text whose notoriety itself bears witness to the perceived improprieties of mixing poetry and theory, Wordsworth offers a description of good poetry as "the spontaneous overflow of powerful feelings." But that element of feeling must be informed by the results of thinking, and thinking "long and deeply." Customary habit and Rousseauvian (Jacobin) sensibility are here yoked together to afford a solution to the problem Schiller and others had addressed in the debate about the beautiful soul—how to preserve moral and aesthetic propriety while bypassing the routinized operations of the conscious will and the deadening rhetoric of mere duty or obedience. While refusing a "systematic defence of the theory upon which these poems are written," and thus conceding the rhetorical or actual disadvantages of theory in itself, Wordsworth here attempts a synthesis of the otherwise antagonistic principles of Burke and Paine.[12] With Burke he stands for custom and tradition, for the habitual conventions of a relatively immobile and of course quite unrevolutionary subculture: the inhabitants of the remoter rural areas with some actual or imaginary property in the land they inhabit. But with Paine, and against the hierarchical ambitions of Burke, he finds in this immobility an image of democratic social life, devoid of "social vanity," speaking a plain language in which the "gross and violent stimulants" (whether Gothic or chivalric) have no place, and defining an authentic human nature not in terms of education or social rank but in a receptivity to "the grand elementary principle of pleasure."[13] This is no rationalist radicalism, setting forth the rights of man in propositional form; and, by refusing the positive evaluation of the commercial society that was for Paine the foundation of political promise as well as the undeniable way of the future, Wordsworth risks and perhaps performs the lapse into nostalgia. But he takes over the Painite commitment to ordinary language and to the construction of a democratic universalism, here one of feeling, or thought-in-feeling, rather than of pure ratiocination. The image of the rural commonwealth of independent owner-occupiers living under a subsistence regime, of the sort that Wordsworth describes in "Michael" and half-adumbrates in the 1800 preface and elsewhere, could be argued to have been hopelessly out of date as a description of Westmoreland in 1800, and therefore covertly reactionary—a paradise that can only be proposed as such because it has been lost.[14] But Wordsworth's commitment to the language of ordinary persons "in the middle and lower classes of society" was definitely perceived as a radical challenge by a whole generation of reviewers; and by representing those ordinary persons as definitely the protagonists and perhaps the potential readers of polite poetry, it definitely worked against any notion of "the peculiarity and exaltation of the Poet's character."[15] Furthermore, the suggestion that extreme states of physical or mental distress in such persons as beggars, mad mothers, and abandoned women might produce vivid examples of normal human responses was a definite desentimentalizing of the dialectic of identity in difference that kept apart the respectable and nonrespectable elements of society. Wordsworth's contributions to *Lyrical Ballads* certainly rebuke any excessive pride in human reason, and as such might have been received as generically anti-French. But the democratic sentiments at play in his narratives of dispossession are not far removed from the genre of social tragedy that had proved popular in republican France (witness the success of *Paul et Virginie*). Wordsworth explicitly deplores the sad effects of those "sickly and stupid German tragedies that causes such controversy on the English stage."[16] But his own poems definitely trespass into the territory of the disclaimed melodrama, and they were perceived as so doing.[17] At the same time, he is careful to signal his likely contempt for the "meddling intellect," with its "fifty years of reason," and to suggest his disapproval of the "joyless forms" of the republican fêtes that have supplanted a "living calendar."[18]

The thesis of the preface to *Lyrical Ballads*, wherein the volatile potential of the passions is steadied by an interaction with natural forms and forces to the degree that it becomes the basis for possible consensus, is an attempt to reconcile the universality that the radicals of the 1790s had sought only in reason with the spontaneity and particularity of the sympathetic imagination. Under the proper enabling and restraining conditions provided by limited kinds of social and geographical environments, the personal can become or appear as the general, and the individual can embody the best potential of the species. This emphasis on social-geographical determination is modified in the critical texts of 1815 into a psychological analysis of the poetic faculties. But Wordsworth's idiosyncratically formulated ruralist "civic humanism" does survive; as late as 1825 Hazlitt, who was perhaps the poet's most severe as well as his most astute critic, could pronounce that his muse remained a "levelling" one.[19]

To argue for any kind of radical Wordsworth is to go against the grain of most of the best recent criticism—by Jerome McGann, James Chandler, Marjorie Levinson, and Alan Liu, for instance—and to appear to regress to the more traditional consensus figuring the poet as a youthful republican who turned into a middle-aged Tory.[20] The recent criticism, with its emphasis on the covertly reactionary elements in the apparently democratic young Wordsworth, has set out to put the conservatism back into the early career and, in some cases, to disavow completely any radical or countercultural integrity, conscious or otherwise, in the early writings. This is, I think, to go too far, and to render those writings too coherent and too thoroughly a figment of the needs of our post-Althusserian generation, reading back the inevitability of defeat or corruption with a very large authority given to hindsight, and indeed to our own acceptance of disempowerment. Wordsworth's democratic ideology was never a simple, uncompounded thing and never expressed itself as simply identical with any of the available models provided by Paine, Godwin, Mackintosh, Spence, or others. It sought, or found itself obliged to produce, a distinct articulation, not only out of a compulsion to achieve some sort of originality (itself a marketable gesture at the time) but also in response to the pressures directed at poetry itself.

I would not claim that Wordsworth could not have been a radical revolutionary, that he was a revolutionary spirit beaten down by some generic spirit (or economy) of the age. But I would propose that his aptitude for poetry involved him in a determining interaction with the very definite constraints imposed upon that genre, to a degree that any incipient republicanism would have been likely to develop (in a person of his precise disposition and biographical experience) exactly as it did: into a complicated and sometimes inexplicit marriage of different tendencies and aspirations. He could certainly have been more direct in his poeticized politics than he was. After all, John Jordan has persuasively shown that there were, in and around 1798, various kinds of explicitly political poetry against war and slavery and social injustice. And he has suggested also that we should not take simplicity alone as a restrictively "Jacobin" signature: it had become as good as a convention.[21] Furthermore, if we read back from what became of Wordsworth's attempt at articulating a democratic phenomenology of feelings and perceptions, shared by small communities in specific locations, we may tend to regard it as little more than an ideology of sentimental localism and domesticity, offered as a haven in a heartless world rather than as an alternative social model with definite economic and aesthetic implications. To do so would, however, be to miss the distinctness of the initiatives he set going between 1798 and 1805. Famously, Wordsworth himself seems to have been unable to resolve, except by retreat into dogma, the tensions between his own model of an owner-occupier commonwealth and the statewide, delocalized and urban-based democratic movements that carried forth the political and economic ambitions of the ordinary persons on whose behalf he had originally written.

As Wordsworth's republican gestures were moderate and complex, to the extent that they can even be credibly denied by many critics, so too his stand "against method" was seldom as explicit and extreme as that of the counterrevolutionary right.[22] Matthew Arnold put about the notion that this poet was no philosopher, and many since have accepted the model of weak-mindedness as a defining characteristic of Romanticism in general and of Wordsworth in particular. Critics have generally missed the social-economic requirements that are written into the early accounts of the imagination, and they have similarly over-endorsed the anti-intellectual and antirationalist elements of those same accounts. Where Wordsworth writes against Jacobinism, for example, he does not always write against reason. The early text of *The*

Borderers is a rebuke of the Jacobin personality and the "strong inconti-
nence in crime" that power-hungry personalities can give way to; but
this is no simple identification of reason with criminality. Indeed it is
Rivers's hostility toward rather than his respect for the rules of "moralists and saints and lawgivers" that makes him a villain.[23] He identifies
his own psychotic drive to complete independence with an ethic of social freedom, and he is in fact a creature of passion rather than of reason. At the same time, the very unpredictability of his passions can be
read as a warning against accepting any rational paradigm as adequate
to the description of human nature.

In this respect Wordsworth definitely signals his differences from
the Paines and the Priestleys who believed that human affairs were indeed subject to rational perfectibility. He endorses thereby the image of
the necessary complexity of the human that would become more and
more visibly the very hallmark of the generically literary approach. In
the 1799 draft of what would become *The Prelude* the cry of "hard task to
analyse a soul" again limits the role of "analytic industry" and of "geometric rules" and makes a virtue of its willingness to complicate the
"unity" of its argument by describing things that cannot be "regularly
classed."[24] By this time, after Pitt's dalliance with Benthamite principles
for reforming the poor law, this negation of Wordsworth's is directed as
much against the utilitarian as against the radical rationalist argument.
At the same time, he remains, as he does throughout the later drafts of
the poem, friendly toward mathematical models that are understood
simply as such and limited to mathematical contexts. Geometry appears
as evidence of "an independent world / Created out of pure intelligence," and the retrospective narration transcribes the appeal of the
"clear / And solid evidence" of mathematics as fitting consolation for
the disappointments of Godwinism.[25]

Any judgments we might make about the professions of *The Prelude*
are of course problematized by their being intermediate and recollected; they always invite the suspicion of irony and distance, even
where they do not seem to require or confirm them, and they can always
be read as indicative of a more enlightened state of mind in the present
tense of the writing itself. But Wordsworth never negates a positive
function for mathematical intelligence within what he sees as its proper
limits, even as he consistently prefers to discover an ordering principle
in nature, in the "forms distinct" that defend him from "disjoining, join-
ing things / Without the light of knowledge."[26] Nature here performs
the function of a method, adjudicating the connections he makes by a
consistent standard. It is not abstract method, and it is one not articu-
lable except within the sphere of a performing self aroused to imagina-

tive perception. If this is far from the ready and easy way of the Ramist and radical rationalist traditions, it is equally at a distance from the Burkean endorsement of mere habit upheld by acquiescence in the social and political establishments. Nature is more to Wordsworth than mere second nature.

Even in *The Excursion,* a poem whose political conservatism is so often taken for granted, Wordsworth refuses any complete denunciation of reason and of the rational instinct. The finest moments in the Wanderer's early education are reported as those in which "thought was not," moments of relief from "his intellect / And from the stillness of abstracted thought." It is the Wanderer who dismisses Voltaire as a mere "scoffer" driven by "impious pride."[27] But the "equitable law" and "mild paternal sway" that the Solitary had seen promised in the fall of the Bastille are never negated in themselves. The Wanderer's reiterated prescription for coping with life's vicissitudes is one that enters also into Wordsworth's nondramatic writings in midcareer: obedience to "duty" as the (Kantian) product of "abstract intelligence" beyond the confines of "space and time." But the dramatic tension of *The Excursion* consists not least in the juxtaposition of the Solitary's recounted idealism, sympathetic by virtue of tragedies both personal and historical, with the Wanderer's rather bleak and impregnable faith—a faith that visibly fails to create any enduring consensus at the end of the poem. The narrator's own intrusion of buoyant nationalism—"Hail to the State of England!"—is uncontextualized by any but the most attenuated hints of his poetic personality, which on this occasion finds its anchor in the established church and in the particular figure of the Pastor.[28] The Wanderer's severe metaphysics is not the single authority in the poem, and if it is respected it is at the same time presented as a standard that few can match, or perhaps would want to match. Wordsworth's "Ode to Duty," which more than any other poem prefigures the Wanderer's attitudes, tos and fros between the barely repressed appeals of instinctual delight and the (maternal) reproofs of a consistent ethical law without ever quite settling into acceptance.[29]

It would be hard to argue that Wordsworth's poetry did not become more generally conservative as the poet aged and found himself more frequently rewarded for his talents. His dismay at the spectacle of a working class "trained to theoretic feud" is drearily conformable with a series of similar reservations by bewildered Tories from the 1820s on.[30] In the early poetry, however, Wordsworth's position remains somewhat to the left of the nationalist consensus, if we take that consensus to be typified by Burke (though this should perhaps be queried) and by a general disapproval of the claims of all rational endeavor and all democratizing sympathies. He claims to have gloried in his existence as an "Englishman," one "born in a land the name of which appeared/ To licence some unruliness of mind," but he never trespassed into the kinds of rhapsodies to chivalry and aristocracy that attracted such pointed criticism to Burke's writings. The hindsight of the 1830s allowed for an expressed respect for Burke as the exploder of "upstart Theory," and these sentiments figure also in the published poem of 1850. But the endorsement is late and limited (and first appeared, indeed, along with a parallel tribute to Burke's liberal enemy Charles James Fox).

Wordsworth's preferred renderings of "nature," "experience," and "truth" are definitely Baconian in their relation to context-bound and situated perceptions rather than to the abstractions of a "logic and minute analysis" that can indeed preclude error but never create truth. The attempt to promote poetry as the synthesis of the emotional and the scientific nevertheless prevents him from endorsing the strong anti-rationalist rhetoric of the counterrevolution. He proposes instead a remaking of reason by passion, so that passion becomes "highest reason in a soul sublime" or "reason in her most exalted mood."[31] But this attempted reidentification of the very two faculties that the ideological reaction to 1789 had specified as either tragically separate or (in the Jacobin personality) misguidedly combined had to cause problems for Wordsworth's readers, especially since his poetic argument is not marked by a Coleridgean endorsement of a corresponding social and political hierarchy (this remaining, I would say, the critical difference between the two writers). We might say that Wordsworth fudges the question; or we might say that he seeks to explore a literary politics that is not clearly committed either to a Burkean political order or to the radical agrarian alternative provided by Thomas Spence—a politics, indeed, that is arguably enacted solely in the sphere of the literary experience, while the exact limits of that sphere are either not understood or not specified.

Understandably, it was not the doctrinal ingenuity of Wordsworth's political-economic imagination that found a place in a radical tradition. Its complexity and its inexplicit articulation have proven too literary and anachronistic for the political theorists (for it could never deal sympathetically with urbanization, the primary given factor in nineteenth-century political life) and too unfamiliar for the practitioners of a literary criticism that Wordsworth himself in many ways helped to create. Finally, such subversive effects as the poetry has had have been derived more from its declared commitment to ordinary language (in "theory," as it were) than from the intricate and ambivalent democracy of rural sympathizers whose lives the poems themselves record. This challenge was felt by the generation of 1800, and it is felt to this day by a literary-critical academy that still functions in part to preserve a visible priority for the display of *special* language skills. Nonetheless, it is hard not to register the view that we are here speaking of a radical *literature* rather than a *radical* literature; that is, the shock of the Wordsworthian is one most tellingly felt within the subculture of the literary, whose relation to any wider or more general culture is itself, and ineluctably, the subject of concern and skepticism. This condition itself seems to refute the general claims that theory might make for a comprehensive application across a diversified (local and global) society. In the writings of William Blake, which most readers would agree to be more explicitly political than those of Wordsworth, we encounter another though not unrelated version of the aspiration to a radical literature.

The Struggle with Albion's Angels: William Blake

No one, it would seem, doubts Blake's revolutionary aspirations. Blake's writings are required reading for anyone engaged in the search for a radical literature, and passages from them are regularly encountered in left-activist manifestos. Upon close inspection we can, however, see that Blake's radical initiative is not unmarked by tensions of its own, even as they are addressed in a more directly libidinal and challenging way than can be contained within any Wordsworthian category of imagination.

Like most of the poets, Blake is no Painite radical. He has what has come to be regarded as the standard Romantic antipathy toward rational systems and abstract propositions. The misguided angels who are in fact truly demonic are those who converse in "Analytics" and speak of themselves as the "only wise . . . with a confident insolence sprouting from systematic reasoning." First causes are not to be looked for in general principles but in acts of imagination: "What is now proved was once, only imagin'd." In a play on the contemporary habit of landscaping, Blake finds that the "crooked roads without Improvement, are roads of Genius." The ready and easy way is here given no credit: genius dawdles, dilates and digresses, precluding accusations of passive femininity largely by its primitive and unpredictable energies. Blake is hostile to any (Ramist) single method, seeing there only the single vision of the state of Ulro. His energies come from a dialectic, from a conflict of contraries that must not be reduced. Whoever tries to "reconcile" the Prolific and the Devourers (one instance of this conflict) "seeks to destroy existence."[32] Religion tries to do just this, and so does rational method. Indeed, Blake finds rational method to be the corrupt core of the orthodox Judeo-Christian tradition: it is Urizen who perverts a "fiery joy" into the "ten commands" and initiates a negative mythology wherein mystery masquerades as "Science."[33]

Blake, however, shares with Paine and with others among the dissenting radicals a belief in the inevitability and desirability of revolution, and in its necessary origin in mental rather than in empirical-historical events. As Paine wrote of France in 1789: "The mind of the nation had changed beforehand, and the new order of things had naturally followed the new order of thoughts." Paine locates the terms of this change of mind in rational-utilitarian instincts: "reason and common interest."[34] Blake's specification of the motivational energies of human nature is much more inspirational and libidinal: desire and imagination, with their attendant and inevitable shadow faculties that bring with them suffering and confusion as well as love and pleasure. In his early prophetic works Blake deploys the language of light against the reactionary sublime of darkness and obscurity, very much in the manner of Paine, Price and Barlow, and the other radicals. But he never omits from the reckoning a necessary confrontation with that same darkness and despair as part of the rites of passage of his prophetic protagonists. *America,* engraved in 1793, maintains a relatively straightforward optimism about the birth of a new global political order, and sublime confusion is indeed here the rhetoric of tyranny and of melancholic self-deception. But the motif of erotic liberation in which the political is couched is complicated from the start by the rape (by Orc of the daughter of Urthona) that sets going the revolutionary process itself. The onset of light and of new beginnings is never, for Blake, merely a static, innocent, rational enlightenment but a fiery turmoil of released libido through which all vocabularies are redefined.

Blake's very visible stand against method is not always easy to contextualize. We are surely right to read his antirationalist polemic as an anti-Enlightenment gesture, and also as a rejection of the kinds of radicalism associated with the French and British "Jacobins." But, as Margaret Jacob has persuasively argued, the figure of Newton, frequently invoked by Blake as the demon of rational system, was also associated with the established church and with the official philosophy of the Royal Society. In this respect Newton might have been an image of "the rejection of republican and democratic forms of government" and of "libertine and pantheistic modes of Enlightenment."[35] Newtonianism and scientific method could then have appeared to Blake as doubly compromised and as a false image of the radical imagination, superficially challenging but covertly co-opted by the established interests. Donald

Ault has shown in great detail the complexity of Blake's response to Newton, arguing for a recognition of Newton as no mere mathematical rationalist but a complex and even contradictory exponent of scientific, theological, and occultist paradigms. He suggests that Blake identified Newton and Descartes, two figures usually imaged as antithetical by the British tradition, as "co-conspirators" against the imagination, while he also worked within and between their systems and vocabularies, recognizing them not just as objective enemies but as incarnations of the repressive (and hence ultimately redeemable) energies within even the imaginative self.[36]

The dialectical nature of Blake's presentation of almost everything is certainly a feature of the prophetic books as well as of the more famous *Songs*. A belief in the possibility of absolute difference or complete rejection is consistently presented by Blake as itself the symptom of an alienated mind. This wholistic doctrine, with its faith in the synthesizing powers of visionary love, has been proposed as the core of Blake's connection to the seventeenth-century radicals.[37] Thus, for him, reason has a place but only a place. (For Winstanley, we recall, it had been a positive agent, acting against the mysteries of the "imagination.") The fantasy that what is properly a part might become the whole is Urizen's original error, just as the gradual reincorporation of Urizen is perhaps the dominant narrative component of Blake's writings taken as a whole.

Even in *The Book of Urizen*, arguably Blake's darkest and most bitterly self-critical poem, the dialectic of reincorporation appears simultaneously with that of separation, both in Los's agonies over the binding-down of the law-giving patriarch, and in Fuzon's expedition to a possible promised land. W. J. T. Mitchell has made the interesting and, I think, convincing case for this poem as a rejection not just of reason but of that phase of the French Revolution associated with the influence of Condorcet. Mitchell argues for placing Blake within a tradition of Romantic opposition to *writing* in its identity as the operative mode of rationalist revolution. He sees in Urizen a satirical image of "textual man," even a "neo-Burkean caricature of revolutionary rationalism."[38] In particular, he sees the famous frontispiece to the poem as a composite image of Rousseau and Condorcet, famous respectively for self-absorption and rational-textual idealism. Mitchell's argument works to position Blake's reaction to the later phases of the French Revolution as very much in the mainstream of British dissent, though it never becomes Burkean in any extended sense. Condorcet's *An Authentic Copy of a New Plan of the French Constitution* had been translated in 1793, the year before Blake engraved his poem. And Urizen himself, in the frontispiece, is shown as a blind or slumbering copyist (and perhaps as an

engraver) hunched down with his back to a pair of upright tablets looking very like those on which the *Déclaration des droits de l'homme* were inscribed and represented as such in popular prints of the revolutionary
period. Condorcet did make statements suggesting a preference for
Urizenic simplicity over, for example, the liberal cultural relativism associated with Montesquieu.[39] In his writings on education, however, he
was adamant that the public authority did *not* have the right to decide
"where truth resides or where error is to be found," as he was outspoken in his opposition to the "dark fanaticism" of a state religion.
Even the constitution, as he described it in 1791, was to be open to re-
evaluation and correction. He made this explicit again in 1793, arguing
for "a constitutional mode of subjecting the constitution itself to reform
at fixed intervals."[40]

   That Condorcet himself was no mere Urizen-figure does not of
course mean that Blake might not have thought of him as such. In
so doing he would merely have been participating in what we have seen
to be a nationalist mythology reducing all things French to violent
extremes of reason and passion. And Blake did reproduce that mythology, at times in quite parochial ways. Edward Duffy has, for instance,
noted that, "of the fourteen Rousseau entries in the *Blake Concordance*,
not a single one allows Jean-Jacques to stand free of Voltaire."[41] We
have seen that the two apparently antithetical qualities of aristocratic
rationalism and bourgeois sentimentality were indeed the twin demons
of the British image of France, as they were also located side by side in
the Panthéon by the French themselves. But this degree of specificity
was probably not envisaged by most of their abusers, who intoned these
names as signifiers of all that was bad about the French. The French
constitution of 1791 did in fact allow for its own reformation. But, for
Blake in 1794, it could well have been the entire governmental ideal
that had come under suspicion, and he could have found its shortcom-
ings as much in the old regime of prerevolutionary France as in the de-
liberations of the early 1790s. In May 1788 Louis XVI had announced
that a great state required "one king, one law, one registration"—
almost exactly the Urizenic "one King, one God, one Law" that Blake
would satirize six years later.[42] *The Book of Urizen* could then be a compound critique of the recent political scene, as it is of the accumulated
creation myths of both Christian and pagan history; it might be read as
an address to the repetition compulsion in French political culture that
others besides Blake found evidenced in the course of the Revolution.
If Urizen is a Robespierre figure in his self-propelled separation from
the trammels of consensus politics, then he is also the sign of a cycle of
tyranny coming full circle.

The Book of Urizen, for all its cosmological scope, does then seem to suggest a special relation between the fantasy of rational control and the problems of French politics. In the later prophetic books the critique of instrumental reason lies at the heart of Blake's attack on the general conditions of modernity itself. Like Wordsworth he upbraids those who "murder by analyzing"; like Coleridge he asserts that "he who would do good to another, must do it in Minute Particulars," and not in abstract obedience to some ideal of "General Good." In *Jerusalem*'s extended statement against the "abstract objecting power" we can trace the ultimate lineaments of Blake's case against system and method, whether rationalist or utilitarian.[43] Here, more thoroughly than ever, social renovation is imaged in terms of a personalized release of erotic and imaginative energies. Implicitly this is a critique of the myths of the national character, although it is presented as the restoration of a very British Albion. The final night of *The Four Zoas* had redeemed Urizen out of "cold abstraction" and "self destroying beast formd Science"; and the end of "Mystery" that comes with the last judgment is also the end of the belief in an absolute, reified dichotomy of reason and passion. Urizen had begun by giving way to a fantasy of choice: "I have sought for a joy without pain, / For a solid without fluctuation."[44] This illusory quest was also that of the French, according to so many of their British critics. The eventual reunification of reason *with* passion and imagination is thus, in a way, both an example of the British "middle way" and a deconstruction of the rhetoric that had allowed for the differentiation of Britain from France. The two terms of the "Jacobin" personality are no longer schizophrenically alienated from each other and productive of violent metamophoses. In blending rather than yoking together by violence the rational and the erotic, Blake's last judgment might be thought to include the French under its redemptive umbrella. We will never know, since Blake did not make specific any extension of his model beyond that of a renovated Britain. And hardly anyone read these books to provide additional comment. Just as Wordsworth's campaign on behalf of the language of ordinary persons had its major effects on the literary subculture rather than on national political life, so it must be said that the radical potential of Blake's writings remained almost entirely unrealized in their own generation, for reasons both of doctrinal obscurity and productive scarcity. Although David Erdman, in his monumental *Blake: Prophet against Empire,* has traced precise political references throughout the writings, they are sufficiently transformed into sublime allegory to remain both obscure and debatable. Blake's attack on single vision, moreover, included also, in its choice of a composite art, an attack on the narrowly textualist habits of the readers of poetry. For all these reasons, the books that all might read were in fact read by very few. As literary critics we have become used to identifying a kind of radical effect in the afterlife of texts, available long after their original writers and readers have passed away. Blake has fared better here; and it is no accident that the first great articulation in British literature of exactly this idea of deferred redemption comes from his great contemporary, Shelley.

Eroticism and Futurity: Shelley and Keats

If Blake presents us with a dialectic of expression and restraint, imagination and reason, that is finally given apocalyptic power in the last judgment, then it is still eros that contains logos, and not the other way round. The subsumption of the historical by the psychosomatic is finally achieved by acts of love rather than by moments of achieved rational insight of the sort that conclude, for example, Hegel's *Phenomenology of Spirit* and *Encyclopaedia*. And we may take this distinction as typifying the respective fates of literature and philosophy as they define for themselves places in the discursive economy of modern European culture. (Hence this is the distinction deliberately eroded by Nietzsche, Freud, and Derrida, to name but three). Blake's universalized subjectivity claims to preserve a place for minute particulars and even announces them as the sine qua non of authenticity; but it is quite devoid of the *historically* personalized idiosyncrasies of Rousseau's *Confessions* (and even, in milder forms, of Wordsworth's *Prelude*), which made that book so threatening to any idea of consensus or even of continuous identity. As such Blake's paradigm really manages to avoid history, in any of the senses that made it so problematic for those not fully confident of the potential identity of individual and species that the sublime allegory promised to exemplify. And thus it occupies a particularly *literary* space in its alternative to those kinds of objectivity now more and more identified with philosophy and the unimaginative sciences: system, method, and theory.

Within that space it nonetheless exploits very fully the subversive potential of the erotic. Blake's case for the uncontainable personality calls forth an uncontainable style, "variety in every line," and a declaration of nonrestraint: "Poetry Fetter'd, Fetters the Human Race."[45] And its emphasis on the libidinal, which was (as Christopher Hill and A. L. Morton have shown) a strong element in English radical Protestantism, does indicate and exemplify one kind of radicalism available to literature, a radicalism now founded not in the generation of systems but in the subversion of all systems. Insofar as the tendency to systematic rationalization was identified as a prominent feature of the post-Romantic world, literature's general stance against method also positioned it in opposition to the entire project of modernization. This "conservative" predisposition has remained evident among both writers and critics of literature, although it has recently passed over into a different formation, wherein it has been reenergized by an alliance with the antimethodical ethic of postmodernism.

In its more extreme incarnations, in the writings of Blake, Shelley, Hardy, Joyce, and Lawrence (which yet stop short of the further extremes represented by the genres of the perverse and of perceived pornography), literary eroticism has been received as a genuine challenge to its middle-class readers, both professional and general. The task for such writers as Shelley and Blake may be thought of as requiring some strategy whereby the accepted Romantic imperative to self-invention and self-creation can be directed away from any lapse into the more banal vocabularies of the national character, themselves functioning within a rhetoric of freedom and self-expression. By the techniques precluding their popularity, as well as by the political-erotic content of their writings, Blake and Shelley have avoided such easy incorporation, in a way that Wordsworth has not. While Blake's imaging of a revolutionary erotic is mostly shadowed by the experience of the fall as at least a temporary (and temporal) obstacle, Shelley's comparative freedom from the inheritances of Christian culture at first seems to provide a more consistently paradisal prospect. But the strain of transcendentalism in Shelley's densest and most thoroughly worked poetry can position its resolutions just as far beyond the "stain of earthliness" as does Blake's Christianity.[46] His most overtly rationalist poem, the early *Queen Mab*, went unpublished except in a limited edition for private circulation. Its visibly didactic component—the poem has as many pages of footnotes as of verse—does not, however, make it a simple manifesto for the rationalist position. It believes in "Reason's voice" and looks forward to a time when "reason and passion" will cease to be antagonists (this was also Blake's project), but its case against tyranny and war is informed also by clear pantheist and neoplatonist doctrines.[47]

The poem begins and ends, moreover, with framing references to the element of erotic love that will more and more compose the terms of Shelley's envisioned alternative to a merely rational, systematic reform of the sort henceforth commanded largely by the utilitarians. Shelley remained a profoundly intellectualized poet, whose sources and inspirations in a range of scientific and philosophical doctrines cannot be denied.[48] Their incorporation into a complex ethics of love and epistemology of metaphor renders them, however, at once difficult to follow and themselves transformed into a distinctly psycholiterary language.[49] This language is marked by a dialectic of affirmation and retraction that never allows Shelley's work to emerge into utopianism or simple idealism. In "Alastor," a poem that in many ways parallels *The Book of Thel* and *The Book of Urizen*, it is self-absorption that precludes sexual-social harmony. The same syndrome arguable afflicts "Epipsychidion" in a more explicitly personalized context. *The Revolt of Islam* (1818) suggests that the terms of any proper revolution are to be looked for in the emancipation of women and the universal reign of love within a somewhat Wordsworthian but far more eroticized single "human heart."

But even here Shelley takes conscious refuge in the imprecision of the literary. While wishing to further a "liberal and comprehensive morality" and the cause of "liberty and justice," his preface nonetheless eschews any attempt at "methodical and systematic argument" and promises a poem that will be "narrative, not didactic." Mary Shelley's note also begins by assuring us that, despite the poet's extraordinary "logical exactness of reason," his primary commitment is to the imagination and to poetry. Whatever alliances Shelley sought to make between "Science, and her sister Poesy"—and he did so seek—it seems that poetry was to remain the senior partner and the ultimate principle of cultural synthesis, as the argument of *A Defence of Poetry* makes clear.[50] Poetry's principal executor is love, an anarchistic rejuvenating energy whose linguistic analogue is metaphor. The materials of science are its tools but not its essence. Didactically simplified, Shelley's ideas here come quite close to those of Erasmus Darwin and to the Enlightenment materialists upon whom they both drew.[51] His and Mary's sensitivity to accusations of didacticism suggests an awareness of the debates that *The Botanic Garden* had aroused: the poem was denounced as at once too doctrinal, and hence unpoetic, and as immoral. The suggestiveness of poetry is what appeals to Shelley as an alternative to the more explicit, propositional language of science and philosophy. At the same time, his recourse to suggestiveness, and to a complicated allegorical-symbolic apparatus, denies him the satisfactions as well as the encumbrances of clear communication. *Prometheus Unbound* again denies any attempt at "a reasoned system" and positively discredits the "didactic."[52] And again, its challenging subsumption of culture and science within an ethic of universal love is mediated through the poem's sheer difficulty, which is of an order that makes it possible to take quite seriously Shelley's own assertion that it was meant only for "the more select classes of poetical readers."[53] Like Blake, Shelley writes himself out of a general audience for his most meditated poetry; and as with

Blake, that gesture is at once chosen and enforced. It is hard to say, for instance, to what degree the calling into question of the very medium of communication, in language and syntax, is a *chosen* priority, in a world where the entire project of poetry was contextualized in such conflicting ways: as individualist and "original," as imprecise, as apolitical, and as feminized.

Not for nothing, then, does *A Defence of Poetry* make the case for the necessary latency of all truly poetical effects at such times as the poetic-creative principle is at odds with the priorities of its cultural-historical matrix. Shelley clearly hoped for better from his own, contemporary moment. But he provided, as insurance, the theory that would explain its failures without diminishing the claims that could be made for the creative imagination in its primary incarnation, poetry. To the best of my knowledge, Shelley's is the first sustained exposition of a field of inquiry we now call "reader response." He is interested in how literary items are received and in how they could be said to be "understood" or "misunderstood." In his extended argument, the doctrinal and the didactic become disguises or distractions, along with the languages of systems and the enchantments of theory. What makes *A Defence of Poetry* so enduringly modern, despite its platonizing moments, is its recognition of the desperate need to find a place for literature in a discursive landscape that would deny it any effect, and certainly any radical effect, as the price of its exemption from certain kinds of punishment or inquisition. What we now recognize as "cultural criticism" has not extricated itself from these dilemmas and paradoxes, for it continues to have to respond to determinations very similar to those perceived by Shelley.

Shelley's ideal of renovation by way of the imaginative-erotic is, then, placed in a relation to general history that is incipiently adversarial. These larger, general pressures are also symptomatized as individual attributes, as in "Epipsychidion," which attempts a personal, biographical application of ideals that are more easily held simply as ideals, for future rather than present incarnation. The case for a nonanalytic pleasure principle wherein "each part exceeds the whole" must be made against the incumbent limits of existing selves, here including not just the proverbially hostile critics but the denizens of the Shelley circle itself.[54] If one of the implications of "The Triumph of Life" is that a failure in self-knowledge brings down all knowledge, then it is not clear that Shelley ever convinces himself that he has, except momentarily or in imagination, passed beyond the mystery of self. His location of that mystery within the vocabulary of the erotic makes him, like Blake, prescient of the culture of psychoanalysis that in so many ways comes to share with literature the work of privatizing critical reflection. We are back once again with the legacy and instance of Rousseau's *Confessions*, where the integrity of all pronouncements is queried by their emanation from an interested but unpredictable subjectivity.

Similar questions devolve from the poetry of Keats, which also explores the conflicts that arise in the construction and expression of personality, and especially in the sphere of the erotic. Keats's interest in the positive applications of imprecision, and his apparent commitment to an ethic of tolerant uncertainty, have been canonized as the incarnation of a normative Romantic aesthetic. But there are complications. Passions are mixed and unpredictable and cannot be methodically anatomized; but they are not readily envisaged as the medium of any general social reform. Philosophy may indeed clip an angel's wings, but it is not clear how far the angel would fly even if unburdened by it. The love of Isabella and Lorenzo is no match for the cruelty of her brothers, backed by superior social power; the resolution of "The Eve of St. Agnes" is to say the least indecisive; and only Lamia, a supernatural being whose contact with mortal life proves tragic, has the talent to achieve the Urizenic ideal and to "unperplex bliss from its neighbour pain."[55] Keats displays the standard Romantic impatience with the neoclassical and Enlightenment restraints, despising "rusty laws lined out with wretched rule," but he has nothing simple to put in their place. Given that nothing can reveal "the dark mysteries of human souls / To clear conceiving," it is a dynamical sublime, a "vast idea" alone, that gives a justification for the language of poetry.[56]

This embrace of the indeterminate is, however, not always, or even commonly, an occasion for celebration. Reflecting as it does on any prospect for apprehending or employing a determinate selfhood, an achieved identity, it casts radical doubt on the credibility of the commonplace self-other relations that we assume and find necessary in the conduct of ordinary life. Keats's narrative persona as poet or author frequently slides into that of his protagonists, who similarly merge with and into one another. There is a fairly constant confusion as to who is who (especially apparent in "Endymion"), where is where, and who says or does what to whom. The erosion of ego identity, so often celebrated by latterday commentators, is in Keats's poetry mostly allied with the traumatic. Nor is ego identity itself a desired state. Any celebration of an aesthetic state wherein we do not know whether we "wake or sleep," "what flowers" are at our feet, or why we "sojourn here"—and there are countless examples of poets and protagonists thus teased out of thought—needs to be set against the insistence on the recurrence of a "sole self" whose integrity is not so much the source of ontological self-confidence as of simple loneliness or sensory deprivation, "alone and palely loitering."[57]

We may suggest, then, that Keats's confident impatience with what he perceived as an Enlightenment ideology of "clear conceiving" was not matched by any convincing confidence in the alternative values, to self and to society, of vast conjecture, or even of a humbler passiveness. Perhaps it is this fastidious agnosticism, knowing as it does the deficiencies of both extremes and knowing also the implausibility or impossibility of any comforting compromise between the two (for Keats has no truck with British common sense), that explains the strange suspensions of the end of "Lamia": Lycius and Lamia are both at fault, and both innocent. Both die, as Keats erases any clear distinction between mortal and immortal beings, of the sort that would allow us a moral judgment. If Keats had made it clear that Lamia lived on to prey again on young men, then we would have a tale of female vampirism. By making her wholly human—she too sighs a "death-breath"—in a secular parody of Christ's incarnation and fate as one finally, fully forsaken, Keats deprives the gender system of its traditional valencies of innocent boy and knowing woman.[58] Lamia's terror at public exposure need not be read merely as fear of philosophy's cold eye but can be received as grief for the end of emotional reciprocity and total (if tortured) mutuality. Apollonius, in Keats's careful construction, is no hero; Lamia is no heroine; and Lycius, the one in the middle, between reason and passion, male philosophy and female passion, is no golden mean. Nor does the poem offer a hint of how disaster might be avoided, given the corrupted core of a human nature that cannot resist, in Lycius, commodity culture and its compulsion to display. In a world where both passion and knowledge seem both destructive and self-destructive, there is no way out, and apparently no option of simply cultivating one's own garden.

Recent criticism has tended to explore the troubled themes and narratives of Keats's longer romances, as if the traditionally celebrated odes have been canonized to the point of inertia or passive acceptance. But the same deliberate dissatisfactions may be argued there too, in the bizarrely decadent admonitions of "Ode on Melancholy," in the incipiently parodic pseudo-philosophics and stylistic excesses of "Ode on a Grecian Urn," and in the momentarily gratifying but patently inept confusion of species with individual ("Thou wast not born for death, immortal bird") that marks "Ode to a Nightingale."[59] Keats is confident of what he is against, which in terms of this study we may call Enlightenment method, but quite unsure about what he can be comfortably for.

The culture of feeling and intuition that some Romantic writers and many more subsequent literary critics have specified as the very humanness of their "Romanticism" is deconstructed by Keats even before it gets going. (It is also deconstructed by Wordsworth in the sphere of empirical encounter, where misunderstandings replace communication, by Shelley in the abstraction of desire itself, and by Byron always.) Keats thus implants the terms of a recognition that the very vocabulary of what will be "literature" for the nineteenth and twentieth centuries may be poisoned at the source, held back from complete decadence (where it is held back) only by refusing the commitment to fixation. Imperfection, incompletion, and frustration, in the coexistent spheres of the philosophical, the formal, the social and the sexual, are not to be recuperated as the symptoms of a self-accepting humanness but rather persist within the paradigm of the trauma. The Enlightenment paradigm has gone, but nothing has appeared to take its place.

The notoriously difficult argument of "The Fall of Hyperion," one of Keats's most direct efforts at posing the question of the nature and use of poetry, fails to make unambiguously clear the relative merits of poets and dreamers, bringers of balm and vexers of the world, as it also obscures any clear statement of where he places himself in this contrast.[60] Its difficult logic appears to place the narrator below the rank of poet, in the publicly recognized sense, and yet as one rewarded with the vision because of his extradition from earthly gratifications. In making worldly impotence the very qualification for the attainment of aesthetic insight, Keats here appears to accept the verdict of his near-complete "feminization" and to try to turn necessity to virtue.[61] Imprecision and disempowerment fail to produce either a finished poem or an argued condition of earthly satisfaction. Similarly, in so much of his poetry, the erotic component survives as a measure of failure and frustration rather than as any index of a better world to come.

The Romantic project, at least as evidenced in Blake, Shelley, and Keats, may be summarized as follows, as it concerns the relation between the literary and the erotic: the search for a consensual and thus potentially reformist or revolutionary language steers clear of the (anyway unmarketable) systematic and didactic only to run aground on a form of inwardness whose variations are beyond prescription and sometimes even description. This does not mean that its radical challenge was not felt, and widely opposed by a middling restriction of the literary to the delineation of moderate feeling and common sense manners. Indeed, much of subsequent literary history may be read as the record of the containment processes applied to the likes of Hardy, Joyce, and Lawrence as they reactivated the challenge that the erotic could present to the gradualist paradigms of the national (literary) character. (Wordsworth offended in a different way, departing from the middle course in the other direction, toward an abstracted coldness and near-extinction of all rhetoric of feeling.) The "Jacobin" novel of the 1790s, as authored by Godwin, Mary Hays, and others, failed by virtue of its overindulgence in the language of reason and philosophy. That recourse has been denied to literature ever since. Systems, propositions, and theories have been more and more associated with cold-blooded social reformers and would-be radical politicians.

The other side of the British myth of the French revolutionaries, their libidinal self-indulgence, has proved harder to exclude completely from the national idea of literature, because its very locus in the unsystematic and unpredictable nature of the erotic has rendered it superficially adaptable to the modes of feminized imprecision that also define what is held to be *literature* in the first place. Both extremes, however, have been consistently at war with a model of British common sense embodied in English common feeling, dominantly the property of a sensitized middle class but occasionally available also to exemplary members of the aristocracy and the working class, at such moments as they are able to cast aside the restraints of privilege and poverty respectively. The model of the national literature that has been most formative in the schools and universities, and in the culture at large, privileges compromise over adherence to absolute principle, and is thus a Burkean construction. In its preference for particularity over general statement, intuition over proposition, practice over principle, and modest muddle over magisterial method, it has severely restrained the emergency of any radical vocabulary, whether rational or erotic. The British reaction to the French Revolution was a critical component in the construction and reconstruction of this tradition.

8

THOUGHTS ON THE PRESENT
DISCONTENTS

A Revolution That Will Not Finish

Throughout this study I have implied and occasionally indicated some definite relations between the debate over theory and method in the immediate aftermath of the French Revolution and related controversies in our contemporary educational and political discourses, most particularly in Britain but also in the United States. I hope I have adequately justified the claim made in my introduction: that the French Revolution is not "finished," and that its legacies, ideological and institutional, cannot be sensibly dismissed as no longer relevant to our arguments about ourselves and our opportunities. Indeed, it is at once analytically confirming and practically disappointing to see so much evidence of how direct and uncritical the reproduction of the rhetoric of the 1790s can be.

Any number of examples might come from Britain, which is more explicit than the United States about its ideological divisions and has been, at least until very recently, more insecure about its international role and reputation. It is also, given the strains of maintaining a class culture, more visibly anxious about the commonality of its traditional "common sense," and thus perhaps more often given to overstatement of its claims. Relatively trivial instances of the continuation of the myth of the national character can be found all over literary criticism and literary journalism. Here is John Bayley, holder of a prestigious Oxford chair and frequent mentor to the literary layperson (the much-debated "English common reader"), reviewing David Lodge's *After Bakhtin* and opining that "consciously or unconsciously, Literary Theory [*sic*] aspires to the condition of utopianism, which may explain its attraction for students who are more interested in the comforts of solutions than in those of literature itself."[1] This compulsive fetishization of complexity is almost statutory in British English departments, and it sits (or tries to sit) like a dead weight over any attempt to expand its own much-touted ethic of liberal open-mindedness to questions of theory. Almost any issue of the *Times Literary Supplement* will suffice for evidence of the more or less constant diatribe against theory (and usually against France or America, or both). In one recent such issue, James Wood ex-postulates against "the rust of theory (the creeping stain of pseudo-analysis, the blisters of jargon)" and sees a "vulgarity" in "the glee of critics let off the hook of literature and allowed to splash in the ruthless abstractions of philosophy."[2] Here is the ghost of Robespierre, the coldest of the ruthless abstractionists. Elsewhere it might be Stalin, also available for reincarnation as a Marxist, a feminist, a deconstructionist. This kind of rhetoric has had an especially long and vigorous life in Britain, as this book has shown. But the most lurid among recent ex-amples of the revolt against theory probably come from the United States, where the battle goes on all the more passionately perhaps be-cause its fortunes have, not long since, seemed to flow in the other di-rection. David Lehman's dismally belated *Signs of the Times,* which might more accurately be received as the signs of about ten years ago, mounts its attack on theory behind an interpretation of the fall of Paul de Man's reputation. Here, by way of monotonous invocations of a schoolboy's *1984* and occasional appeals to right-thinking conservative-liberal aca-demics, Lehman berates what he sees as a "debased idiom" ruining those who should be "the professionally appointed curators of our liter-ature" and raises the flag for something called literature "in its own right." Theory in general, and deconstruction in particular, are but "a squiggle of fancy French mustard on the hot dog of a banal observa-tion."[3]

Nativism and populism go hand in hand even more theatrically in Camille Paglia's orations, where they are spiced with a strong measure of erotic primitivism and rock and roll. As I write, Paglia has just pub-lished two different sections of the same essay (also published elsewhere) in two of the most widely read literary-academic newspapers, the *New York Times Book Review* and the *Chronicle of Higher Education.* Grasping Mrs. Thatcher's recently laid to rest broom—"It is time to clean house"—Paglia preaches the gospel of general humanities studies against spe-cialization and touts the nativist energies of an America "which leaped far beyond European thought from the moment we invented Holly-wood." Foucault becomes an "absolute ninny," American interest in whom is "revolting" since French preoccupation with the "decentered subject" is merely the result of being "crushed by Germany" in World War II (which "we," after all, won, apparently with the help of the au-thor's uncles).[4] Scholars should talk to "non academics" instead of to each other, and they should look to American popular culture instead of to "death-by-sludge French theorists" for their insights into "multiple discourses."[5] Absurd as these utterances may seem to many professional intellectuals, they are agreed with by others, and they are the reading matter of a large section of the concerned public. And they are merely the latest scrambling of the "common culture" rhetoric that has been ongoing throughout the 1980s. Paglia's theorists and "academic leftists" (as usual, the two go together, according to the shorthand whose persistence this book has tried to explain) are sexless corporate creatures, "strutting wannabes, timorous nerds who missed the 60s while they were grade-grubbing in the library and brown-nosing the senior faculty."[6]

Even where one is not tempted to trace the anatomy of paranoia, as in Michael Albert's essay in the leftist *Z Magazine,* "theory" is still construed merely as a good career move—"big bucks, big status"—and upbraided for its failure of popular intelligibility.[7] There is clearly a cultural iceberg beneath this pinnacle of resentment and disapproval, whereby the fact that some theorists make good salaries (though hardly significant in relation to those in law, engineering, and medical schools) becomes symptomatic of the total bad faith of systematic thinking in the humanities. Theorists, like Jacobins, are seen as betraying a cause, that of a common culture and a common vocabulary (neither of which has ever existed in complex societies).

For all these critics and commentators who will have nothing to do with theory, the proper literary response remains a function of an unpredictable intuition, usually "human": but how predictable it is! Brian Doyle, echoing Perry Anderson, suggests that English studies has functioned within the national culture by providing a symbolic rather than a theoretical totality, "a substitute for any 'theory' of the national life in the form of an imponderable base from which the quality of the national life can be assessed."[8] The famous debate between ancients and moderns has taken a new form but hardly a new direction. Shaftesbury's preference for the *"virtuoso"* over the "scholar," and for the "primitive simplicity" of "rude nature" over "improved sophistry and pedantic learning," is reincarnated in the cultivated insouciance and spontaneity of the conventional literary critic.[9] Like Mackintosh's ideal politician, in a passage already quoted, the critic must be constantly alert to the "minute" and the "evanescent," to things that are "perpetually changing their form, and varying their combinations" in "endless variety."[10] The method to be employed can only come from contemplation of the thing it is to be employed upon: the customary must be customized.

Matthew Arnold, in so many ways a founding father of university teaching in the humanities, argued in "The Study of Poetry" for the priority of a tact, sense, and feeling that cannot be defined "in the abstract . . . for we should thereby be darkening the question, not clearing it."[11] In "The Function of Criticism at the Present Time" he proposed that the tragic flaw of the French Revolution was its attempt to give "immediate political and practical application" to "ideas of the reason."[12] So spectacular was this error that it has, Arnold regrets, worked to confirm the British in their contempt for ideas in themselves, and in a stubborn anti-intellectualism. Arnold imagined the study of literature as another middle ground, a way of encouraging attention to ideas in facts, and facts imbued with ideas. But with I. A. Richards the balance tips away from law and theory toward an emphasis on the psychologically healthy effects of polymorphous reponse itself. After the dreadful evidence, in 1914–18, of what technology could accomplish, the whole scientific-rational enterprise came to be, in the minds of many humanists, tainted with the reputation of a merely instrumental reason. Literature and literary response were reciprocally imagined as our single ray of hope, both for the individual mind and for the national culture. This new incentive went along with what we have seen to be a traditional denigration of science and of "ideas" in the definition of the national literature. For T. S. Eliot, Henry James's "superior intelligence" was evidenced in his possession of "a mind so fine that no idea could violate it," a famous phrase that has most often been taken to suggest that no idea should even *enter* such a mind.[13]

Even Raymond Williams, one of the greatest socialist critics of this century, turns to Orwell and to Cobbett, those splenetically patriotic democrats whose egalitarianism was often expressed as hostility to system and to the foreign, as instances of the possibilities and achievements of a literary politics (though Williams did have strong reservations about Orwell). Williams's early participation in the culture of the national character was such as to allow him to approve even those on the opposite side of the political fence—Burke and Carlyle—because they seemed to him to have been in touch with an "experienced" or a "complex" reality. He later attributed such oversights, or incomplete accounts, to the "general condition of thought in this country"—a condition that allowed others to accuse him, when he did move toward a more general analytic mode, of having "got into theory."[14]

Williams's gestures "against theory" were always nuanced and implicit, and they were later adjusted into more positive estimations. But the socialist tradition contains far more tendentious and splenetic instances of a British nationalist antipathy to systematic paradigms. E. P.

Thompson's notorious attack on Althusser and his British followers did make some telling points in its passionate defense of a "real history," but it also reproduced all the traits of the British national character as we have described it: a monotonous contempt for "Grand Theory," for a model that is seen (unconvincingly) as trying to "swallow reality in one gulp," and a corresponding worship of something mystically called "experience," along with a general disregard for anything done by the French. The slur of Stalinism (a phenomenon that Althusser, if anything, critiques while seeking to explain), the vulgar antiacademicism— for Althusser, we are told, "beguiled half the *lumpen-intelligentsia* of Oxbridge"—and the identification of the theoretical demon with "one of the dottiest moments in the Enlightenment" all place Thompson squarely in the tradition of British common sense.[15] No one should be able to look back at the contexts of the time (1978) without some sympathy for Thompson's frustrations and some discomfort with the pious theoreticisms he was opposing. But the rhetorical conjunctions among Althusser, theory, France, and Stalin played only to the most uncritically nationalist strains in the socialist movement, and they functioned as real inhibitions on any serious debate within it. Thompson's faith in such nontheorizable paradigms as "literature" (of course), "real" history, and "a certain kind of disciplined moral critique" remains unanalyzed in its assurance that the fact can always trump the theory.[16] The incommensurable priorities of Thompson and the British Althusserians were from the first symptoms of a broader schism within the British left that has not yet healed, if it ever can heal. Ironically, and some would say tragically, that schism may have assisted in the maintenance of an extended period of right-wing government that is even more opportunistically committed to the rhetoric of patriotism and of the British way of doing things. The degree to which the language of common sense is, precisely, *shared* by Thompson and by his avowed enemies on the conservative right is an index of the seriousness of the problem. Its unanalyzed dominance has allowed, for instance, the conservative command of the *language* of patriotic common sense to mask the introduction of one of the most mechanistically "rationalist" legislations in British political history: the so-called poll tax.

The language of contemporary Britain, and above all of contemporary metropolitan England, thus remains very much affected by the debates of the 1790s and their specification of theory and method as fundamentally antagonistic to the British national character. We see these notions in the small print of academic monographs—as when Stanley Jones dismisses the agrarian radical Thomas Spence as merely the author of "ineffectual half-crazed theorizings"—and in the larger print of the national political life.[17] Then–Prime Minister Thatcher's response to the end of the cold war famously included the convening of a panel of "experts" to discuss the implications of a reunited Germany. Charles Powell's memorandum of the meeting, leaked to the press, turned out to abound in negative references to the national character of the Germans. Surprisingly these consisted less of the standard references to law-and-order Prussians obsessed with bureaucracy and order than of much older mythologies, those whose genesis has been traced in chapter 4 of this study. This panel of experts meeting in the summer of 1990 found the Germans to be self-obsessed, with a "strong inclination to self-pity and a longing to be liked," and guilty of both "aggressiveness" and "sentimentality," mediated by an "inferiority complex." While some of the panelists felt that today's Germans were quite different from their ancestors, others opined that "a lot had still not changed."[18] The elements of these myths are derived, interestingly less from Bismarck than from the sorrowing Werther, and thus from the same series of national traits that Coleridge described in the early nineteenth century. The experts, it seems, have read their literature.

   An equally vivid instance of the power of such traditions may be traced in the debate, also in 1990, over a British constitution. Larry Siedentop argued that, now more than ever, reliance on an unwritten constitution is "dangerously complacent" in the light of the displacement of traditional political and cultural forms by purely economistic models (Thatcherism) with strong but undeclared centralizing tendencies.[19] He is no Painite radical but simply advises a clarification of practice in the interests of a general understanding of the whole of which economics is but a part. In response, the ever-willing Roger Scruton called Siedentop "more liberal than socialist"; but even this moderate case (oddly positive, as Scruton rightly points out, about the class system) is enough to rouse his antagonist to the defense of a threatened monarchy and of a myth of organic evolution that "began at the Conquest" and whose implications are "gloriously displayed in our nineteenth-century novels." All this, of course, with the obligatory reference to Stalin.[20] Edmund Burke is no ghost here, unless a living ghost, as the survival of British social life in the face of economic decline is to be hoped for principally in the existence of an unwritten constitution. This same Edmund Burke functioned also as a heroic precursor for cold-war America, a defender of the values of the free world against the dark night of Russian communism.[21]

   Even more recently, the revelation of the full extent of the miscarriage of justice against the Birmingham Six (six Irishmen falsely convicted of murder but only released after seventeen years and various show retrials) led Anthony Lewis to suggest that the "absence of a constitution" has encouraged British judges to "think less of individual interests and more of the state's," as it has also allowed for hostility to freedom of speech and of the press.[22] Lewis here speaks for the potential benefits of a theorized politics.

The acceptance of a myth of the national character and the national interest that is significantly founded in a contempt for theory and system is not just, then, a symptom of literary criticism; it pervades the entire society in which that literary criticism finds its audience. Occasional foreign commentators, ever since Voltaire, Montesquieu, and de Staël, have looked to the British with a worshipful eye and admired a constitution that is, like the mind of Shakespeare in his plays, at once everywhere and nowhere. This has only further consolidated the national self-esteem. Not for nothing has a distinguished British sociologist, W. G. Runciman, titled one of his books *Confessions of a Reluctant Theorist*. Gerald Newman has argued that the intelligentsia, far from standing in any critical or skeptical relation to the myth of the national character, has in general been most assiduous in promoting it. He attributes this to the facility with which the paradigm could be deployed in the interests of middle-class intellectuals opposing themselves to a "Frenchified" ruling class—an observation that, if correct, certainly helps to explain the persistence of nativist elements even in the British socialist tradition.[23] Lord Kames at once universalized the culture of patriotism—"almost every nation hate their neighbors, without knowing why"—and admitted its excessive power among the English, rendering them "extremely averse to naturalize foreigners."[24] And Mme de Staël, who liked the English, still noted that their cherished liberty was founded in the rejection of "every thing that comes from strangers, both in literature and politics."[25]

Even the rigorous Hume, we recall, could permit himself the opinion (albeit in a footnote) that, "since nature has implanted in every one a superior affection to his own country, we never expect any regard to distant nations, where a competition arises."[26] John Stuart Mill, perhaps reacting against the internationalist tradition in which he was himself nurtured, saw in Coleridge a proper attention to the "national character," one consisting not least in a "highly salutary shrinking from all extremes."[27] Burke of course went further, announcing that "nation is a moral essence, not a geographical arrangement, or a denomination of the nomenclator."[28] And yet, in making it thus, Burke calls attention to the *unnatural* composition of the nation, as requiring some moral identity, an earned participation. As we have seen, he regarded theory

as a cosmopolitan, internationalist initiative that could only survive by
breaking down the local and national structures (imaginary structures)
upon which his own preferred political order depended. Questions of
"theoretic truth and falsehood," he rightly divined, are not "governed
by circumstances any more than by places."[29] Thus, in the heady days
of the early 1790s, the *Anti-Jacobin* saw in *"French PHILANTHROPY"* the
death of every "patriot passion":

> Taught in her school to imbibe thy mawkish strain,
> CONDORCET, filtered through the dregs of PAINE,
> Each pert adept disowns a Briton's part,
> And plucks the name of ENGLAND from his heart.[30]

As the nineteenth century progresses we find an increasing tendency to
identify this model of the "nation" with a corresponding notion of
"race." Mainstream Enlightenment thinkers generally held to a belief
in a single human species, modified by climate and culture; in the nineteenth century, models of "racial" hierarchy became more common.[31]
By 1914 references to English literature as an emanation of the British
or Saxon "race" figured significantly in literary criticism.[32] While they
have since disappeared (at least in explicit forms) from literary criticism, they remain with us even when divorced from any biological associations.[33]

Literary criticism, at least as often as literature itself and sometimes
more so, has in its consensual forms (for there were always exceptions)
conspired very readily in the celebration and publication of the national
character. But criticism has other potentials, which have come dramatically to the fore with the professionalization of the discipline and
the entrance into it of nonestablishment interests and subgroups. Insofar as criticism is a descriptive-interpretative rather than a spontaneous
language, it can be more open than literature itself to the possibilities of
theory and method, and more sympathetic to general statements. The
"theory wars" occurring in today's humanities departments are to some
degree a mediated response to the tensions generated by the French
Revolution and by the English Revolution of the 1640s. With the advent
of a postmodern position for theory itself, rational method has almost
become the signature of an improper power, or aspiration to power, a
masculine dream of reason that can only be for everyone else a nightmare. Theory and method, allies for so long in the critique of nationalism and of the national myth of common sense, are perhaps now more
forcefully disambiguated than ever before. Theory, in short, tells us of
nothing less than the improprieties of method. This makes it all the

more important that, in the search for an effectively radical contemporary form, criticism be reminded of the history of these relations.

The Problem of Theory in the Postmodern

While the narrative of this book has been largely concerned with the history that was written by the winners, it is important to remind ourselves that the tradition of radical cosmopolitanism that was associated with Enlightenment theory has never been completely submerged. Those who for various reasons contested the terms of the nationalist consensus were able to turn to it for rhetorical identity, and they did so. William Godwin declared roundly:

A nation is an arbitrary term. Which is most properly termed a nation, the Russian empire, or a canton of Berne? Or is everything a nation upon which accident shall bestow that appellation?[34]

Condorcet saw rational liberty as entailing above all the "abolition of inequality between nations"—the very inequality that made credible the image of nationality to begin with.[35] Against Hume and his kind, Richard Price argued that "a narrower interest ought always to give way to a more extensive interest," since we are all "citizens of the world."[36] The equivalent of this attitude in literature and aesthetics was what we would now have to call a "comparatist" perspective. Gibbon saw in the reading of literature the opportunity to become, "by turns, a Greek, a Roman, the disciple of Zeno and of Epicurus." As he crossed national and historical boundaries, so he also refused the compartmentalization of disciplines that has become so familiar in modern universities: to understand Virgil is to understand not just literature but the history, geography, politics, and culture of Rome.[37] Contesting what was already by the turn of the eighteenth century a nationalist ideology of spontaneity, John Dennis argued that poetry could hardly be "without Rule and Order" since it comprehended within it the arts of logic, ethics, eloquence, painting, and music. It is to be appreciated not at the expense of other forms of expression but precisely in its relations with them. Those who must make other things "little in order to make poetry great" forget that poetry functions by way of its connections to logic and philosophy, and not at their expense. Speaking of *Paradise Lost*, he reminds us that "the poem that has done most Honour to England is Three Fourths of it metaphysicks."[38]

The knowledge of classical languages and literatures and the command of specialized fields of knowledge that defined the eighteenth century's image of cosmopolitanism (at least before radical rationalism proposed its key to all mythologies) were bound to render that image unacceptable to a bourgeois readership, and perhaps unobtainable by that readership. A model of the national character as a generalist one, publicized in the national language, would prove much more companionable. The internationalism of radical reason was open to denunciation in the 1790s as a French idea, and the attack on "narrow and slavish patriotism" that the reformist utilitarians mounted was, as we have seen, very much at odds with the literary interest. It too, moreover, spoke the language of a political "liberty" that was "one and indivisible" and therefore antipathetic to localist sentiments.[39]

The cosmopolitan ideal did not fare very well in the nineteenth and twentieth centuries. In the academy the degree of its failure may be measured in the incidence of such belated concepts as "comparative" literature and "interdisciplinary" studies, gestures condemned to work against the grain of the received categories of inquiry. It is hard not to conclude that much of the animus directed against Paul de Man, even before the notorious revelations of his wartime career, was a function of his internationalism and his commitment to a seriously *comparative* literature. In the Enlightenment tradition, de Man threatened any literary criticism founded in the "screen of received ideas" that passes for "humanistic knowledge," delivered in the rhetoric of moral indignation and religiosity.[40] Literature especially has been principally conceived as a national and often nationalist entity; it has been proposed as the last refuge of liberal-mindedness even as it has required narrower and narrower qualifications for its understanding, with very obvious consequences for the profession of criticism and for the educational state apparatus. Above all, it has eschewed theory, received once again as a threat to local and particular interests and insights, just as it had been by Edmund Burke.

Are things changing? Perry Anderson, looking back at his own formative essay of 1968, "Components of the National Culture," regrets the "theoretical triumphalism" of those times but finds that the profoundly antiacademic initiatives of the Thatcher governments have worked to displace the culture of the center somewhat to the left and toward the embrace of theory. The academic media have become Americanized, a tendency visibly represented in the wide circulation of the corporate-liberal mentality carried in the *New York Review of Books*.[41] But at the same time, Anderson updates his earlier and bleaker analysis by finding a renewed British appetite for theory in the work of anthropologists, sociologists, and even literary critics. His troublingly eclectic list of the new British "theorists" does, however, lack a certain conviction, not least in the context of the antitheoretical backlash whose emergence he also chronicles.[42]

Far from suggesting any end to the revolt against theory, I would argue that the debate itself has taken a new turn, one wherein the inherited regimens of "for and against" have become confusingly intermixed. The always fragile boundaries keeping literature and literary criticism within its own special pastures are working perhaps less efficiently than ever before. Feminism, deconstruction, and cultural studies have so affected the professional attitude to literature that the old liberal consensus appears to survive, where it does survive, largely by inertia (though I can imagine that a strong turn to the right could well restore life to that old consensus). It is too early to say whether this new identity for literary studies will work to displace it from its pedestal as the "central" discipline in the humanities—a pedestal that was, after all, set up to fulfill specifically imprecise functions—or whether it will prove to be central to some newly emerging political-educational consensus.

The debate within and around the postmodern brings forward many of the questions involved in this choice of futures (not, of course, that there is any simple "choice"). Whether as style, attitude, or movement (for this too is in question), the invocation of postmodernity brings with it both a new cosmopolitanism and a series of anxieties about what that cosmopolitanism might now intend and depend upon. For its advocates, the postmodern condition is an acceptance and celebration of difference and diversity—sexual, national, aesthetic, political. For its left-wing critics, these same symptoms are implausibly imaged as sharable by all; they should rather be understood as the ideological self-image of a first-world generation, one that reproduces rather than critiques the terms of corporate-industrial multinationalism. Fredric Jameson worries that the postmodern has displaced the modernist critique of the commodity by "the consumption of sheer commodification as a process," thus remaining "only the reflex and the concomitant of yet another systemic modification of capitalism itself." At the same time, he deems unavailable "the luxury of the old-fashioned ideological critique, the indignant moral denunciation of the other": we must rather attempt to think the incidence of "catastrophe and progress altogether" as itself the symptom of "the social restructuring of late capitalism as a system."[43]

Postmodern attitudes seem to share with the inherited "common sense" doctrines a distrust of totalizing explanations and a faith in the integrity of microscopic detail. For this reason they can be taken to stand "against theory," where theory is understood to require general analysis according to generalizing principles. But the fetishization of difference that informs postmodern rhetoric is not founded on any defense of traditional nationalist mythologies. On the contrary, it insists on the incommensurability of its components, which are fragmented and mutually competitive precisely because of the local determinations of class, gender, and ethnicity. Instead of a culture, we have subcultures, parts that never organically compose a whole and can be made to seem coherent only by vigorous repression. This acceptance of differently interested subject-positions can be used in the cause of an activist, oppositional politics, and is thus used. However, to the degree that difference remains only a subject of celebration or identification rather than of analysis and critique, it can support a covertly reproductive strategy whose hallmark is a merely belligerent unwillingness that anyone should speak for or about anyone else. The task is not so much to decide in some essential sense what postmodernism *is*, as to distinguish the various uses its languages are put to, both as epistemology and as style.

This task is very much under way and will surely remain topical for some time to come. Seamus Deane has queried the postmodern "simulacrum of pluralism" that merely makes a "mystique" of diversity while reproducing the "concealed imperialism of the multinational."[44] Critics like Deane, Jameson, and Edward Said have eloquently registered the degree to which what looks like a repressive image of nationalism to first-world radicals can seem like a liberating or positive incentive for stateless cultures like Palestine, or misstated ones like Ireland. We would be ill advised to fix ourselves to a strict perspective on the postmodern when its rhetorics and attitudes can be and have been put to such widely different uses. Some care is thus required for any useful assessment of the place of theory within it.

Perhaps the most important and widely interrogated contemporary version of the "theory problem" is to be found in feminist debate. The range of critical and methodological alternatives within what is loosely known as feminism is at least as great as that within postmodernism, and it would be similarly reductive to specify any one component as primary or typical. British Marxist feminists especially have held fast to theoretical approaches and languages. One strand of contemporary feminist argument, dominantly French but popular also in the United States, does, however, accept the coding of reason and sensibility (to use the older terms) as respectively masculine and feminine (or even male and female) and tries to counter the received preferences by articulating an alternative feminine hierarchy headed by fluidity, contextuality, and the body. Luce Irigaray, for instance, seeks to give voice to the enigma that woman has always been in the male ordering of nature, and to put her in control of a language that is, in the received male sense of the term, nontheoretical.[45] Others disavow such distinctions and set out to "rehabilitate the true meaning of theory" in feminist terms, as signifying "any discourse that attempts to draw political conclusions, that offers a strategy or tactics to the feminist movement."[46]

As the excluded interest returns to present its challenge, there is a decision to be made about whether or not to call it "theory." In the United States this argument has been affected by the peculiar turn given to that term by Paul de Man—scholastic, masculinist, objectivist, and largely apolitical. Many feminists are suspicious of what is called theory, and they have reason to be so given its traditional associations with rational, masculine method (an association Wollstonecraft challenged but could not destroy). Coleridge identified the "power of abstraction" as the main distinction between man and beast, accessible only by the suppression of instinct and passion and of the "despotism of the eye" that had always been associated with the female.[47] For Hazlitt, the signature of avoiding effeminacy of character was being able to go "the shortest and most effectual way to work" to attain one's ends, eschewing the serpentine pleasures of digression and delay.[48] This rhetorical hegemony—and there are countless examples—almost seems to demand that feminists refuse the claims of theory, when they are advanced on such terms. Thus Naomi Schor, arguing for the force of "detail" in the subversion of a male rationalist ideal and aesthetic of the sublime that she finds to be premised on "the absence of all particularity," sees in the Enlightenment paradigm only the attributes of "the phallocentric cultural order."[49]

These reservations about the masculine birth of theory are important ones, and forceful not least because of their conjunction with the contextual preferences of a postmodernist rhetoric whose compatible affiliation with the marginal may be read as the signal of its own deliberately feminized position. Judith Newton indeed argues that much of what has come to be known as the postmodern, and the new historicism in particular, was itself generated by "the theoretical breaks of the second wave of the women's movement, by feminist criticism of male-centered knowledges for their assumption of 'objectivity.'"[50] But the postmodern has also taken over much from the male theorists of the Frankfurt School, who were also suspicious of the implications of coherent narratives, whether scientific, sociological, or fictional. After Horkheimer and Adorno, reason comes to us in the clothing of instrumental reason, with all the historical tragedies that term conjures up.

But in such cases as the revolt against reason takes the form of a fetish-ization of "detail," we should be concerned about what sort of relation is here implied to the received Anglo-American literary culture and to its own profoundly antitheoretical biases. This tradition has never had a "male-centered knowledge" or anything other than a hostile attitude to the notion of "objectivity." On the contrary, it has consistently advanced the superiority of what we now recognize as feminized positionalities.

The intended alternatives to masculine reason proposed by some feminists and postmodernists thus need to be tested out for any latent or unrecognized identification with the empiricisms of the received ed-ucational and political consensus. As we have seen, the sphere of litera-ture and literary criticism has itself been so thoroughly feminized that its male practitioners have commonly felt the need to engage in aggres-sive remasculinization of their languages—through modernism, pro-fessionalization, and perhaps theory itself.[51] So acutely felt was the feminization of the literary that Irving Babbitt, who was adamantly op-posed to the professionalization of literary criticism and the dominance of the philological method, declared himself to be even more con-cerned about the implications of the predominance of the dilettante:

> The man who took literature seriously would be suspected of effeminacy. The really virile thing is to be an electrical engineer. One already sees the time when the typical teacher of literature will be some young dilettante who will interpret Keats and Shelley to a class of girls.[52]

The New Critics turned away from Keats and Shelley in response to ex-actly these fears, preferring the intellectual rigors of Donne and the metaphysicals. Any argument against theory, feminist or otherwise, would be well advised to ask itself what relation it intends to the in-place feminization of intuition and sensibility that has, for over two hundred years, been associated with the literary. Mary Wollstonecraft sensed ex-actly this when she made her case for a gender-neutral faculty of reason that women could possess without betraying their sex; we must now wonder whether that same faculty can be possessed without identifica-tion with the destructive technologies of a more developed phase of modernity. A number of Marxist feminists have taken up Wollstone-craft's task.

We are, then, at an interesting point in the history of theory, one where, as I have said, the warning that theory often announces is against the pretensions and aspirations of method itself. Terry Eagleton, who has done more than most to defend and demonstrate the claims of theory, now looks back on his own earlier work as characterized by "a certain fetishism of method" and an overvaluing of the "systematic" which he now recognizes as "very male." But, in coming out against method, Eagleton preserves a place for theory as a usefully "unnameable" practice able to avoid the "stale identity of longer established discourses." Pluralism (not eclecticism) of method is now a positive tactic, provided that consistency of political goal be maintained.[53]

This is one approach to the dilemmas of theory, which Fredric Jameson also senses in imaging the theorist as now condemned to walk a "tightrope":

Language can . . . no longer be true; but it can certainly be false; and the mission of theoretical discourse thus becomes a kind of search-and-destroy operation in which linguistic misconceptions are remorselessly identified and stigmatized, in the hopes that a theoretical discourse negative and critical enough will not itself become the target of such linguistic demystification in its turn. The hope is, of course, vain.[54]

In their different ways both Jameson and Eagleton demonstrate a definite anxiety about the prospects for theory in a generation seemingly hostile to totality. Neither of them suggests the collapse into empiricism that haunts E. P. Thompson's preferred alternative to Grand Theory. Instead they draw, directly or implicitly, on the formulations of problems and solutions published by Horkheimer and Adorno in the 1940s, in an analysis of the fate of reason that is still worth recollecting for the 1990s.

The co-authored *Dialectic of Enlightenment* is well known for its denunciations of the "indefatigable self-destructiveness of enlightenment" and of "rationalism." At the same time, the twentieth-century culture of barbarism is blamed not on the excess but on the "weakness of the modern theoretical faculty."[55] Theory might, then—as long as it is critical theory—offer a way forward beyond the defunct and disastrous paradigms of enlightenment. In his *Eclipse of Reason,* less well known despite being written in English, Horkheimer lays out the problem very clearly. The "objective reason" that was the motivating faculty in the Enlightenment demystification of religion, with its dream of the complete rational perspicuity of man and nature, is no longer available except as hopeless anachronism. It vanished in its own critique of metaphysics, a critique so total as to come to include "the objective concept of reason itself." The bourgeois ideal of tolerance eroded all absolutist claims, including those of reason, and created the contemporary culture of "relativism." So we are now governed by "subjective reason," a pragmatist faculty with no objectivist aspiration, with the result that it remains completely "harnessed to the social process." This world is ruled by functionalism and instrumentality, with truth revealed as merely "habit" and understanding as simply "conduct."[56]

Thus, if the European Enlightenment has failed, its demise hideously evident in the death camps, so too has American pragmatism, whose experimentalist ideology Horkheimer regards as little more than the "counterpart of modern industrialism." Subjective reason's fetishization of experimental science is antiphilosophical, and because that science is itself wholly within the "social process" nothing based upon it can have a critical function. What Horkheimer sees coming and most fears is a society without critique, without any place for an authentic or useful theory. There can be no going back, for "the transition from objective to subjective reason was not an accident, and the process of development of ideas cannot arbitrarily at any given moment be reversed."[57] This analysis of the 1940s works very well for the 1990s in its adumbration of the dilemmas of theory within the postmodern. "There is no royal road to definition"; definitions take on meaning only "in the course of a historical process"; all abstractions imply "a misrepresentation of concrete existence." Critical theory henceforth can work neither with objective or subjective reason, conceived of as a choice, but only with their "mutual critique" and by its own "self-critique" in the "continuous theoretical effort of developing philosophical truth."[58]

Horkheimer is arguing here for a strategy that has, in various analogous languages, become almost normal doctrine among the postmodern avant-garde. As such, it often seems to produce a theory that leads us out of the temptation to theory itself, insofar as such theory is dominated by the fantasy of rational completion. But Horkheimer says something else of considerable interest for the narrative of this book:

Since isolated subjective reason in our time is triumphing everywhere, with fatal results, the critique must necessarily be carried on with an emphasis on objective reason rather than on the remnants of subjectivist philosophy, whose genuine traditions, in the light of advanced subjectivization, now in themselves appear as objectivistic and romantic.[59]

In other words, he says that the very unfashionable and anachronistic status of objective reason should encourage us to go against the grain and to seek out avenues for exploring it, not in hopes that it can, like some deposed monarch, be restored intact to its original authority, but because its extinction will put an end to the dialectic and thus eventually to critical theory itself.

Horkheimer's advice, if followed, would seem to put us in the odd position of appealing for something we cannot wholeheartedly defend or even wholly identify: a contemporary analogue of the objective reason that disappeared forever with the Enlightenment. After Marx, Freud, and Nietzsche, among so many others, there can be no going back to a world-model whose perfect order is "theoretically self-evident for each imaginable subject endowed with intelligence."[60] Those of us who choose this route will thus be in the position of invoking something we "know not what," a utopian projection that is, like Shelley's favorite horrors, shapeless. But if a renewal of attention to the modalities and possibilities of objective reason be indeed part of the task, then it can do no harm to know something of their history. If there is any use to this extended analysis of what many have been content to admit as a truism—that the Romantics, and the British, don't much like theory, and that the Americans have a very turbulent relationship with it— then it will be as a contribution to this history. An informed account of who we are now, and what we believe, can only be assisted by a recognition of the terms and implications of past choices about theory and method in their perceived relations to the social order. For those of us who specialize in literary matters, this history is especially critical, for it has not just affected but largely created the academic subculture of literary studies. An understanding of the cultural formations that accompanied the heyday and subsequent decline of a British empire is important in itself. It may also not be out of place in our contemporary efforts to understand the different but not unrelated crises in the image and the history of an American "nation" and an American empire.

NOTES

Most footnotes give only abbreviated bibliographical information. Full citations may be found in the bibliography.

Introduction

1. George Will, "Literary Politics," p. 72.
2. Daniel Harris, "AIDS and Theory," p. 1.
3. *Pearson's Political Dictionary*, p. 15.
4. See especially *From Columbus to Castro: The History of the Caribbean, 1492–1969*.
5. *The Philosophy of the Enlightenment*, p. 2.
6. For a guide to the complexities of various historical evaluations of *theory*, in the context of the reciprocal invention of *praxis*, see Raymond Williams, *Keywords*, pp. 316–18.
7. *The Example of France a Warning to Britain*, pp. 2–3, 79.
8. Sieyès, *What Is the Third Estate?* pp. 171–72.
9. For a brief account and bibliography, see the afterword by Margaret Ferguson in Howard and O'Connor, eds., *Shakespeare Reproduced*.
10. See my "New Brooms at Fawlty Towers."
11. Gadamer, *Philosophical Hermeneutics*, p. 40.
12. *Against Method*, pp. 45, 27.
13. "Traveling Theory," in *The World, the Text, the Critic*.
14. See *The Order of Things*, pp. 303–43.
15. "Components of the National Culture," p. 47.
16. *Miscellaneous Works*, p. 178.
17. Cited in Raymond Williams, *Marxism and Literature*, p. 57.

Chapter One

1. *Reflections on the Revolution in France*, p. 92.
2. *The Rights of Nature* 1:13.
3. *Remarks on the Letter of the Rt. Hon. Edmund Burke*, p. 44.
4. *Complete Writings* 1:315.
5. Cited in Ong, *Ramus, Method, and the Decay of Dialogue*, p. 191.

6. Ramus, trans. MacIlmaine, *The Logike*, p. 12.

7. Richardson, *The Logicians School-Master*, pp. 329, 333.

8. Grafton and Jardine, *From Humanism to the Humanities*, pp. 181–82.

9. Ibid., p. 178.

10. Perry Miller, *The New England Mind*, p. 147ff., contends that Puritanism was dominantly a realist theology, seeking to do away with the kinds of social hierarchy that were associated with the nominalist acceptance of the need for *interpreting* the mind-world relation. For the Puritans, he suggests, the commonest knowledge was the truest knowledge. For a more ambivalent view of Ramus's own position, see Ong, *Ramus*, pp. 208–9, 225–69 passim.

11. Ramus, trans. Fage, *Dialectica*, preface.

12. Ramus, trans. Bedwell, *The Way to Geometry*, preface.

13. *The Artes of Logike and Rethorike*, cited in Howell, *Logic and Rhetoric in England*, p. 220. For a general account of the popularity of Ramism, see Neal Gilbert, *Renaissance Concepts of Method*, esp. pp. 66–73, 129–44.

14. See Grafton and Jardine, *From Humanism to the Humanities*, pp. 168–69.

15. *The Massacre at Paris*, scene 9, p. 118.

16. *The Lawyers Logike*, cited in Ralph Pomeroy, "The Ramist as Fallacy-Hunter," pp. 232.

17. Richardson, *The Logician's School-Master*, p. 34; Miller, *The New England Mind*, p. 127. For other renderings of *disserendi*, see Ong, *Ramus*, p. 180. Milton's (late) Ramist logic, interestingly, preferred *ratiocinandi* as the goal of logic; see Milton, *A Fuller Course in the Art of Logic*, p. 218.

18. See Graves, *Peter Ramus and the Educational Reformation of the Sixteenth Century;* and Ramus, *Avertissements sur la réformation de l'université de Paris.*

19. Compagnon, "1555, 13 September," p. 217.

20. See Graves, *Peter Ramus*, pp. 124–25.

21. Ong, *Ramus*, p. 310.

22. *Logike*, p. 15.

23. See, for example, Gareth Stedman Jones, *Languages of Class.*

24. *The Great Instauration*, in *Works* 4:15, 32–33.

25. See *Intellectual Origins of the English Revolution*, pp. 85–130.

26. *Philosophical Works* 1:2, 69.

27. Ibid. 1:32, 55. Compare 1:91.

28. *Essays on the Law of Nature*, p. 136.

29. *An Essay Concerning Human Understanding*, p. 45.

30. Ibid., pp. 13, 670, 671.

31. See Howell, *Logic and Rhetoric in England*, pp. 260–63, 388ff. For the general reaction against Ramism on empiricist principles, see pp. 16–28.

32. For an argument that this style devolves from Locke's understanding of the genre of the "essay," see Rosalie Colie, "The Essayist in his Essay."

33. *Works* 7:139, 146, 152.

34. Such, in various ways, is the argument of, among others, Shapin and Shaffer, *Leviathan and the Air-Pump;* Schouls, *The Imposition of Method;* and Hunter, *Science and Society in Restoration England.*

35. On the Ranters, see Christopher Hill, *The World Turned Upside Down*, pp. 184–258, and *A Tinker and a Poor Man*, 381–82; A. L. Morton, *The World of the Ranters*. On the Levellers, see Hill, *The World Turned Upside Down*, pp. 107–50; Morton, *The World of the Ranters*, pp. 197–219, and *The Matter of Britain*, pp. 73–82.

36. Hill, *The World Turned Upside Down*, p. 361.

37. See Keith Thomas, *Religion and the Decline of Magic*, pp. 341–42, 443–45.

38. Wolfe, ed., *Leveller Manifestoes*, p. 160.

39. Ibid., p. 124.

40. Cited in Hill, *The World Turned Upside Down*, pp. 139–41, 148.

41. Winstanley, *Law of Freedom*, pp. 77, 251.

42. Walzer, *The Revolution of the Saints*, p. 290.

43. See, for example, *The Case of the Armie* (1647), in Wolfe, *Leveller Manifestoes*, p. 198ff; and Hill, *The World Turned Upside Down*, p. 72.

44. Cited in Hill, *The World Turned Upside Down*, p. 72.

45. Ibid., pp. 306–23.

46. See, respectively, Morton, *The World of the Ranters*, p. 71; Hill, *The World Turned Upside Down*, pp. 215, 237.

47. Ibid., p. 61; Blake, *Complete Poetry and Prose*, pp. 57, 499. On the general relation between the 1640s and the 1790s, see Carl Cone, *The English Jacobins*, pp. 1–14; and E. P. Thompson, *The Making of the English Working Class*.

48. Crabbe, *Poetical Works*, p. 103. On the relation between Methodism and Puritanism, see Henry Abelove, *The Evangelist of Desire*, pp. 87–95.

49. "On the Ignorance and Vulgarity of the Methodists," *Examiner* 19 (8 May 1808): 303.

50. Lyles, *Methodism Mocked*, p. 22. Southey's *Life of Wesley*, p. 27, favors this explanation.

51. See Lyles, *Methodism Mocked*, pp. 82–84, and Abelove, *The Evangelist of Desire*, pp. 96–109, who suggests that Wesley's rules met with a rather mixed reception within the movement.

52. Halévy, *The Birth of Methodism in England*, p. 44.

53. Ong, "Peter Ramus and the Naming of Methodism," p. 235 and generally. Howell, *Eighteenth-Century British Logic and Rhetoric*, p. 58, identifies Wesley's text as a translation of Henry Aldrich's *Artis Logicae Compendium* (1691); for an account of Aldrich, see pp. 42–60.

54. *Encyclopaedia Britannica* 2:204.

55. *Poetical Works*, pp. 104, 124.

56. Lyles, *Methodism Mocked*, p. 23.

57. *The Round Table*, in *Complete Works* 4:58.

58. Boswell, *Life of Johnson*, p. 443.

59. Thompson, *The Making of the English Working Class*, p. 40.

60. Crabbe, *Poetical Works*, p. 122; Hunt, "On the Ignorance and Vulgarity of the Methodists," p. 301.

61. *Examiner* 21 (22 May 1808): 334.

62. See *Irony and Authority in Romantic Poetry*.

63. Wordsworth, *Prose Works* 1:118. For a different thesis about the importance of Methodism to Romanticism, see Richard Brantley, *Locke, Wesley, and the Method of English Romanticism*.

64. *Prose Works* 1:116–17.

65. *Humphry Clinker*, pp. 75, 95.

66. See *The Making of the English Working Class*, pp. 385–440.

67. "On the Indecencies and Profane Raptures of Methodism," *Examiner* 33 (14 August 1808): 524–25, and 33 (28 August 1808): 555–57.

68. *Thelyphthora* 1:xx, xxi.

69. For Blake in relation to the seventeenth century, see Morton, *The Matter of Britain*, pp. 98–121; for an account of the relation between Methodism and the seventeenth century, see Thompson, *The Making of the English Working Class*, pp. 24–58.

70. Introduction to Halévy, *The Birth of Methodism*, p. 19.

71. Semmel, *The Methodist Revolution*, p. 124.

72. See Hempton, *Methodism and Politics*, pp. 55–84; and Thompson, *The Making of the English Working Class*, pp. 46–49.

73. See Iain McCalman, *Radical Underworld*, pp. 50–72.

Chapter Two

1. *The Friend* 1:410.

2. *Biographia Literaria* 2:176.

3. *Lectures 1795*, pp. 255–56.

4. See *Anthropology*, pp. 174–82. First published in 1797 (2d ed. 1800), these were the lectures that Kant had been using throughout his career at Königsberg.

5. *Considerations on the Principal Events of the French Revolution* 2:257, 251.

6. See *Reflections on the Philosophy of the History of Mankind*, pp. 3–78.

7. See, for example, John Lucas, *England and Englishness;* Gerald Newman, *The Rise of English Nationalism*. The extensive collection of essays edited by Raphael Samuel under the title *Patriotism* contains much material pertaining to the seventeenth and eighteenth centuries; see, especially, Christopher Hill, "The English Revolution and Patriotism" (1:159–68); Madge Dresser, "Britannia" (3:26–49); Jeannine Surel, "John Bull" (3:3–25). Surel dates the popularity of the image of John Bull from the 1780s, i.e., after the American but before the French Revolution. And Linda Colley, in "Radical Patriotism in Eighteenth-Century England" (1:169–87), argues that the radicals had found it difficult to claim the rhetoric of patriotism after 1779–80 because of France's siding with America and besmirching "democracy" with popery.

8. "Of National Characters," in *Essays*, pp. 116–17.

9. *Anthropology*, p. 174.

10. *The Friend* 1:419.

11. *The Great Instauration*, in *Works* 4:19.

12. *Intellectual Origins of the English Revolution,* pp. 85–130. Hill notes that more of Bacon's works were published in 1640–41 than in all the fourteen years since his death (p. 116). Charles Webster, *The Great Instauration,* p. xv, also finds that Bacon was of "overwhelming significance among Puritan intellectuals." And Richard Foster Jones, *Ancients and Moderns,* also identifies Bacon as "the chief inspiration in the revolt from the past," seeing him as "firmly installed" by the Commonwealth as "the dominant influence of the day" (pp. 48, 280). The assumption of a strong connection between Puritanism and Baconianism has, however, been disputed; see Michael Hunter, *Science and Society in Restoration England,* pp. 31, 112ff.

13. "The Masculine Birth of Time," in Farrington, *The Philosophy of Francis Bacon,* p. 64.

14. *Francis Bacon and the Style of Science,* p. 1.

15. *Works* 4:26–27.

16. *History of the Royal Society,* p. 113.

17. This is a familiar but contested hypothesis. The association of Protestantism (of which Puritanism was a strong form) with the rise of rational method (and hence of science) was most forcefully and famously adduced by Max Weber in *The Protestant Ethic and the Spirit of Capitalism.* Stressing the power of "religious forces" in the formation of culture and of economic practice in the early modern period (p. 155), against what he saw as the economism of Marxist analysis, Weber specified Protestantism as the exemplary origin of rationalism. The further application of this model to the relation between Puritanism and science was carried out by Robert K. Merton; see *Puritanism and the Rise of Modern Science,* ed. I. Bernard Cohen.

18. *Probability and Certainty in Seventeenth-Century England,* pp. 16, 68, etc. See also Hunter, *Science and Society in Restoration England,* who finds that the links between science and the mercantile community were "disappointing" (p. 5); that the Royal Society by no means typified that science (pp. 32–58); and that Descartes and Hobbes were more important to the evolution of the mechanical philosophy than was Bacon (p. 16). Hunter cites John Worthington complaining to Henry More in 1667 that Cambridge students are "idolizing the French Philosophy" and "enravisht" with Cartesianism (p. 181). Steven Shapin and Simon Shaffer, in *Leviathan and the Air-Pump,* also make clear that the experimental method was by no means uncontested, and they argue that its eventual popular recognition was much dependent upon "certain social and discursive conventions" and "a special form of social organization" (p. 22). In proposing that the much-vaunted "matter of fact" must be read as a "social as well as an intellectual category" (p. 69), Shapin and Shaffer offer evidence that is very pertinent to an understanding of the mythology of the British national character.

19. See Margaret Jacob, *The Newtonians and the English Revolution;* and J. R. Jacob, *Robert Boyle and the English Revolution.*

20. *Opticks,* p. 404.

21. *Elements of Sir Isaac Newton's Philosophy,* pp. 3, 78, 8, 155.

22. *Characteristics* 1:168–69.

23. Ibid. 2:226, 236, 240, 347.

24. This is the thesis of Isaac Kramnick's *The Rage of Edmund Burke*. Kramnick sees in Burke's writings a "pivotal insight" into the "transformation from the aristocratic to the bourgeois world" and an epitome of "the love/hate ambivalence that the assertive bourgeoisie felt toward their aristocratic betters" (pp. xii, 8). He describes this syndrome in terms that are simultaneously economic, cultural, and sexual-psychoanalytic.

25. *Characteristics* 2:161. See also 2:206–7, where Shaftesbury identifies bigotry and excess enthusiasm with method, with a reduction of everything to "article and proposition" at the expense of hitherto sacred "mysteries."

26. *Enquiries*, pp. 163–64.

27. L. L. Laudan, "Thomas Reid and the Newtonian Turn of British Methodological Thought," pp. 106, 116.

28. *Essays on the Intellectual Powers of Man*, p. 46.

29. *Inquiry*, pp. 9–10, 262–63.

30. *Inquiry*, p. 32. Compare pp. 37, 268.

31. *Essay on the First Principles of Government*, pp. 24, 4, 8.

32. *Letters to the Rt. Hon. Edmund Burke*, pp. iv, 144.

33. *Description of a New Chart of History*, pp. 11–12.

34. *An Address to the Inhabitants of Birmingham*, p. 44.

35. *A Letter to Jacob Bryant*, p. 34.

36. Preface to Collins, *Philosophical Inquiry*, p. iv.

37. *An Examination of Dr. Reid's Inquiry*, pp. 201, 1.

38. *The Conduct to be Observed by Dissenters*, p. 10.

39. See *An Answer to Mr. Paine's Age of Reason*. For endorsements of Hobbes, see *A Letter to Jacob Bryant; A Free Discussion of the Doctrines of Materialism*, pp. xxv–xxvi.; and *The Doctrine of Philosophical Necessity Illustrated*, pp. xxvi–xxvii.

40. *The Doctrine of Philosophical Necessity Illustrated*, p. xxvii.

41. *The Newtonians and the English Revolution*, p. 53. See 52–71 for Jacob's account; and also Christopher Hill, "Thomas Hobbes and the Revolution in Political Thought," in *Puritanism and Revolution*, pp. 275–98.

42. *Leviathan*, in *English Works* 3:23–24.

43. *Travels* 1:119, iv.

44. *Political Disquisitions* 1:xvi, xxi, 1.

45. *Vindiciae Gallicae*, pp. vii, 115, 113.

46. *Anti-Jacobin Review*, n.s. 1 (1799): 109–10.

47. *Pursuits of Literature*, p. 276.

48. *Patriot* 1 (1792): 136–37.

49. David Williams, *Lessons to a Young Prince*, p. 9.

50. *Advice to the Privileged Orders*, pp. 2, 1. Sieyès reasoned that the physical sciences could afford a merely inductive method because the facts they assembled were already organized by an orderly nature. Since no such order exists in the affairs of men, "principles" are required. See *Vues sur les moyens d'exécution . . .* , pp. 28–30.

51. *Advice to the Privileged Orders*, pp. 15, 27.

52. Rous, *Thoughts on Government,* p. 7.

53. *Vindiciae Gallicae,* p. 123.

54. *Temperate Comments,* p. 20; James Parkinson, *Knave's-Acre Association* (1793); Thomas Cooper, *A Reply to Mr. Burke's Invective,* pp. 66, 82.

55. *Enquiry Concerning Political Justice,* pp. 67, 69, 158, 160.

56. Olivia Smith, *The Politics of Language,* pp. 1–67, has attributed Paine's complex reception to a linguistic phenomenon, arguing that there was in the early 1790s no constituency for a language above vulgarity but below refinement among the politically active middle classes. I would doubt that this circumstance, even if credible, would have been as important in discouraging positive affiliations as Paine's attitudes to religion and patriotism.

57. *Complete Writings* 1:276, 278–79, 331.

58. *Reflections,* pp. 285–88 and passim.

59. *Letters to Burke,* p. 16. See also Belsham, *Historic Memoir,* p. 64.

60. See Sieyès, *Quelques idées de constitution* (1789). The plan did call for eighty *départements* (with Paris as the 81st) containing 720 *communes.* Paris would have nine "districts" each containing nine "*quartiers,*" i.e., eighty-one in all. Nine was, in other words, something of a magic number. All of this allowed Burke the satirical opportunity to imagine a citizen belonging to "Chequer, no. 71" (*Reflections,* p. 315).

61. See Webster, *The Great Instauration,* pp. 535–39, for a reprint of the text of Woods's *Ten to One.*

62. "A Digression on Madness," in *A Tale of a Tub,* pp. 166–67.

63. *Reflections,* pp. 136, 138. Burke's anti-Semitism often goes without mention. Note the further references to "Jews and jobbers" and to "the Jews in Change Alley" (pp. 144, 204).

64. *Reflections,* pp. 281–82. For a discussion of Coleridge's "imagination" as a Burkean faculty, see my "Coleridge on Wordsworth and the Form of Poetry."

65. See *History of the Royal Society,* pp. 89–90, and the discussion earlier in this chapter.

66. *Works* 4:16, 95, 113.

67. Ibid. 5:233, 343, 345.

68. Ibid. 6:63, 60.

69. *Lectures, 1795,* pp. 325–26. Compare pp. 62–63.

70. *Collected Letters* 1:179–80.

71. *Lectures, 1795,* p. 5.

72. *Lay Sermons,* pp. 23–24, 49–50.

73. *Biographia Literaria* 1:285.

74. See, again, my "Coleridge on Wordsworth and the Form of Poetry."

75. *The Example of France,* p. 79.

Chapter Three

1. Christopher Hill, "The Norman Yoke," in *Puritanism and Revolution,* pp. 50–122.

2. *Travels in France* 1:iv.

3. *Enquiry into the State of the Public Mind,* p. 20.

4. *Vindiciae Gallicae,* pp. 117, 118.

5. *British Mercury* 2 (1799): 339.

6. *Philosophical Works* 1:80, 85.

7. I have analyzed and perhaps overemphasized this syndrome in "Putting One's House in Order: The Foundations of Descartes's Method" (1977). The language of a radical solipsism does register in the *Discourse,* where it is in tension with the suggestion that a shared reality may emerge from the proper exercise of reason. One might propose this visible play between solipsist and universalist potentials as itself the symptom of an emergent and unstable subject position.

8. Marjorie Nicolson, "The Early Stage of Cartesianism in England," p. 369.

9. Hilda L. Smith, *Reason's Disciples,* pp. 6, 11–12, 17, 118–39.

10. See, for example, Yvon Belaval, "La crise de géométrisation" (1952). A typical view is C. C. Gillispie, *The Edge of Objectivity,* p. 94, who finds that Cartesian science created the "impression of arrogance which an excessively mathematical temper is likely to convey. It was too ambitious. It overestimated the function of scientific explanation. It tried . . . to explain both the behavior and the reason in things by a single generalization."

11. *Elements of Sir Isaac Newton's Philosophy,* pp. 6, 8, 78, 134.

12. Margaret C. Jacob, *The Radical Enlightenment,* p. 46f; Peter A. Schouls, *The Imposition of Method,* p. 8ff., and *Descartes and the Enlightenment.*

13. *Diderot and Descartes,* pp. 24–26, 62, 134, and passim.

14. *Man a Machine,* pp. 111, 142–43, 158. See also the editor's note on pp. 165–66.

15. *Preliminary Discourse,* pp. 6–7, 25, 74.

16. See Charles C. Gillispie, "The *Encyclopédie* and the Jacobin Philosophy of Science" (1959), p. 269f. But, again, see also Vartanian, *Diderot and Descartes.*

17. *Encyclopédie* 5:643A. The first edition of *Encyclopaedia Britannica* (1771) refers to its French predecessor as trying to explain, "as much as possible, the order and connection of human knowledge" (2:301).

18. Ong, *Ramus,* pp. 295–318, makes a case for the Ramist heritage in this respect. A. H. T. Levi, "Ethics and the Encyclopedia in the Sixteenth Century" (1976), finds that Descartes's *The Passions of the Soul* is the only "imaginatively powerful and logically rigorous realization of the encyclopedic dream" in the seventeenth century (p. 171).

19. See Robert Darnton, *The Business of Enlightenment,* pp. 416–59. However, Darnton also argues that the *Méthodique* was in fact much less radical than its precursor, appearing "virtually as an official publication" (p. 454).

20. *Man a Machine,* p. 149.

21. *A Treatise on Man* 1:134f., 290; 2:14.

22. *De l'esprit,* p. xix.

23. *De l'esprit,* pp. 198, 426, 480; *Treatise* 1:12.

24. *De l'esprit,* p. 333; *Treatise* 2:339–40, 1:261, 229; *De l'esprit,* p. 10.

25. *Nature* 2:598, 429.

26. *Traité des sistêmes*, pp. 409, 417, 418; my translation. On Condillac's post-humous reputation, see W. R. Albury, "The Order of Ideas: Condillac's Method of Analysis as a Political Instrument in the French Revolution" (1986).

27. *Essay Concerning Human Knowledge*, p. 323; *Logic*, 269 (compare *Traité*, 100–101), 41, 43, 71.

28. *Traité*, pp. 2–6, 24.

29. *Logic*, pp. 93, 219, 112–13.

30. *Traité*, pp. 1–2.

31. *Logic*, pp. 73, 83, 87, 335.

32. See *Logic*, p. 27.

33. *Logic*, pp. 299, 199, 205.

34. See Van Duzer, *Contributions of the Ideologues*, pp. 97–99. For a detailed account of Condorcet's career, see Keith M. Baker, *Condorcet;* and L. Pearce Williams, "The Politics of Science in the French Revolution" (1959). Baker (p. 391ff.) identifies Condorcet as one of the earliest users (if not the originator) of the term "social science."

35. *Selected Writings*, pp. 235, 237, 211.

36. Ibid., pp. 225, 237, 5.

37. Ibid., pp. 93, 111, 262, 80, 290.

38. "Reflections on the English Revolution" (1792), pp. 44, 43.

39. "Observations de Condorcet," in Destutt De Tracy, *Commentaire sur l'Esprit des Lois*, p. 406.

40. *Selected Writings*, p. 178–79.

41. "Thoughts on French Affairs," in *Works* 4:356, 358.

42. *Selected Writings,* pp. 231–32. Compare Volney, *Volney's Ruins*, pp. 72–73, where print is seen as the means by which "science will become a vulgar possession" and "the human race will become one great society."

43. *Selected Writings*, pp. 277–78; compare 296.

44. Ibid., p. 238. Many of the mathematicized social reforms entertained by the early French republic were in fact extensions of the schemes put forward in the last years of the old regime. But Condorcet was involved, both before and after 1789. See Baker, *Condorcet*, pp. 65–67.

45. Cited in Van Duzer, *Contributions of the Ideologues*, p. 151.

46. *Pursuits of Literature*, p. 204.

47. *Sober Reflections*, pp. 74, 77. The notion of the Jacobins as consistently anti-intellectual has become familiar but has been challenged by L. Pearce Williams, "Science in the French Revolution." On Marat's antiestablishment "science," see C. C. Gillispie, *Science and Polity*, pp. 290–330.

48. *Rousseau and the French Revolution*, p. 172. See, among others, Daniel Mornet, *Les origines intellectuelles de la Révolution Française*, pp. 92–94; Jean Roussel, *Jean-Jacques Rousseau en France*. Sieyès in fact used the phrase "general will" (volonté générale) in his *Déclaration des droits de l'homme* (1789), p. 11, and it appeared in the Declaration of Rights voted in by the National Assembly in August 1789; see Roberts and Cobb, *French Revolution Documents* 1:172–73. There is a counterargument suggesting the indirect influence of *The Social Contract* in

the prerevolutionary period; for a summary of the debate, see Sarah Maza, "Politics, Culture, and the Origins of the French Revolution" (1989), p. 714.

49. "De degré de l'influence qu'a eu la philosophie," *Mercure britannique* 2:362; my translation. Gwyn Williams, *Artisans and Sans-Culottes,* p. 31, notes only one new edition of *The Social Contract* between 1762 and 1789, and thirty-two in the next ten years, including a "proliferation" of pocket editions from 1792 on. On the reading of Voltaire, see R. S. Crane, "Diffusion of Voltaire's Writings in England, 1750–1800" (1923). Among the two hundred private libraries whose holdings he surveyed, Crane found that 80 percent contained something by Voltaire, 50 percent something of Pope, and 23 percent something by Rousseau.

50. *Miscellaneous Works* 5:60, 109; 3:23; 5:88.

51. Cassirer, *The Question of Jean-Jacques Rousseau,* 124; Rousseau, *Miscellaneous Works* 5:36–37.

52. *Miscellaneous Works* 5:77, 1:24, 3:14, 23.

53. *Miscellaneous Works* 2:243–44; *Reveries,* pp. 52–53; *Miscellaneous Works* 5:173–83. Similarly, the Savoyard priest is not "pledged to the support of any system" (*Émile,* p. 240).

54. *Reveries,* pp. 33, 35; *Confessions,* p. 17. Rousseau's hyperbolic assertion of singularity may be read as the sign of an effort at bourgeois self-promotion, and as such it would have constituted a kind of typicality with which his readers could hardly have failed to identify.

55. *Émile,* 170, 277. For Kant's mandate, see "An Answer to the Question, What Is Enlightenment?" in Kant, *On History,* p. 3.

56. *Eloisa* 3:50–51.

57. *Confessions,* p. 479; *Reveries,* p. 79.

58. *Strictures on the Modern System of Female Education,* pp. 22, 26; *"Mary" and "The Wrongs of Woman,"* p. 88; *Memoirs of Emma Courtney,* p. 25.

59. *Discourse on the Love of our Country,* p. 36.

60. *An Answer to Mr. Paine's Age of Reason,* pp. 36–37. Seamus Deane, "The Reputation of the French *Philosophes*" (1975), p. 276ff., has argued that there was no "liberal" acceptance of Rousseau before at least the 1820s.

61. "Letter to a Member of the National Assembly," in *Works* 4:26, 25, 31, 27. Abstract benevolence is criticized in exactly these terms in Coleridge's poem of 1795, "Reflections on Having Left a Place of Retirement" (*Coleridge: Poetical Works,* p. 107). One can further imagine the effect of such language on the young Wordsworth, who would indeed abandon a child in 1792. Wordsworth's relation to Rousseau is a much debated question. See, among others, Jacques Voisine, *J-J Rousseau en Angleterre,* pp. 202–22; Margery Sabin, *English Romanticism and the French Tradition,* pp. 32–47; James Chandler, *Wordsworth's Second Nature,* pp. 93–109; W. J. T. Mitchell, "Influence, Autobiography, and Literary History" (1990); David Simpson, "Public Virtues, Private Vices: Reading Between the Lines of Wordsworth's 'Anecdote for Fathers.'" Voisine, pp. 223–40, makes the interesting suggestion that Charles Lloyd might have been the mediator of Rousseau's ideas to the Wordsworth circle.

62. *Rousseau in England,* esp. pp. 46–53. For other accounts of Rousseau's

reception in Britain, see Roddier, *J-J Rousseau en Angleterre au XVIIIe siècle;* Voisine, *J-J Rousseau en Angleterre;* Joan McDonald, *Rousseau and the French Revolution;* Seamus Deane, "The Reputation of the French *Philosophes*" (1975), and *The French Revolution and Enlightenment in England,* esp. pp. 58–71.

63. See Voisine, *J-J Rousseau En Angleterre,* pp. 143–50; David Williams, *Lessons to a Young Prince,* p. 59.

64. *Anti-Jacobin Review and Magazine* 1 (1799): 360.

65. Thelwall, *Sober Reflections,* pp. 71–77; Sieyès, *Vues sur les moyens d'exécution,* p. 8.

66. As, for example, by William Blake, *Complete Poetry and Prose,* p. 477. On Voltaire's British reputation, see Schilling, *Conservative England and the the Case Against Voltaire;* and Seamus Deane, "John Bull and Voltaire" (1971).

67. *Complete Writings* 1:300.

68. *Reflections,* pp. 211–13.

69. See, for example, Pierre Trahard, *La sensibilité révolutionnaire,* pp. 5–8. For a review of the early British histories, see Hedva Ben-Israel, *English Historians and the French Revolution.*

70. See, especially, Lynn Hunt, *Politics, Culture, and Class in the French Revolution.*

71. Roberts and Cobb, *French Revolution Documents* 1:396.

72. Ben-Israel, *English Historians and the French Revolution,* p. 53; *Anti-Jacobin Review* 25 (1807): 450.

73. *Lay Sermons,* pp. 14–15.

74. *Vindiciae Gallicae,* pp. 15–17.

75. See, for example, Norman Hampson, *A Social History of the French Revolution,* pp. 250–51, where it is argued that there was little actual transfer of property, that more aristocrats escaped than suffered the guillotine, and that most of the violence was directed against ordinary citizens.

76. Roberts and Cobb, *French Revolution Documents* 1:347.

77. *Rousseau and Romanticism,* p. x.

Chapter Four

1. *Anthropology,* pp. 179–81.

2. *Biographia Literaria* 2:197, 194, 191.

3. Ibid. 2:183, 185, 190, 212.

4. *The Friend* 1:421–23.

5. *The Watchman,* pp. 89–92.

6. *History of the Royal Society,* p. 127.

7. Donald R. Kelley, *The Beginning of Ideology,* p. 146. Compare Burke, *Reflections,* p. 262.

8. Ong, *Ramus,* pp. 296–301.

9. *Don Juan* 1:64, in *Don Juan,* ed. Marchand, p. 24.

10. *The British Critic* 1 (1793); ibid. 14 (1799): 67–69.

11. "Thoughts on French Affairs," in *Works* 4:343, 355, 328, 330. For an account of the conspiracy theories in relation to the construction of the national

character, see Seamus Deane, *The French Revolution and Enlightenment in England*, pp. 21–42.

12. See Mornet, *Les origines intellectuelles de la Révolution Française*, pp. 357–87; and Margaret Jacob, *The Radical Enlightenment*, p. 109f.

13. *The Radical Enlightenment*, pp. 225, 156. Thomas Paine wrote a supplement to *The Age of Reason*, unpublished until an edited version in 1810 and a complete text in 1818, in which he argued for the origins of freemasonry in Druid sun worship; see *Complete Writings* 2:830–41.

14. *The British Critic* 5 (1795): 471.

15. *Memoirs Illustrating the History of Jacobinism* 1:iv.

16. *Proofs of a Conspiracy*, pp. 65, 243.

17. *Proofs of the Real Existence of Illuminism*, pp. iii, 287, 157, 191, 83–84.

18. Thomas Atkinson, *An Oblique View of the Grand Conspiracy* (1798); William Hamilton Reid, *The Rise and Dissolution of the Infidel Societies* (1800); Robert Clifford, *Application of Barruel's Memoirs* (1798).

19. *Mercure britannique* 2 (1799): 498–99, 487, 489.

20. *European Magazine* 32 (1797): 105; *Analytical Review* 26 (1797): 234.

21. Mounier, *De l'influence attribuée aux philosophes*, pp. 118, 49; *Anti-Jacobin Review* 11 (1802): 336, 348.

22. For a brief account see Lefèbvre, *The French Revolution* 2:32–34.

23. *Anti-Jacobin Review* 7 (1801): 516.

24. *Monthly Magazine* 3 (1798): 515.

25. *Critical Remarks on Pizarro,* p. iv.

26. L. F. Thompson, *Kotzebue*, p. 58. See pp. 55–108 for an account of Kotzebue in England.

27. Ibid., pp. 109–69.

28. *Sheridan and Kotzebue*, pp. 67, 68.

29. Appendix to Kotzebue, *The Natural Son*, p. 82.

30. *Prose Works* 1:128, 126, 130, 124.

31. *Critical Remarks on Pizarro*, p. 47.

32. *British Critic* 12 (1798): 598–600; *European Magazine* 34 (1798): 256.

33. *Anti-Jacobin Review* 3 (1799): 155, 440; 9 (1801): 78.

34. Kotzebue, *The Natural Son*, p. v.

35. Kotzebue, *Lover's Vows*, p. iii; idem, *The Natural Son*, 36.

36. *Anti-Jacobin Review* 21 (1805): 142.

37. See Jonathan Arac, "The Media of Sublimity"; Michael Hays, "Comedy as Being/Comedy as Idea."

38. *German Museum* 1 (1800): 382. Compare Wordsworth's account of the creation of "excitement" by the "gross and violent stimulants" rendered effective only because of a prior state of "almost savage torpor" (*Prose Works* 1:128). Both Schiller and Wordsworth here draw attention to the negative effects of a society founded in the division of labor.

39. William Preston, "Reflections on the Late German Writers," pp. 70, 67, 79, 17, 24, 29, 28.

40. *Strictures on the Modern System of Female Education*, pp. 29, 33.

41. "Reflections on the Late German Writers," pp. 38, 37.

42. *Monthly Magazine* 5: (1798): 173, 174.

43. *Lectures on the Theory of Language,* p. 283.

44. *Analytical Review* 25 (1797): 22.

45. *British Critic* 8 (1796): 150. For an account of Kant's reception in England, see Wellek, *Immanuel Kant In England.*

46. *European Magazine* 37 (1800): 285.

47. *German Museum* 1: (1800): 57, 71.

48. *Analytical Review* 26 (1797): 85–86; *Anti-Jacobin Review* 5 (1800), 347, 339; 6(1800): 570.

49. *Law of Freedom,* p. 222.

50. *Critique of Pure Reason,* pp. 13, 32.

51. Ibid., pp. 9, 10, 11.

52. Ibid., pp. 32, 20, 22.

53. Ibid., pp. 25, 33–34.

54. *A General and Introductory View of Professor Kant's Principles,* pp. 231–32, 57–58.

55. *Elements of the Critical Philosophy,* pp. 1, 23, 76, 115, 124–25.

56. "On Grace and Dignity," in *Works* 9:203, 205, 208.

57. *Enquiries,* pp. 280, 303, 172; compare pp. 286–87.

58. *Reveries,* p. 68; *Émile,* pp. 276, 249. Compare *Miscellaneous Works* 1:54, 3:249.

59. *Reveries,* pp. 68, 73, 96–97.

60. *Sorrows of Young Werther,* p. 27.

61. Ibid., pp. 26, 30, 95, 71.

62. *Examiner* 4 (24 January 1808): 63.

63. *Sense and Sensibility,* pp. 42, 98.

64. Simpson, *Origins of Modern Critical Thought,* p. 28.

65. *Anti-Jacobin Review* 4 (1799): viii–ix.

66. Ibid. 4 (1799), xii; 5 (1800): 349; 4 (1799): xiii.

67. Ibid. 5 (1800): 434; 4 (1799): xiii. See also 6 (1800): 574, where there is an explicit criticism of the poets' own visit to Germany.

68. Ibid. 6 (1800): 565, 569–70; compare 1 (1799): 729. Ibid. 2 (1799): 283.

69. *European Magazine* 24 (1793): 11–13.

70. Hazlitt, *Works* 11:34.

71. Jackson, *Coleridge: The Critical Heritage,* p. 224.

72. *Romantics, Rebels, and Reactionaries,* pp. 115, 121.

73. *Nightmare Abbey,* p. 67.

74. The failure to distinguish different historical phases and political applications of this Romantic irony informs, I'm afraid to say, my own *Irony and Authority in Romantic Poetry,* which treats the reflexive method largely as a formal-aesthetic strategy.

75. Deane, "The Reputation of the French *Philosophes*," p. 285ff.

76. *Germany* 1:4, 137ff., 222, 276.

77. Ibid. 2:259; 3:81, 87–88, 90, 95.

78. *Ibid.* 1:37–42; 3:165, 135, 168.
79. Ibid. 3:302, 213, 205.
80. Ibid. 3:202, 1:19.

Chapter Five

1. *The Lawyers Logike,* cited in Howell, *Logic and Rhetoric in England, 1500–1700,* p. 225.

2. See, especially, Marlon Ross, *The Contours of Masculine Desire;* Peter De Bolla, *The Discourse of the Sublime,* pp. 230–78; and the essays collected in Anne Mellor, ed., *Romanticism and Feminism.* See also Jerome Christensen, *Practicing Enlightenment,* pp. 94–119, where the feminization of literary culture is read through a close analysis of Hume's style and method.

3. *The World Turned Upside Down,* pp. 306–23.

4. Keith Thomas, "The Puritans and Adultery," points out that only four such sentences were imposed during the lifetime of this law (1650–60), and only one carried out; but he affirms that noncapital prosecutions for "fornication" were quite common. In "Women and the Civil War Sects" Thomas argues that the Puritans could not be described as making any coordinated efforts toward the liberation of women, but provides impressive documentation of the degree to which women were numerically dominant in the sects themselves.

5. It is, however, the powerful argument of Mary Nyquist, "The Genesis of Gendered Subjectivity," that no anachronistic feminism should be read into Milton's argument, which remains, for her, clearly within the conventions of masculinist ideology.

6. *Works* 4:284. For general accounts of the masculinist inclination of seventeenth-century science, see Brian Easlea, *Science and Sexual Oppression,* and *Witch-Hunting, Magic, and the New Philosophy.*

7. *History of the Royal Society,* preface, p. 18.

8. Cited in Ong, *Ramus,* p. 214. On the traditional masculinization of logic, and the reciprocal feminization of rhetoric, see Patricia Parker, *Literary Fat Ladies,* esp. pp. 95–125.

9. *The Rights of Nature* 1:2; *Sober Reflections,* 36, 63.

10. *Vindiciae Gallicae,* pp. 309, 164, 165.

11. *Complete Writings* 1: 286, 354, 338.

12. *Historical and Moral View of the French Revolution,* pp. 12, v. The entire rhetoric of this text is built around the opposition between effeminate aristocracy and manly philosophy; see, e.g., pp. 21, 31, 245–48.

13. *Vindication of the Rights of Men,* p. 6. Compare pp. 27, 44–45.

14. *Vindication of the Rights of Woman,* pp. 113, 105.

15. *Memoirs of Mary Wollstonecraft,* pp. 54, 55, 73, 125, 56.

16. *The Proper Lady and the Woman Writer,* pp. 48–113.

17. *The Female Reader,* pp. vi, ix, iii.

18. *Vindication of the Rights of Woman,* pp. 22, 185, 39, 54.

19. The conventions are magisterially described in Pocock, *The Machiavellian Moment.*

20. *Vindication of the Rights of Woman,* pp. 35, 37, 56, 177, 140–41. This attack on monarchy and property distinguishes Wollstonecraft from her seventeenth- and eighteenth-century feminist predecessors, most of whom (at least in the elite tradition) managed to preserve royalist affiliations while arguing for the rights of women. Catherine Gallagher, in "Embracing the Absolute," addresses this apparent paradox and suggests that the image of absolutism might have appealed to such women as one of freedom from constraint; but class identities must surely have accounted for some of these instances. See also Hilda Smith, *Reason's Disciples,* and Rae Blanchard, "Richard Steele and the Status of Women," on the traditions of rationalist and Cartesian feminism.

21. *The Proper Lady and the Woman Writer,* pp. 109, 27.

22. *Vindication of the Rights of Woman,* p. 9.

23. I have no space to pursue this case, but it is hard not to suspect that the stylistic shifts signaled in such passages as "Modesty . . . may I unblamed presume" and "But, I have tripped unawares on faery ground" (pp. 121, 124) are not self-consciously mock-heroic, as they commonly are in Fielding, Cowper, and other writers.

24. *Posthumous Works* 3:62, 94; compare p. 81.

25. Ibid. 3:52–53, 60, 128.

26. Ibid. 4:42, 47; compare *Vindication of the Rights of Woman,* pp. 3–4.

27. *Posthumous Works* 1:52. Compare *Vindication of the Rights of Woman,* pp. 30–31, and p. 75, where a distinction is made between "strong, persevering passions" and "romantic wavering feelings"—hardly the argumentation of a "female Werter." See also *Thoughts on the Education of Daughters,* pp. 112, 116, and passim.

28. *A Historical and Moral View of . . . the French Revolution,* pp. v, 31, 12.

29. Ibid., pp. 356, 406, 357, 355.

30. The Marquis d'Argens, cited in Vartanian, *Diderot and Descartes,* p. 31. See, again, Marjorie Nicolson, "The Early Stage of Cartesianism in England"; Hilda Smith, *Reason's Disciples;* and the discussion of Descartes in chapter 3, above.

31. *Plan for the Conduct of Female Education,* p. 40ff.

32. *Zoonomia,* pp. xv, 1, 2.

33. *Poetical Works* 1:186.

34. Ibid. 3:59n. Compare 3:249: "Mankind was originally of both sexes united."

35. Ibid. 3:175, 3, 4.

36. Edmonds, *Poetry of the Anti-Jacobin,* p. 150ff.

37. Polwhele, *The Unsex'd Females,* pp. 7n., 9, 10n., 14, 15. For an account of the revolutionary associations of late eighteenth-century botany, see Alan Bewell, "'Jacobin Plants': Botany as Social Theory in the 1790s"; and Marilyn Butler, *Romantics, Rebels, and Reactionaries,* pp. 129–37. See also Vartanian, "La Mettrie, Diderot, and Sexology in the Enlightenment." Other popular "science" of the time, Mesmerism, was also seen to be a sexualized communication especially available to women; see Gillispie, *Science and Polity in France,* pp. 261–89.

38. See, among recent studies, Hagstrum, *Sex and Sensibility;* Mullan, *Sentiment and Sociability;* and Conger, ed., *Sensibility in Transformation.*

39. "Reflections on the Late German Writers," p. 43.

40. *The Unsex'd Females,* p. v.

41. See James Turner, "The Properties of Libertinism," for an excellent introductory survey and bibliography.

42. Mathias, *Pursuits of Literature,* p. 158; Knight, *Remains of the Worship of Priapus,* p. 142ff. For a brief and dominantly psychoanalytic reading of the image of the liberty cap, see Neil Hertz, *The End of the Line,* pp. 179–91. The evidence in Payne Knight and elsewhere suggests a perfectly conscious use of the Phrygian cap as phallic image.

43. *The Progress of Civil Society,* pp. 6, 133, 141, 148.

44. *An Essay on Woman,* p. 5. Margaret Jacob, in *The Radical Enlightenment,* pp. 206–8, suggests that the homosexual associations of freemasonry, which had certain phallicist inclinations, are to be read as a reaction to the new bourgeois cult of domesticity.

45. See Iain McCalman, *Radical Underworld,* pp. 204–31; David Erdman, *Commerce des Lumières,* p. 52ff.; and Robert Darnton, "Philosophy Under the Cloak."

46. *De l'esprit,* pp. 281n., 120.

47. Mirabaud, *Nature* 2:538; *Volney's Ruins,* pp. 202–4; Price, *A Discourse on the Love of our Country,* p. 36.

48. *A Political Dictionary,* pp. 170, 118.

49. *Vues sur les moyens d'exécution,* p. 32ff.; *What Is the Third Estate?* p. 74.

50. *Travels,* 1:281.

51. *Selected Writings,* 97ff., 274–75.

52. See Olwen Hufton, "Women in Revolution, 1789–1796."

53. Wollstonecraft, *An Historical and Moral View.* p. 425f.

54. Landes, *Women and the Public Sphere in the Age of the French Revolution;* Levy, Applewhite, and Johnson, *Women in Revolutionary Paris, 1789–95.* On the displacement of Marianne by Hercules as the Jacobin icon, see Lynn Hunt, "Hercules and the Radical Image in the French Revolution." See also David Williams, "The Politics of Feminism in the French Enlightenment."

55. See Elisabeth Roudinesco, *Théroigne de Méricourt,* pp. 4, 7.

56. Cited in Levy, Applewhite, and Johnson, *Women in Revolutionary Paris,* p. 90.

57. For an account of her career, see Landes, *Women in the Public Sphere,* pp. 124–27.

58. Amar is cited in Hampson. *A Social History of the French Revolution,* p. 212–13. I refer to *A Critical Dictionary of the French Revolution,* ed. François Furet and Mona Ozouf.

59. Roberts and Cobb, *French Revolutionary Documents* 1:349, 2:342.

60. Hunt, "The Unstable Boundaries of the French Revolution," pp. 33, 34.

61. *A Political Dictionary,* p. 17.

62. *Reflections on the Revolution in France,* pp. 164.

63. "Letter to a Member of the National Assembly," in *Works* 4:31.

64. See, for example, *Works* 5:313–16. The basic study of the imagery of the Revolution debate is still James T. Boulton's *The Language of Politics in the Age of Wilkes and Burke.*

65. *The Bloody Buoy*, pp. ix–xi, 51 and passim.

66. *Vindication of the Rights of Brutes*, p. 76.

67. *Poetry of the Anti-Jacobin*, p. 281; Mathias, *Pursuits of Literature*, p. 15; Courtenay, *Philosophical Reflections*, p. 40ff.

68. Pigott, *The Female Jockey Club*, pp. 2–3; Spence, *The Rights of Infants*, p. 8. and *The Restorer of Society*, pp. 14–15.

69. *Letters Written in France* (1791), p. 29.

70. See, among others, David Punter, "1789: The Sex of Revolution."

71. See note 2, above.

72. *Strictures on Female Education*, pp. 4–5, i, 13.

73. *Letters for Literary Ladies*, p. 45.

74. *Works* 1:210, 211.

75. *Adeline Mowbray*, pp. 2–3, 41–42, 255. Sophia King's *Waldorf; or, the Dangers of Philosophy* (1798) specifies in its subtitle the point to be taken.

76. Pigott, *The Female Jockey Club*, pp. 123, 197; Polwhele, *The Unsex'd Females*, p. 37ff. For an account of the bluestockings, see Bouten, *Mary Wollstonecraft and the Beginnings of Female Emancipation*, pp. 98–128.

77. *Vindication of the Rights of Woman*, p. 105.

78. *Observations on the Reflections*, pp. 93, 54, 5.

79. *Loose Remarks on Certain Positions*, pp. 1, 26, 37.

80. *A History of England*, 5:6, 8; 6:vii.

81. *Letters on Education*, p. vi.

82. *Memoirs of Emma Courtney*, pp. xvii, 6, 61, 135.

83. Ibid., pp. 122, 126.

84. *Appeal to the Men of Great Britain*, pp. v–vi, 105, 127, 187, 239.

85. *Female Biography* 1:iii–iv.

86. *Letters* 1:563.

87. *Memoirs of Modern Philosophers* 1:11, 182.

88. *Letters Containing a Sketch of the Politics of France* 1:174ff., 213–15.

89. *Sketches of the State of Manners and Opinions* 2:50, 53, 60, 63.

90. Ibid. 2:83, 186–87.

91. *Lay Sermons*, pp. 61–62.

92. This is one of the themes of my *Wordsworth's Historical Imagination.*

93. Barbauld, preface to *The Poetical Works of William Collins*, pp. vii–viii.

94. *The Female Reader*, pp. ix–x.

Chapter Six

1. Frank Lentricchia, "Patriarchy Against Itself." See also the ensuing debate in *Critical Inquiry* 14 (1987–88): 379–413.

2. See Margaret W. Ferguson, *Trials of Desire*, pp. 18–53 (on du Bellay); see also pp. 159–62, where Sidney's career is interpreted as a crisis in an aristocrat's frustrated, militant masculinity.

3. See, for example, W. J. T. Mitchell, *Iconology,* pp. 116–49; and Frances Ferguson, "The Sublime of Edmund Burke." See also Peter de Bolla, *Discourse of the Sublime.*

4. *Philosophical Enquiry,* pp. 4, 53.

5. Ibid., pp. 60, 63, 78, 62.

6. Ibid., pp. 39, 43, 57, 86.

7. Ibid., pp. 67, 95.

8. *Spectator,* no. 412, p. 372.

9. *Reflections on the Revolution in France,* pp. 175–77.

10. Hobbes, *English Works* 1:2, 3:693, 700. Compare Winstanley, *Law of Freedom,* p. 353.

11. Cited in Christopher Hill, *The World Turned Upside Down,* pp. 365–66. Compare Bacon, *Works* 4:364.

12. Examples are numerous and commonplace. See, among many others, Paine, *Complete Writings* 2:859; Condillac, *Traité des sistêmes,* p. 56ff; Helvétius, *Treatise on Man* 1:viii, 2:239–40; Holbach, *Common Sense,* pp. 13, 16, 96; Condorcet, *Selected Writings,* p. 5.

13. *Complete Poetry and Prose of William Blake,* p. 38.

14. Barlow, *The Conspiracy of Kings,* p. 12; Towers, *Thoughts on the Commencement,* p. 88; Mackintosh, *Vindiciae Gallicae,* p. v. See also Catherine Macaulay, *Observations on the Reflections,* 34; Wollstonecraft, *An Historical and Moral View of the French Revolution,* pp. 224–28, 425; *Vindication of the Rights of Woman,* p. 154.

15. *Vindiciae Gallicae,* p. 7.

16. Hays, *Appeal to the Men of Great Britain,* pp. 47, 97, 100. See also David Punter, "1789: The Sex of Revolution."

17. *Vindication of the Rights of Men,* pp. 2, 5, 34, 137 and passim.

18. *Prose Works* 1:116, 128.

19. *Culture and Society,* p. 69.

20. *The New England Mind: The Seventeenth Century,* pp. 144–45.

21. See Ong, *Ramus,* pp. 281–83; and Sharratt, "Peter Ramus and the Reform of the University," pp. 16–19.

22. Wordsworth, *Poetical Works* 4:57; Bacon, *Works* 1:663 (cited in Miller, *The New England Mind,* p. 127).

23. *Of Dramatic Poesy* 1:17, 56, 59, 76.

24. Vickers, ed., *Shakespeare: The Critical Heritage,* 1:46, 2:279, 317.

25. *Iliad* 1:214–15.

26. *Characteristics* 2:347.

27. Ibid. 1:214–15.

28. Lamb, *Complete Works,* p. 299. On this subject, see Jonathan Arac, "The Media of Sublimity."

29. Beattie, *An Essay on the Nature and Immutability of Truth,* pp. 24–25, 43, 448–49, 450.

30. *Characteristics* 2:257.

31. See, for example, *The Friend* 1:450ff.

32. I merely note here that the often supposed hegemony of the spoken

over the written that has been found typical of Western metaphysics in general does not always take the same forms at different times; so that, if we wish to suggest that the foundation of the problem of subjectivity as a philosophical inquiry entails also the fetishization of speech as the primary marker of subjectivity, it yet remains evident that particular formations of the problem, and indeed analogous formations outside the language of philosophy, take shape and relate to one another as the result of specific historical determinations.

33. *Thoughts on Man*, pp. 251–52.

34. See, again, Arac, "The Media of Sublimity"; and Michael Hays, "Comedy as Being/Comedy as Idea."

35. Anon, *A Defence of the Political and Parliamentary Conduct of . . . Burke*, p. 6.

36. *Miscellaneous Works*, pp. 26, 27, 30, 32.

37. Ibid., pp. 170–71, 178, 167.

38. Coleridge, *Biographia Literaria* 2:16; Burke, *Reflections*, p. 241.

39. *Biographia Literaria* 1:9, 2:59–60.

40. *The Works of Alexander Pope* 3:150n., 88n., 166n.

41. *Characteristics* 2:5–6.

42. *Prose Works* 1:120, 148, 141.

43. *Poetry and Prose*, pp. 503, 484–85.

44. Ibid., pp. 502, 508.

45. See Annette Cafarelli, *Prose in the Age of Poets*, for an account of the rise of biography, and an argument for its appeal as an immethodical version of cultural history.

46. See Foucault, *The Order of Things*, esp. 303–43.

47. *Confessions*, p. 478; *Reveries*, pp. 76, 77, 79.

48. *Poetical Works* 2:261; *The Prelude*, p. 124 (1805, 3:644–48).

49. *Biographia Literaria* 1:13, 22.

50. For an introduction, see Halévy, *The Growth of Philosophic Radicalism*.

51. Shaftesbury, *Characteristics* 1:46; Hume, *Enquiries*, pp. 189, 204, 163. Compare p. 231. Hume located benevolence and the desire for approbation as prior to and different from self-love and hence as the sources of utility.

52. Helvétius, *Treatise on Man* 1:12ff. Compare Bentham, *Introduction to the Principles of Morals and of Legislation*, p. 50ff.

53. Ian Hacking, *The Emergence of Probability*, p. 176, gives Hume's *Treatise* of 1739 the credit for originating the epistemology of probabilism. Douglas Lane Patey, in *Probability and Literary Form*, pp. 23–34, argues an exemplary role for Locke. See also Stephen Stigler, *The History of Statistics*.

54. *Mill on Bentham and Coleridge*, pp. 42, 93.

55. *Works* 1:238, 245, 295; *Introduction to the Principles of Morals and of Legislation*, p. 11.

56. *Works* 1:235n., 180. Like Ramus, Bentham also favored classification by dichotomies; see Halévy, *The Growth of Philosophic Radicalism*, pp. 60–62.

57. *Works* 2:494–95, 501. For an account of Bentham's relations to the

Lansdowne circle and to the English Jacobins, see Halévy, *The Growth of Philosophic Radicalism*, pp. 164–203.

58. *Works* 2:521–22, 1:358–62, 4:407–18. But for a much more radical view of the "constitution," see 2:442.

59. "The Press—Coleridge, Southey, Wordsworth and Bentham," in *Complete Works*, 19:205.

60. *Introduction to the Principles of Morals and of Legislation*, p. 9; *Works* 2:459, 462, 463.

61. *Works* 1:236n., 269, 295.

62. *Probability and Literary Form*, pp. 176ff., 220–51.

63. John Brewer, *The Sinews of Power*, offers a detailed account of the development of bureaucracy through the eighteenth century. He notes, for example, that the Excise had a "Method" for training its offers (pp. 94, 225).

64. *Westminster Review* 1 (January 1824): 10, 9, 11, 12.

65. Ibid., pp. 10–11.

66. *The Influence of Literature upon Society* 2:218, 229.

67. "Signs of the Times," in *Works* 27:76, 68, 74.

Chapter Seven

1. *Tom Jones*, pp. 101, 373.

2. *Letters Written in France*, p. 70ff.; compare *Sketches of the State of Manners and Opinions*, p. 299.

3. See Condorcet, *Selected Writings*, pp. 13–14, 242–43; Mackintosh, *Vindiciae Gallicae*, p. 200.

4. *Poetical Works* 1:iii, 45, 55.

5. Barbauld, ed., *Pleasures of Imagination*, pp. 2–3.

6. *Spectator*, no. 411, p. 370.

7. *Biographia Literaria* 2:15–16, 27.

8. *The Influence of Literature upon Society* 1:45.

9. Hayley, *An Essay on Epic Poetry*, pp. 13, 18.

10. *Miscellaneous Works* 2:133–34.

11. I have in mind here the widespread effects, and at times the apparent intention, of Jerome McGann's influential *The Romantic Ideology*.

12. *Prose Works* 1:126, 148.

13. Ibid. 1:124, 128, 140.

14. For more on "Michael," see my *Wordsworth's Historical Imagination*, pp. 141–49.

15. *Prose Works* 1:116, 162.

16. Ibid. 1:128.

17. See Mary Jacobus, *Tradition and Experiment in Wordsworth's "Lyrical Ballads."*

18. *Poetical Works* 4:57, 60.

19. *Complete Works* 11:87.

20. Jerome McGann, *The Romantic Ideology;* James Chandler, *Wordsworth's*

Second Nature; Marjorie Levinson, *Wordsworth's Great Period Poems;* Alan Liu, *Wordsworth: The Sense of History.*

21. John Jordan, *Why the "Lyrical Ballads"?* pp. 84–102, 128–54.

22. The seminal argument against the idea of an anti-intellectual Wordsworth is Raymond Dexter Havens, *The Mind of a Poet.* See also Geoffrey Durrant, *Wordsworth and the Great System.*

23. *The Borderers,* pp. 204, 210.

24. *The Prelude,* pp. 20, 25, 19, 7.

25. Ibid., pp. 194, 408, 296–98.

26. Ibid., p. 322.

27. *The Excursion* 1:213, 291–92; 2:483, 486 (*Poetical Works* 5:15, 17, 59).

28. Ibid., 3:715–16, 4:73–76, 6:6 (*Poetical Works* 5:101, 112, 186).

29. *Poetical Works* 4:83–86.

30. "The Warning," *Poetical Works* 4:113.

31. *The Prelude,* pp. 255, 404, 422, 154, 468.

32. *Complete Poetry and Prose,* pp. 42, 36, 38, 40.

33. Ibid., pp. 54, 78.

34. *Complete Writings* 1:298, 446.

35. Jacob, *The Radical Enlightenment,* pp. 93, 94. See the same author's *The Newtonians and the English Revolution.*

36. *Visionary Physics,* p. 22ff.

37. See A. L. Morton, *The Everlasting Gospel,* also printed in *The Matter of Britain,* pp. 83–121.

38. "Visible Language: Blake's Wond'rous Art of Writing," pp. 56, 59.

39. See, for example, *Selected Writings,* pp. 80, 235, 237.

40. Ibid., pp. 127, 130, 132, 178. Bentham agreed with this, and so did Godwin, in arguing the need for a "flexible and unrestrained" legislation to match the volatile qualities of human nature (*Enquiry Concerning Political Justice,* p. 604).

41. *Rousseau in England,* p. 157. On the popular conflation of the two figures, see also Voisine, *J-J Rousseau en Angleterre,* p. 139.

42. Roberts and Cobb, *French Revolutionary Documents* 1:364, 27; Blake, *Complete Poetry and Prose,* p. 72.

43. *Complete Poetry and Prose,* pp. 251, 205, 153.

44. Ibid., pp. 389, 390, 403, 71.

45. Ibid., p. 146.

46. "Queen Mab," line 135, in *Shelley: Poetical Works,* p. 764.

47. *Poetical Works,* pp. 772, 796.

48. The basic studies include Carl Grabo, *A Newton Among Poets* and *The Magic Plant;* James A. Notopoulos, *The Platonism of Shelley;* C. E. Pulos, *The Deep Truth.*

49. See John W. Wright, *Shelley's Myth of Metaphor.*

50. *Poetical Works,* pp. 120, 32, 156, 92.

51. For Shelley's relation to Darwin, see Grabo, *A Newton Among Poets,* pp. 30–79.

52. *Poetical Works*, p. 207.

53. Ibid., p. 207.

54. Ibid., p. 415. For Shelley and the erotic, see Gerald Enscoe, *Eros and the Romantics;* Nathaniel Brown, *Sexuality and Feminism in Shelley;* and William Ulmer, *Shelleyan Eros.*

55. "Lamia," 1:192, in *The Poems of John Keats*, p. 625.

56. "Sleep and Poetry," lines 195, 289–91, in *The Poems of John Keats*, pp. 77, 81.

57. *The Poems of John Keats*, pp. 532, 528, 506, 531, 506.

58. Ibid., p. 648.

59. Ibid., p. 529.

60. See "The Fall of Hyperion," 1:138–215, in *The Poems of John Keats*, pp. 665–71.

61. That this may be the result of a struggle for masculinized empowerment in distinctly bourgeois terms is the convincing thesis of Marjorie Levinson's *Keats's Life of Allegory*. Keats's career predicament may be read as an apt forecast of the dominant social identity of literature for those coming after him: that it will be middle-class, marked neither by aristocratic disinterest nor classless methodicality. The canonization of Keats, correspondingly, has occurred precisely by way of subsequent feminizations; see Susan Wolfson, "Feminizing Keats."

Chapter Eight

1. John Bayley, review of *After Bakhtin*, in *TLS*, 10–19 August 1990, p. 840.

2. James Wood, "Literature Its Own Best Theory?"

3. David Lehman, *Signs of the Times*, pp. 85–86, 260, 22.

4. Camille Paglia, "Ninnies, Pedants, Tyrants, and Other Academics," pp. 1, 29, 33.

5. Paglia, "Academe Has to Recover Its Spiritual Roots," pp. B1–B2.

6. "Ninnies, Pedants, Tyrants," p. 29.

7. Michael Albert, "Getting By," p. 15.

8. Brian Doyle, *English and Englishness*, pp. 39–40.

9. Shaftesbury, *Characteristics* 1:214–15.

10. Mackintosh, *Miscellaneous Writings*, pp. 179, 180.

11. *Essays in Criticism: Second Series*, p. 15.

12. *Essays in Criticism*, p. 11.

13. *The Egoist* 5:2.

14. See *Politics and Letters*, pp. 105–7, 114, 134.

15. *The Poverty of Theory*, pp. 46, 44, 98, 170, 180.

16. Ibid., p. 176.

17. Stanley Jones, *Hazlitt: A Life*, p. 235.

18. Charles Powell, "Be Nice to the Germans."

19. "Thatcherism and the Constitution."

20. Roger Scruton, "Safer Unstated."

21. See Kramnick, *The Rage of Edmund Burke*, pp. 42–51.

22. "Bill of Wrongs."

23. *The Rise of English Nationalism*, pp. 49–60, 163–65.

24. *Sketches of the History of Man* 2:187, 189.

25. *The Influence of Literature Upon Society* 1:299. See also 2:6, 217, where a case is made for some of the French virtues of "conciseness" and some moderately systematic thinking.

26. *Enquiries*, p. 225.

27. *On Bentham and Coleridge*, pp. 132, 134.

28. "Letters on a Regicide Peace," in *Works* 5:326.

29. *Works* 4:319. On the theory of international conspiracy see, again, Seamus Deane, *The French Revolution and Enlightenment in England*, pp. 21–42.

30. Edmonds, *Poetry of the Anti-Jacobin*, p. 274.

31. See Nancy Stepan, *The Idea of Race in Science*, pp. 1–19.

32. See Chris Baldick, *The Social Mission of English Criticism*, pp. 218–21. For an account of the uses of English literature in the governing of India (part of the official education after 1835) see Gauri Viswanathan, *Masks of Conquest*.

33. See the pertinent remarks on "cultural racism" by Paul Gilroy, "One Nation under a Groove," pp. 269–70.

34. *Enquiry Concerning Political Justice*, p. 262 (book 4, chap. 1).

35. *Selected Writings*, p. 258.

36. *A Discourse on the Love of our Country*, p. 10.

37. *An Essay on the Study of Literature*, pp. 91, 30.

38. *The Critical Works of John Dennis*, 1:336; 2:297.

39. *Westminster Review* 1 (1824): 3.

40. *The Resistance to Theory*, pp. 23, 21, 26.

41. "A Culture in Contraflow: I," pp. 41, 46, 49–50.

42. "A Culture in Contraflow: II," pp. 123–30.

43. *Postmodernism*, pp. x, xii, 46–47, 62.

44. Deane et al., eds., *Nationalism, Colonialism, and Literature*, pp. 18–19.

45. See, especially, her *Speculum de l'autre femme*.

46. Elaine Marks and Isabelle de Courtivron, ed., *New French Feminisms*, p. 213.

47. *Logic*, pp. 242–43.

48. "On Effeminacy of Character," in *Works* 8:253.

49. *Reading in Detail*, pp. 3–4. On the relation of theory to the phallic order, see also Neil Hertz, *The End of the Line*, e.g., pp. 169, 177–78. Much recent work suggests that the question of theory and of what Christine Di Stefano calls the "enlightened modernist legacy" for feminism is at the forefront of contemporary concerns. See Di Stefano, "Dilemmas of Difference," p. 66; Sandra Harding, "Feminism, Science, and the Anti-Enlightenment Critiques"; and other essays in the volume that reprints them. For a positive view of the rationalist enterprise, see also Sabine Lovibond, "Feminism and Postmodernism."

50. Judith Newton, "History as Usual?" p. 153.

51. See Doyle, *English and Englishness*, pp. 69–73.

52. Cited in Graff and Warner, ed., *The Origins of Literary Studies in America*, p. 112.

53. Terry Eagleton, *The Significance of Theory*, pp. 76, 88, 83.

54. Fredric Jameson, *Postmodernism,* pp. 392–93.

55. Horkheimer and Adorno, *Dialectic of Enlightenment,* pp. xi, xvii, 24–25, xiii.

56. Horkheimer, *Eclipse of Reason,* pp. 17–18, 19, 21, 30, 48.

57. Ibid., pp. 50, 73, 149, 62.

58. Ibid., pp. 167, 165, 171, 174–75, 180.

59. Ibid., p. 174.

60. Ibid., p. 15.

BIBLIOGRAPHY

Abelove, Henry. *The Evangelist of Desire: John Wesley and the Methodists.* Stanford: Stanford University Press, 1990.

Albert, Michael. "Getting By." *Z Magazine* (May 1991): 14–15.

Albury, W. R. "The Order of Ideas: Condillac's Method of Analysis as a Political Instrument in the French Revolution." Pp. 203–25 in John A. Schuster and Richard R. Yeo, eds., *The Politics and Rhetoric of Scientific Method: Historical Studies.* Dordrecht: D. Reidel, 1986.

Alembert, Jean le Rond d'. *Preliminary Discourse to the Encyclopaedia of Diderot.* Trans. Richard N. Schwab and Walter E. Rex. Indianapolis and New York: Bobbs-Merrill, 1963.

Analytical Review, or History of Literature, Domestic and Foreign. 28 vols. London, 1788–98.

Anderson, Perry. "Components of the National Culture." *New Left Review* 50 (1968): 3–57.

———. "A Culture in Contraflow, I." *New Left Review* 180 (1990): 41–78.

———. "A Culture in Contraflow, II." *New Left Review* 182 (1990): 85–137.

Anon. *Temperate Comments upon Intemperate Reflections; or, a Review of Mr. Burke's Letter.* London: Logographic Press, for J. Walter, 1791.

Anon. *A Defence of the Political and Parliamentary Conduct of the Right Honourable Edmund Burke.* London: D. I. Eaton, at the Cock and Swine, 1794.

Anti-Jacobin Review and Magazine; or, Monthly Political and Literary Censor. 52 vols. London, 1799–1817.

Arac, Jonathan. "The Media of Sublimity: Johnson and Lamb on *King Lear.*" *Studies in Romanticism* 26 (1987): 209–20.

Arnold, Matthew. *Essays in Criticism.* 2d ed. London: Macmillan, 1869.

———. *Essays in Criticism. Second Series.* London: Macmillan, 1935.

[Atkinson, Thomas]. *An Oblique View of the Grand Conspiracy Against Social Order; or, a Candid Inquiry tending to show what Part the Analytical, the Monthly, the Critical Reviews and the New Annual Register have taken in that Conspiracy.* London: J. Wright, 1798.

Ault, Donald D. *Visionary Physics: Blake's Response to Newton.* Chicago and London: University of Chicago Press, 1974.

Austen, Jane. *Sense and Sensibility.* Ed. Tony Tanner. Harmondsworth: Penguin, 1980.

Babbitt, Irving. *Rousseau and Romanticism*. 1919; rpt. Cambridge, Mass.: Riverside, 1930.

Bacon, Francis. *The Works of Francis Bacon*. Collected and ed. James Spedding, Robert Leslie Ellis, and Douglas Denon Heath. 14 vols. London: Longman, 1857–74.

Baker, Keith Michael. *Condorcet: From Natural Philosophy to Social Mathematics*. Chicago and London: University of Chicago Press, 1975.

Baldick, Chris. *The Social Mission of English Criticism, 1848–1932*. 1983; rpt. Oxford: Clarendon, 1987.

Barbauld, Anna Laetitia. *The Pleasures of Imagination. By Mark Akenside. To which is prefixed a Critical Essay on the Poem by Mrs. Barbauld*. London: T. Cadell and W. Davies, 1795.

———. Prefatory essay to *The Poetical Works of William Collins*. London: T. Cadell and W. Davies, 1797.

———. *The Works of Anna Laetitia Barbauld. With a Memoir by Lucy Aikin*. 2 vols. London: Longman, 1825.

Bardsley, Samuel Argent. *Critical Remarks on Pizarro*. London: T. Cadell, 1800.

Barlow, Joel. *The Conspiracy of Kings; a Poem: Addressed to the Inhabitants of Europe, from another Quarter of the Globe*. London: J. Johnson, 1792.

———. *Advice to the Privileged Orders, in the Several States of Europe, resulting from the Necessity and Propriety of a general Revolution in the Principle of Government*. London, rpt. in New York, 1792.

Barruel, Abbé. *The History of the Clergy during the French Revolution. A Work Dedicated to the English Nation*. 3d ed., rev. Dublin, 1795.

———. *Memoirs Illustrating the History of Jacobinism. A Translation from the French of the Abbé Barruel*. 4 vols. London, 1797.

Bayley, John. Review of David Lodge, *After Bakhtin. Times Literary Supplement*, 10–16 August 1990, p. 840.

Beattie, James. *An Essay on the Nature and Immutability of Truth; in Opposition to Sophistry and Skepticism*. Edinburgh, 1770. Facs. ed. Friedrich O. Wolf, in *James Beattie: The Philosophical Works*, vol. 1. Stuttgart-Bad-Canstatt: Frommann-Holzboog, 1973.

Bedwell, William. See Ramus.

Belaval, Yvon. "La crise de géométrisation de l'univers dans la philosophie des Lumières." *Revue internationale de philosophie* 6 (1952): 337–55.

[Belsham, William]. *Historic Memoir on the French Revolution: to which are annexed Strictures on the Reflections of the Rt. Hon. Edmund Burke*. London: C. Dilly, 1791.

Ben-Israel, Hedva. *English Historians and the French Revolution*. Cambridge: Cambridge University Press, 1968.

Bentham, Jeremy. *The Works of Jeremy Bentham*. Ed. John Bowring. 11 vols. Edinburgh: William Tait, 1838–43.

———. *An Introduction to the Principles of Morals and Legislation*. Ed. J. H. Burns and H. L. A. Hart. London: Athlone, 1970.

Bewell, Alan. "'Jacobin Plants': Botany as Social Theory in the 1790s." *Wordsworth Circle* 20 (1989): 132–39.

Blake, William. *The Complete Poetry and Prose of William Blake.* Newly rev. ed., ed. David Erdman. Berkeley and Los Angeles: University of California Press, 1982.

Blanchard, Rae. "Richard Steele and the Status of Women." *Studies in Philology* 26 (1929): 325–55.

Boulton, James T. *The Language of Politics in the Age of Wilkes and Burke.* London and Toronto: Routledge and Kegan Paul and University of Toronto Press, 1963.

Boswell, James. *Life of Johnson.* Ed. R. W. Chapman, corr. ed. J. D. Fleeman. London, Oxford, and New York: Oxford University Press, 1970.

Bouten, J. *Mary Wollstonecraft and the Beginnings of Female Emancipation in France and England.* Paris and Amsterdam, 1922.

Brantley, Richard E. *Locke, Wesley, and the Method of English Romanticism.* Gainesville: University of Florida Press, 1974.

Brewer, John. *The Sinews of Power: War, Money, and the English State, 1688–1783.* New York: Knopf, 1989.

British Critic; a New Review. 41 vols. London, 1793–1813.

Britton, John. *Sheridan and Kotzebue.* London, 1799.

Brooks, Peter. *The Melodramatic Imagination: Balzac, Henry James, Melodrama, and the Mode of Excess.* New Haven and London: Yale University Press, 1976.

Brown, Nathaniel. *Sexuality and Feminism in Shelley.* Cambridge: Harvard University Press, 1979.

Burgh, James. *Political Disquisitions.* 3 vols. Philadelphia: Robert Bell and William Woodhouse, 1775.

Burke, Edmund. *The Works of the Rt. Hon. Edmund Burke.* Rev. ed. 12 vols. Boston: Little, Brown, 1865–67.

———. *Reflections on the Revolution in France.* Ed. Conor Cruise O'Brien. Harmondsworth: Penguin, 1976.

———. *A Philosophical Enquiry into the Origin of our Ideas of the Sublime and Beautiful.* Ed. James T. Boulton. 1958; rpt. Notre Dame and London: University of Notre Dame Press, 1986.

Butler, Marilyn. *Romantics, Rebels, and Reactionaries: English Literature and Its Background, 1760–1830.* Oxford and New York: Oxford University Press, 1982.

Byron, George Gordon, Lord. *Don Juan.* Ed. Leslie A. Marchand. Boston: Houghton Mifflin, 1958.

Cafarelli, Annette Wheeler. *Prose in the Age of Poets: Romanticism and Biographical Narrative from Johnson to De Quincey.* Philadelphia: University of Pennsylvania Press, 1990.

Carlyle, Thomas. *The Works of Thomas Carlyle.* Centenary ed. 30 vols. London: Chapman and Hall, 1896–99.

Cassirer, Ernst. *The Question of Jean-Jacques Rousseau.* Trans. and ed. Peter Gay. 1954; rpt. Bloomington: Indiana University Press, 1963.

Chandler, James K. *Wordsworth's Second Nature: A Study of the Poetry and Politics.* Chicago and London: University of Chicago Press, 1984.

Christensen, Jerome. *Practicing Enlightenment: Hume and the Formation of a Literary Career.* Madison and London: University of Wisconsin Press, 1987.

[Clifford, Hon. Robert]. *Applications of Barruel's Memoirs of Jacobinism to the Secret Societies of Ireland and Great Britain.* By the translator of that work. London: E. Booker, 1798.

[Cobbett, William]. *The Bloody Buoy, thrown out as a Warning to the political Pilots of all Nations; or a faithful Relation of a Multitude of Acts of horrid Barbarity.* . . . By "Peter Porcupine." 3d ed. Philadelphia, 1797.

Cohen, I. Bernard, ed. *Puritanism and the Rise of Modern Science: The Merton Thesis.* New Brunswick and London: Rutgers University Press, 1990.

Coleridge, Samuel Taylor. *Collected Letters of Samuel Taylor Coleridge.* Ed. Earl Leslie Griggs. 6 vols. Oxford: Clarendon, 1956–71.

———. *The Friend.* Ed. Barbara E. Rooke. 2 vols. Princeton and London: Princeton University Press and Routledge and Kegan Paul, 1969.

———. *The Watchman.* Ed. Lewis Patton. Princeton and London: Princeton University Press and Routledge and Kegan Paul, 1970.

———. *Lectures 1795: On Politics and Religion.* Ed. Lewis Patton and Peter Mann. Princeton and London: Princeton University Press and Routledge and Kegan Paul, 1971.

———. *Lay Sermons.* Ed. R. J. White. Princeton and London: Princeton University Press and Routledge and Kegan Paul, 1972.

———. *Coleridge: Poetical Works.* Ed. Ernest Hartley Coleridge. 1912; rpt. Oxford: Oxford University Press, 1980.

———. *Logic.* Ed. J. R. de J. Jackson. Princeton and London: Princeton University Press and Routledge and Kegan Paul, 1981.

———. *Biographia Literaria.* Ed. James Engell and W. Jackson Bate. 2 vols. Princeton and London: Princeton University Press and Routledge and Kegan Paul, 1983.

Colie, Rosalie. "The Essayist in His Essay." Pp. 234–61 in John W. Yolton, ed., *John Locke: Problems and Perspectives.* Cambridge: Cambridge University Press, 1969.

Colley, Linda. "Radical Patriotism in Eighteenth-Century England." Pp. 169–87 in, *Patriotism,* vol.1. (see Samuel).

Compagnon, Antoine. "1555, 13 September. Pierre de la Ramée Receives the Privilege for Publishing his *Dialectique.*" Pp. 216–20 in Denis Hollier et al., eds., *A New History of French Literature.* Cambridge and London: Harvard University Press, 1989.

Condillac, Étienne Bonnot de Mably de. *Traité des Sistêmes, où l'on en démêle les inconvéniens & les avantages.* 2 parts in 1. La Haye: Neaulme, 1749.

———. *An Essay Concerning the Origin of Human Knowledge.* Trans. Thomas Nugent, London, 1756.

———. *La Logique: Logic.* Trans. W. R. Albury. New York: Abaris, 1980.

Condorcet, Marie Jean Antoine Nicholas Caritat, Marquis de. "Reflections on the English Revolution, 1688, and that of the 10th August, 1792." Appended as pp. 37–46 to J. B. d'Aumont, *A Narrative of the Proceedings Leading to the Suspension of the King of the French, on 10th August, 1792.* Manchester, 1792.

———. "Observations de Condorcet, sur le vingt-neuvième livre de L'Esprit des Lois." Pp. 399–432 in A. L. C. Destutt de Tracy, *Commentaire sur l'esprit des lois de Montesquieu, suivi d'observations inédites de Condorcet.* . . . 1798; rpt. Paris, 1819; facs. rpt. Geneva: Slatkine Reprints, 1970.

———. *Condorcet: Selected Writings.* Ed. Keith Michael Baker. Indianapolis: Bobbs-Merrill, 1976.

Cone, Carl B. *The English Jacobins: Reformers in Late Eighteenth-Century England.* New York: Scribner's, 1968.

Conger, Syndy McMillen, ed. *Sensibility in Transformation: Creative Resistance to Sentiment from the Augustans to the Romantics.* Essays in honor of Jean H. Hagstrum. London: Associated University Presses, 1990.

Cooper, Thomas. *A Reply to Mr. Burke's Invective Against Mr. Cooper and Mr. Watt, in the House of Commons, on the 30th of April, 1792.* 2d ed. London: J. Johnson, 1792.

Courtenay, J. *Philosophical Reflections on the Late Revolution in France, and the Conduct of the Dissenters in England, in a Letter to Dr. Priestley.* 2d ed. London, 1790.

Crabbe, George. *The Poetical Works of George Crabbe.* Ed. A. J. and R. M. Carlyle. London: Oxford University Press, 1914.

Crane, R. S. "Diffusion of Voltaire's Writings in England, 1750–1800." *Modern Philology* 20 (1923): 261–74.

Darnton, Robert. *The Business of Enlightenment: A Publishing History of the "Encyclopédie," 1775–1800.* Cambridge and London: Harvard University Press, 1979.

———. "Philosophy Under the Cloak." Pp. 27–49 in Robert Darnton and Daniel Roche, eds., *Revolution in Print: The Press in France, 1775–1800.* Berkeley and Los Angeles: University of California Press, 1989.

Darwin, Erasmus. *Zoonomia; or, the Laws of Organic Life,* vol. 1. New York: J. Swords, 1796.

———. *A Plan for the Conduct of Female Education, in Boarding Schools.* Derby: for J. Johnson, London, 1797.

———. *The Poetical Works of Erasmus Darwin; Containing the Botanic Garden, in two parts; and the Temple of Nature.* 3 vols. London: J. Johnson, 1806.

Deane, Seamus. "John Bull and Voltaire: The Emergence of a Cultural Cliché." *Revue de littérature comparée* 45 (1971): 581–94.

———. "The Reputation of the French *Philosophes* in the Whig Reviews between 1802 and 1824." *Modern Language Review* 70 (1975): 271–90.

———. *The French Revolution and Enlightenment in England, 1789–1832.* Cambridge and London: Harvard University Press, 1988.

———. et al., eds. *Nationalism, Colonialism, and Literature.* Minneapolis: University of Minnesota Press, 1990.

De Bolla, Peter. *The Discourse of the Sublime: Readings in History, Aesthetics, and the Subject.* Oxford: Basil Blackwell, 1989.

de Man, Paul. *The Resistance to Theory.* Minneapolis: University of Minnesota Press, 1986.

Dennis, John. *The Critical Works of John Dennis.* Ed. Edward Niles Hooker. 2 vols. Baltimore and London: Johns Hopkins University Press and Oxford University Press, 1939–43.

Descartes, René. *The Philosophical Works of Descartes.* Trans. Elizabeth S. Haldane and G. R. T. Ross. 2 vols. 1911; rpt. Cambridge: Cambridge University Press, 1973.

de Staël, Madame [Baroness de Staël-Holstein]. *The Influence of Literature upon Society.* Trans. from the French. 2d ed. 2 vols. London: Henry Colburn, [?1812].

———. *Germany; by the Baroness Staël-Holstein.* Trans. from the French. 3 vols. London: John Murray, 1813.

———. *Considerations on the Principal Events of the French Revolution.* Ed. the Duke de Broglie and Baron de Staël. 2 vols. New York, 1818.

Di Stefano, Christine. "Dilemmas of Difference: Feminism, Modernity, and Postmodernism." Pp. 63–83 in Linda Nicolson, ed., *Feminism/Postmodernism.* New York and London: Routledge, 1990.

Doyle, Brian. *English and Englishness.* London and New York: Routledge, 1989.

Dresser, Madge. "Brittania." Pp. 26–49 in *Patriotism,* vol. 3 (see Samuel).

Dryden, John. *"Of Dramatic Poesy" and Other Critical Essays.* Ed. George Watson. 2 vols. London and New York: Dent and Dutton, 1962.

Duffy, Edward. *Rousseau in England: The Context for Shelley's Critique of the Enlightenment.* Berkeley and Los Angeles: University of California Press, 1979.

Durrant, Geoffrey. *Wordsworth and the Great System: A Study of Wordsworth's Poetic Universe.* Cambridge: Cambridge University Press, 1970.

Eagleton, Terry. *The Significance of Theory.* Oxford: Basil Blackwell, 1990.

Easlea, Brian. *Witch-Hunting, Magic, and the New Philosophy; An Introduction to the Debates of the Scientific Revolution, 1450–1750.* Sussex: Harvester, 1980.

———. *Science and Sexual Oppression: Patriarchy's Confrontation with Woman and Nature.* London: Weidenfeld and Nicolson, 1981.

Edgeworth, Maria. *Letters for Literary Ladies, to which is added, an Essay on the Noble Science of Self-Justification.* London: J. Johnson, 1795.

Edmonds, Charles, ed. *Poetry of the Anti-Jacobin.* 3d (enlarged) ed. New York and London: G. P. Putnam's and Sampson Low, 1890.

Eliot, T. S. "In Memory of Henry James." *Egoist: An Individualist Review* 5 (1918): 1–2.

Encyclopaedia Britannica; or, a Dictionary of Arts and Sciences Compiled upon a New Plan. By a Society of Gentlemen in Scotland. 3 vols. Edinburgh, 1771.

Encyclopédie; ou dictionnaire raisonné des sciences, des arts et des metiers. Ed. Denis Diderot and Jean le Rond d'Alembert. 17 vols. Paris, 1751–57.

Encyclopédie méthodique. 192 vols. Paris and Liège, 1787–1832.

Enscoe, Gerald. *Eros and the Romantics: Sexual Love as a Theme in Coleridge, Shelley, and Keats.* The Hague and Paris: Mouton, 1967.

Erdman, David V. *Prophet against Empire: A Poet's Interpretation of the History of His Own Times.* 3d ed. Princeton: Princeton University Press, 1977.

———. *Commerce des Lumières: John Oswald and the British in Paris, 1790–1793.* Columbia: University of Missouri Press, 1986.

European Magazine and London Review. 87 vols. London, 1782–1825.

Fage, R. See Ramus.

Farrington, Benjamin. *Philosophy of Francis Bacon: An Essay on Its Development from 1603 to 1609 with New Translations of Fundamental Texts.* Liverpool: Liverpool University Press, 1964.

Ferguson, Frances. "The Sublime of Edmund Burke, or the Bathos of Experience." *Glyph* 8 (1981): 62–78.

Ferguson, Margaret W. *Trials of Desire: Renaissance Defenses of Poetry.* New Haven and London: Yale University Press, 1983.

———. Afterword, Pp. 273–83 in Jean E. Howard and Marian F. O'Connor, eds., *Shakespeare Reproduced: The Text in History and Ideology.* London and New York: Methuen, 1987.

Feyerabend, Paul. *Against Method: Outline of an Anarchistic Theory of Knowledge.* 1975; rpt. London: Verso, 1978.

Fielding, Henry. *Tom Jones.* Ed. Sheridan Baker. New York and London: Norton, 1973.

Foucault, Michel. *The Order of Things: An Archaeology of the Human Sciences.* 1970; rpt. New York: Random House, 1973.

Furet, François, and Mona Ozouf, eds. *A Critical Dictionary of the French Revolution.* Trans. Arthur Goldhammer. Cambridge and London: Harvard University Press, 1989.

Gadamer, Hans-Georg. *Philosophical Hermeneutics.* Trans. David E. Linge. Berkeley and Los Angeles: University of California Press, 1976.

Gallagher, Catherine. "Embracing the Absolute: The Politics of the Female Subject in Seventeenth-Century England." *Genders* 1 (1988): 24–39.

German Museum, or Monthly Repository of Germany, the North, and the Continent in General. 3 vols. London, 1800–1801.

Gibbon, Edward. *An Essay on the Study of Literature.* Written originally in French; now first translated into English. London: T. Becket and P. A. De Hondt, 1764.

Gilbert, Neal W. *Renaissance Concepts of Method.* New York: Columbia University Press, 1960.

Gillispie, Charles Coulston. "The *Encyclopédie* and the Jacobin Philosophy of Science: A Study in Ideas and Consequences." Pp. 255–89 in Marshall Clagett, ed., *Critical Problems in the History of Science.* Madison: University of Wisconsin Press, 1959.

———. *The Edge of Objectivity: An Essay in the History of Scientific Ideas.* Princeton: Princeton University Press, 1960.

———. *Science and Polity in France at the End of the Old Régime.* Princeton: Princeton University Press, 1980.

Gilroy, Paul. "One Nation under a Groove: The Cultural Politics of 'Race' and

Racism in Britain." Pp. 263–82 in David Theo Goldberg, ed., *Anatomy of Racism*. Minneapolis: University of Minnesota Press, 1990.

Godwin, William. *Thoughts on Man, his Nature, Productions, and Discoveries, Interspersed with some Particulars Respecting the Author*. London: Royal Exchange, 1831.

———. *Memoirs of Mary Wollstonecraft* (1798). Ed. W. Clark Durant. 1927; rpt. New York: Haskell House, 1967.

———. *Enquiry Concerning Political Justice, and its Influence on Modern Morals and Happiness*. Ed. Isaac Kramnick. Harmondsworth: Penguin, 1976.

Goethe, Johann Wolfgang von. *The Sorrows of Young Werther, and Selected Writings*. Trans. Catherine Hutter. New York: Signet Classics, 1962.

Goldmann, Lucien. *The Philosophy of the Enlightenment: The Christian Burgess and the Enlightenment*. Trans. Henry Maas. London: Routledge and Kegan Paul, 1973.

Grabo, Carl. *A Newton among Poets: Shelley's Use of Science in "Prometheus Unbound."* Chapel Hill: University of North Carolina Press, 1930.

———. *The Magic Plant: The Growth of Shelley's Thought*. Chapel Hill: University of North Carolina Press, 1936.

Graff, Gerald, and Michael Warner, eds. *The Origins of Literary Studies in America: A Documentary Anthology*. New York and London: Routledge, 1989.

Grafton, Anthony, and Lisa Jardine. *From Humanism to the Humanities: Education and the Liberal Arts in Fifteenth- and Sixteenth-Century Europe*. Cambridge: Harvard University Press, 1986.

Graves, Frank Pierrepont. *Peter Ramus and the Educational Reformation of the Sixteenth Century*. New York: Macmillan, 1912.

Hacking, Ian. *The Emergence of Probability: A Philosophical Study of Early Ideas about Probability, Induction, and Statistical Inference*. Cambridge: Cambridge University Press, 1975.

Hagstrum, Jean H. *Sex and Sensibility: Ideal and Erotic Love from Milton to Mozart*. Chicago and London: University of Chicago Press, 1980.

Halévy, Élie. *Growth of Philosophic Radicalism*. Trans. Mary Morris. 1955; rpt. Boston: Beacon, 1960.

———. *The Birth of Methodism in England*. Trans and ed. Bernard Semmel. Chicago and London: University of Chicago Press, 1971.

Hamilton, Elizabeth. *Memoirs of Modern Philosophers: A Novel*. 3 vols. London: G. G. and J. Robinson, 1800.

Hampson, Norman. *A Social History of the French Revolution*. 1963; rpt. London and Toronto: Routledge and Kegan Paul and University of Toronto Press, 1976.

Harding, Sandra. "Feminism, Science, and the Anti-Enlightenment Critiques." Pp. 83–106 in Linda Nicolson, ed., *Feminism/Postmodernism*. New York and London: Routledge, 1990.

Harris, Daniel. "AIDS and Theory." *Lingua Franca* 1, no. 5 (June 1991): 1, 16–19.

Havens, Raymond Dexter. *The Mind of a Poet: A Study of Wordsworth's Thought with Particular Reference to "The Prelude."* Baltimore: Johns Hopkins University Press, 1941.

Hayley, William. *An Essay on Epic Poetry* (1782). Facs. ed. Sister M. Celeste Williamson. Gainesville, Fla.: Scholars' Facsimiles and Reprints, 1968.

[Hays, Mary]. *Appeal to the Men of Great Britain in Behalf of Women.* London: J. Johnson, 1798.

Hays, Mary. *Female Biography; or, Memoirs of Illustrious and Celebrated Women, of all Ages and Countries, Alphabetically Arranged.* 1st American ed. 3 vols. Philadelphia, 1807.

———. *Memoirs of Emma Courtney* (1796). London and New York: Pandora, 1987.

Hays, Michael. "Comedy as Being/Comedy as Idea." *Studies in Romanticism* 26 (1987): 221–30.

Hazlitt, William. *The Complete Works of William Hazlitt.* Ed. P. P. Howe. 21 vols. London and Toronto: J. M. Dent, 1930–34.

Helvétius, Claude-Adrien. *De l'esprit; or, Essays on the Mind, and its several Faculties.* Trans. from the French [by William Hooper]. New ed. London: Albion, 1810.

———. *A Treatise on Man; his Intellectual Faculties and his Education. A new and improved edition.* Trans. with additional notes by W. Hooper. 2 vols. London, 1810.

Hempton, David. *Methodism and Politics in British Society, 1750–1850.* London: Hutchinson, 1984.

Herder, J. G. *Reflections on the Philosophy of the History of Mankind.* Trans. T. O. Churchill (1800). Ed. and abridged Frank E. Manuel. Chicago and London: University of Chicago Press, 1968.

Hertz, Neil. *The End of the Line: Essays on Psychoanalysis and the Sublime.* New York: Columbia University Press, 1985.

Hill, Christopher. *Puritanism and Revolution: Studies in the Interpretation of the English Revolution of the Seventeenth Century.* London: Secker and Warburg, 1958.

———. *Intellectual Origins of the English Revolution.* Oxford: Clarendon, 1965.

———. *The World Turned Upside Down: Radical Ideas during the English Revolution.* 1972; rpt. Harmondsworth: Penguin, 1987.

———. "The English Revolution and Patriotism." Pp. 159–68 in *Patriotism,* vol. 1 (see Samuel).

———. *A Tinker and a Poor Man: John Bunyan and His Church, 1628–1688.* New York: Knopf, 1989.

Hobbes, Thomas. *The English Works of Thomas Hobbes.* Ed. Sir William Molesworth. 11 vols. London, 1839–45.

Holbach, Paul Heinrich Dietrich, Baron de [M. de Mirabaud]. *Nature; and her Laws; as applicable to the Happiness of Man living in Society; contrasted with Superstition and Imaginary Systems.* 2 vols. London: W. Hodgson, 1816.

Horkheimer, Max. *Eclipse of Reason.* 1947; rpt. New York: Continuum, 1974.

Horkheimer, Max, and Theodor Adorno. *Dialectic of Enlightenment*. Trans. John Cumming. 1944; rpt. New York: Continuum, 1986.

Howell, Wilbur Samuel. *Logic and Rhetoric in England, 1500–1700*. 1956; rpt. New York: Russell and Russell, 1961.

———. *Eighteenth-Century British Logic and Rhetoric*. Princeton: Princeton University Press, 1971.

Hufton, Olwen. "Women in Revolution, 1789–96." *Past and Present* 53 (1971): 90–108.

Hume, David. *Enquiries Concerning Human Understanding and Concerning the Principles of Morals*. Ed. L. A. Selby-Bigge. 3d ed., rev. P. H. Nidditch. Oxford: Clarendon Press, 1975.

———. *Essays Literary, Moral, and Political* London and New York: Routledge, n.d.

[Hunt, Leigh]. *The Examiner. A Sunday Paper. On Politics, the Domestic Economy, and Theatricals*. London: John Hunt, 1808–9.

Hunt, Leigh. *An Attempt to Show the Folly and Danger of Methodism*. London: J. Hunt, 1809.

Hunt, Lynn. "Hercules and the Radical Image in the French Revolution." *Representations* 2 (1983): 95–117.

———. *Politics, Culture, and Class in the French Revolution*. Berkeley and Los Angeles: University of California Press, 1984.

———. "The Unstable Boundaries of the French Revolution." Pp. 13–45 in Michelle Perrot, ed., *A History of Private Life*, vol. 4, *From the Fires of Revolution to the Great War*. Trans. Arthur Goldhammer. Cambridge and London: Harvard University Press, 1990.

Hunter, Michael. *Science and Society in Restoration England*. Cambridge: Cambridge University Press, 1981.

Irigaray, Luce. *Speculum de l'autre femme*. Paris: Minuit, 1974.

Jackson, J. R. de J., ed. *Coleridge: The Critical Writings*. London: Routledge and Kegan Paul, 1970.

Jacob, J. R. *Robert Boyle and the English Revolution: A Study in Social and Intellectual Change*. New York: Burt Franklin, 1977.

Jacob, Margaret C. *The Newtonians and the English Revolution, 1689–1720*. Ithaca, N.Y., and Hassocks, Sussex: Cornell University Press and Harvester, 1976.

———. *The Radical Enlightenment: Pantheists, Freemasons, and Republicans*. London: Allen and Unwin, 1981.

Jacobus, Mary. *Tradition and Experiment in Wordsworth's "Lyrical Ballads" (1798)*. Oxford: Clarendon, 1976.

Jameson, Fredric. *Postmodernism, or, the Cultural Logic of Late Capitalism*. Durham: Duke University Press, 1991.

Jones, Richard Foster. *Ancients and Moderns: A Study of the Background of the "Battle of the Books."* Washington University Studies, New Series, Language and Literature, no. 6. St. Louis, 1936.

Jones, Stanley. *Hazlitt: A Life. From Winterslow to Frith St.* Oxford: Clarendon Press, 1989.

Jordan, John E. *Why the "Lyrical Ballads"? The Background, Writing, and Character of Wordsworth's 1798 "Lyrical Ballads."* Berkeley and Los Angeles: University of California Press, 1976.

Kames, Henry Home, Lord. *Sketches of the History of Man. Considerably enlarged by the last Additions and Corrections of the Author.* 4 vols. Edinburgh, 1788.

Kant, Immanuel. *Immanuel Kant's Critique of Pure Reason.* Trans. Norman Kemp Smith. 1933; corr. ed. rpt. London: Macmillan, 1973.

———. *On History.* Ed. Lewis White Beck. Indianapolis and New York: Bobbs-Merrill, 1963.

———. *Anthropology from a Practical Point of View.* Trans. Mary J. Gregor. The Hague: Martinus Nijhoff, 1974.

Keats, John. *The Poems of John Keats.* Ed. Miriam Allott. Corr. ed. London: Longman, 1972.

Kelley, Donald R. *The Beginning of Ideology: Consciousness and Society in the French Reformation.* Cambridge: Cambridge University Press, 1981.

King, Sophia. *Waldorf; or, the Dangers of Philosophy.* 2 vols. London: G. G. and J. Robinson, 1798.

Knight, Richard Payne. *An Account of the Remains of the Worship of Priapus, lately existing at Isernia, in the Kingdom of Naples, in two Letters . . . to which is added a Discourse on the Worship of Priapus, and its Connexion with the Mystic Theology of the Ancients.* London: T. Spilsbury, 1786.

———. *The Progress of Civil Society. A Didactic Poem. In Six Books.* London, 1796.

Kotzebue, Augustus von. *Lovers' Vows. A Play in Five Acts.* Trans. from the German by Mrs. Inchbald. London: G. G. and J. Robinson, 1798.

———. *The Natural Son; a Play, in Five Acts* [Lovers' Vows]. Trans. from the German by Anne Plumptre. 5th ed., rev. London: R. Phillips, 1798.

Kramnick, Isaac. *The Rage of Edmund Burke: Portrait of an Ambivalent Conservative.* New York: Basic, 1977.

La Mettrie, Julien Offray de. *Man a Machine.* Ed. Gertrude Carmen Bussey. La Salle, Ill.: Open Court, 1912.

Lamb, Charles. *The Complete Works and Letters of Charles Lamb.* New York: Modern Library, 1935.

Landes, Joan B. *Women and the Public Sphere in the Age of the French Revolution.* Ithaca and London: Cornell University Press, 1988.

Laudan, L. L. "Thomas Reid and the Newtonian Turn of British Methodological Thought". Pp. 103–31 in Robert E. Butts and John W. David, eds., *The Methodological Heritage of Newton.* Toronto: University of Toronto Press, 1970.

Lefèbvre, Georges. *The French Revolution.* Vol. 2, *From 1793 to 1799.* Trans. John Hall Stewart and James Friguglietti. New York: Columbia University Press, 1964.

Lehman, David. *Signs of the Times: Deconstruction and the Fall of Paul de Man.* New York: Poseidon Press, 1991.

Lentricchia, Frank. "Patriarchy against Itself—The Young Manhood of Wallace Stevens." *Critical Inquiry* 13 (1986–87): 742–86.

Levi, A. H. T. "Ethics and the Encyclopedia in the Sixteenth Century". Pp. 170–

84 in Peter Sharratt, ed., *French Renaissance Studies, 1540–70; Humanism and the Encyclopedia.* Edinburgh: Edinburgh University Press, 1976.

Levinson, Marjorie. *Wordsworth's Great Period Poems: Four Essays.* Cambridge: Cambridge University Press, 1986.

———. *Keats's Life of Allegory: The Origins of a Style.* Oxford and New York: Blackwells, 1988.

Levy, Darline Gay, Harriet Branson Applewhite and Mary Durham Johnson, eds. *Women in Revolutionary Paris, 1789–1795: Selected Documents.* Urbana, Chicago, and London: University of Illinois Press, 1979.

Lewis, Anthony. "Bill of Wrongs." *New York Times,* 18 March 1991, p. A11.

Liu, Alan. *Wordsworth: The Sense of History.* Stanford: Stanford University Press, 1989.

Locke, John. *The Works of John Locke.* 10th ed. 10 vols. London: J. Johnson, 1801.

———. *Essays on the Law of Nature.* The Latin text, with translation, introduction, and notes, ed. W. von Leyden. Oxford: Clarendon Press, 1954.

———. *An Essay Concerning Human Understanding.* Ed. Peter H. Nidditch. Corr. ed. Oxford: Clarendon, 1979.

Lofft, Capel. *Remarks on the Letter of the Rt. Hon. Edmund Burke, Concerning the Revolution in France, and on the Procedings of certain Societies in London, relative to that Event.* London, 1790.

Lovibond, Sabina. "Feminism and Postmodernism." *New Left Review* 178 (1989): 5–28.

Lucas, John. *England and Englishness: Ideas of Nationhood in English Poetry, 1688– 1900.* Iowa City: University of Iowa Press, 1990.

Lyles, Albert M. *Methodism Mocked: The Satiric Reaction to Methodism in the Eighteenth Century.* London: Epworth, 1960.

McCalman, Iain. *Radical Underworld: Prophets, Revolutionaries, and Pornographers in London, 1795–1840.* Cambridge: Cambridge University Press, 1988.

[Macaulay (Graham), Catherine]. *Loose Remarks on Certain Positions to be found in Mr. Hobbes' Philosophical Rudiments of Government and Society; with a Short Sketch of a Democratical Form of Government, in a Letter to Signor Paoli.* London, 1767.

———. *Observations on the Reflections of the Rt. Hon. Edmund Burke on the Revolution in France, in a Letter to the Rt. Hon. the Earl of Stanhope.* London: C. Dilly, 1790.

Macaulay (Graham), Catherine. *The History of England, from the Accession of James I to that of the Brunswick Line.* 8 vols. London, 1763–83.

———. *Letters on Education. With Observations on Religious and Metaphysical Subjects.* London: C. Dilly, 1790.

McDonald, Joan. *Rousseau and the French Revolution, 1762–1791.* London: Athlone, 1965.

McGann, Jerome J. *The Romantic Ideology: A Critical Investigation.* Chicago and London: University of Chicago Press, 1983.

MacIlmaine, Roland. See Ramus.

Mackintosh, Sir James. *Vindiciae Gallicae. Defence of the French Revolution and its*

English Admirers against the Accusations of the Rt. Hon. Edmund Burke; Including some Strictures on the late Production of Mons. de Calonne. London: G. J. and J. Robinson, 1791.

—. *The Miscellaneous Works of the Rt. Hon. Sir James Mackintosh.* London: Longman, Brown, Green and Longmans, 1851.

Madan, Martin. *Thelyphthora; or, a Treatise on Female Ruin, in its Causes, Effects, Consequences, Prevention, and Remedy; Considered on the Basis of the Divine Law.* . . . 2d ed., enlarged. 3 vols. London: J. Dodsley, 1781.

Mallet du Pan, J. "Du degré de l'influence qu'a eu la philosophie *françoise* sur la révolution." *Mercure britannique,* 5 vols. in 4 (1798–99), 2:342–70 (no. 14, 10 March 1799).

—. *The British Mercury; or, Historical and Critical Views of the Events of the Present Times.* 2d ed., corr. 3 vols. London, 1799.

Marks, Elaine, and Isabelle De Courtivron, eds. *New French Feminisms: An Anthology.* New York: Schocken, 1981.

Marlowe, Christopher. *"Dido Queen of Carthage" and "The Massacre at Paris."* Ed. H. J. Oliver. London: Methuen, 1968.

[Mathias, T. J.] *Pursuits of Literature. A Satirical Poem in Four Dialogues, with Notes.* 7th ed. Philadelphia, 1800.

Maza, Sarah. "Politics, Culture, and the Origins of the French Revolution." *Journal of Modern History* 61 (1989): 704–23.

Mellor, Anne K., ed. *Romanticism and Feminism.* Bloomington and Indianapolis: Indiana University Press, 1988.

Mill, John Stuart. *Mill on Bentham and Coleridge.* Ed. F. R. Leavis. 1950; rpt. London: Chatto and Windus, 1967.

Miller, David Philip. "Method and the 'Micropolitics' of Science: The Early Years of the Geological and Astronomical Societies of London." Pp. 227–57 in John A. Schuster and Richard R. Yeo, eds., *The Politics and Rhetoric of Scientific Method: Historical Studies.* Dordrecht: D. Reidel, 1986.

Miller, Perry. *The New England Mind: The Seventeenth Century.* 1939; rpt. Boston: Beacon, 1961.

Milton, John. *A Fuller Course in the Art of Logic, Conformed to the Method of Peter Ramus* (1672). Pp. 208–407 in *The Complete Prose Works of John Milton,* vol. 8. Ed. Walter J. Ong. New Haven and London: Yale University Press, 1982.

Mirabaud, M. de. See Holbach.

Mitchell, W. J. T. *Iconology: Image, Text, Ideology.* Chicago and London: University of Chicago Press, 1986.

—. "Visible Language: Blake's Wond'rous Art of Writing." Pp. 46–86 in Morris Eaves and Michael Fischer, eds., *Romanticism and Contemporary Criticism.* Ithaca and London: Cornell University Press, 1986.

—. "Influence, Autobiography, and Literary History: Rousseau's *Confessions* and Wordsworth's *The Prelude.*" *ELH* 57 (1990): 643–64.

Monthly Magazine and British Register. 60 vols. London, 1796–1826.

More, Hannah. *Strictures on the Modern System of Female Education, with a View of the Principles and Conduct prevalent among Women of Rank and Fortune.* 5th ed. Dublin, 1800.

Mornet, Daniel. *Les origines intellectuelles de la Révolution Française, 1715–1787*. 1933; 5th ed. Paris, 1954.

Morton, A. L. *The Matter of Britain: Essays in a Living Culture*. London: Lawrence and Wishart, 1966.

———. *The Everlasting Gospel: A Study in the Sources of William Blake*. New York: Haskell House, 1966.

———. *The World of the Ranters: Religious Radicalism in the English Revolution*. London: Lawrence and Wishart, 1970.

Mounier, J. J. *De l'influence attribuée aux Philosophes, aux Franc-Maçons et aux Illuminés sur la Révolution de France*. Tübingen: J. Cotta, 1801.

Mullan, John. *Sentiment and Sociability: The Language of Feeling in the Eighteenth Century*. Oxford: Clarendon, 1988.

Newman, Gerald. *The Rise of English Nationalism: A Cultural History, 1740–1830*. New York: St. Martin's, 1987.

Newton, Sir Isaac. *Opticks; or, a Treatise on the Reflections, Refractions, Inflections and Colours of Light*. 4th ed. London, 1730; rpt. New York: Dover, 1952.

Newton, Judith Lowder. "History as Usual? Feminism and the 'New Historicism.'" Pp. 152–67 in H. Aram Veeser, ed., *The New Historicism*. New York and London: Routledge, 1989.

Nicolson, Marjorie. "The Early Stage of Cartesianism in England." *Studies in Philology* 26 (1929): 356–74.

Nitsch, F. A. *A General and Introductory View of Professor Kant's Principles concerning Man, the World, and the Deity, submitted to the Consideration of the Learned*. London, 1796.

Notopoulos, James A. *The Platonism of Shelley: A Study in Platonism and the Poetic Mind*. Durham: Duke University Press, 1949.

Nyquist, Mary. "The Genesis of Gendered Subjectivity in the Divorce Tracts and in *Paradise Lost*." Pp. 99–127 in Mary Nyquist and Margaret W. Ferguson, eds., *Remembering Milton: Essays on the Texts and the Tradition*. New York and London: Methuen, 1988.

Ong, Walter J. "Peter Ramus and the Naming of Methodism: Mediaeval Science through Renaissance Homilectic." *Journal of the History of Ideas* 14 (1953): 235–48.

———. *Ramus, Method, and the Decay of Dialogue: From the Art of Discourse to the Art of Reason*. 1958; rpt. Cambridge and London: Harvard University Press, 1983.

Opie, Amelia. *Adeline Mowbray. The Mother and Daughter*. (1802). London, Boston, Henley: Pandora, 1986.

Paglia, Camille. "Ninnies, Pedants, Tyrants, and Other Academics". *New York Times Book Review*, 5 May 1991, Pp. 1, 29, 33.

———. "Academe Has to Recover Its Spiritual Roots and Overthrow the Ossified Political Establishment of Invested Self-Interest." *Chronicle of Higher Education* 37, no. 34 (8 May 1991): B1–B2.

Paine, Thomas. *The Complete Writings of Thomas Paine*. Ed. Philip S. Foner. 2 vols. New York: Citadel, 1945.

Parker, Patricia. *Literary Fat Ladies: Rhetoric, Gender, Property.* London and New York: Methuen, 1987.

[Parkinson, James]. *Knave's-Acre Association.* By "Old Hubert." London: T. Spence, 1793.

Patey, Douglas Lane. *Probability and Literary Form: Philosophic Theory and Literary Practice in the Augustan Age.* Cambridge: Cambridge University Press, 1984.

The Patriot; or, Political, Moral and Philosophical Repository. 3 vols. London, 1792–93.

Payson, Seth A. M. *Proofs of the Real Existence and Dangerous Tendency of Illuminism.* Charlestown, 1802.

Peacock, Thomas Love. *Nightmare Abbey, Crochet Castle.* Ed. Raymond Wright. Harmondsworth: Penguin, 1969.

Pearson, Joseph. *Pearson's Political Dictionary; containing Remarks, Definitions, Explanations, and Customs Political and Parliamentary; but more particularly appertaining to the House of Commons.* London: J. S. Jordan, 1792.

[Pigott, Charles]. *The Female Jockey Club; or, a Sketch of the Manners of the Age.* London: D. I. Eaton, 1794.

Pigott, Charles. *A Political Dictionary: Explaining the True Meaning of Words.* London: D. I. Eaton, 1795.

Pocock, J. G. A. *The Machiavellian Moment: Florentine Political Thought and the Atlantic Republican Tradition.* Princeton: Princeton University Press, 1975.

Polwhele, Richard. *The Unsex'd Females; a Poem, addressed to the Author of the Pursuits of Literature; to which is added a Sketch of the Private and Public Character of P. Pindar.* New York: republished by William Cobbett, 1800.

Pomeroy, Ralph S. "The Ramist as Fallacy-Hunter: Abraham Fraunce and *The Lawiers Logike.*" *Renaissance Quarterly* 40 (1987): 224–46.

Poovey, Mary. *The Proper Lady and the Woman Writer: Ideology as Style in the Works of Mary Wollstonecraft, Mary Shelley, and Jane Austen.* Chicago and London: University of Chicago Press, 1984.

Pope, Alexander. *The Iliad of Homer; the Odyssey of Homer.* Trans. Alexander Pope; new ed. with notes by Gilbert Wakefield. 9 vols. London, 1806.

Powell, Charles. "Be Nice to the Germans." *New York Times,* 20 July 1990, p. A15.

Preston, William. "Reflections on the Peculiarity of Style and Manner in the late German Writers whose Works have appeared in English, and on the Tendency of their Productions." Pp. 15–79 in *The Transactions of the Royal Irish Academy,* vol. 8, *Polite Literature.* Dublin, 1802.

Price, Richard. *A Discourse on the Love of our Country, delivered on November 4, 1789, at the Meeting-House in the Old Jewry, to the Society for Commemorating the Revolution in Great Britain.* London, 1789.

[Priestley, Joseph]. *An Address to the Inhabitants of Birmingham, upon the Necessity of their attending to the Philosophy of Mind, previous to their forming a just or complete Theory of Education; upon the Influence of Education, and its relative Value.* By "a Patriot." Birmingham: M. Swinney, [?1790].

Priestley, Joseph. *A Course of Lectures on the Theory of Language and Universal Grammar.* Warrington: W. Eyres, 1762.

―――. *An Essay on the First Principles of Government; and on the Nature of Civil, Political and Religious Liberty.* London: J. Dodsley, T. Cadell, J. Johnson, 1768.

―――. *An Examination of Dr. Reid's Inquiry into the Human Mind on the Principles of Common Sense, Dr. Beattie's Essay on the Nature and Immutability of Truth, and Dr. Oswald's Appeal to Common Sense in behalf of Religion.* London: J. Johnson, 1774.

―――. *The Doctrine of Philosophical Necessity Illustrated.* London: J. Johnson, 1777.

―――. *A Free Discussion of the Doctrines of Materialism, and Philosophical Necessity, in a Correspondence between Dr. Price and Dr. Priestley.* London: J. Johnson, 1778.

―――. *A Letter to Jacob Bryant Esq., in Defence of Philosophical Necessity.* London: H. Baldwin, 1780.

―――. *A Description of a New Chart of History, containing a View of the Principal Revolutions of Empire that have taken place in the World.* 6th ed., corr. London: J. Johnson, 1786.

―――. *The Conduct to be observed by Dissenters in order to procure the Repeal of the Corporation and Test Acts, recommended in a Sermon, preached before the Congregations of the Old and New Meetings, at Birmingham, November 5th, 1789.* Birmingham: J. Thompson; sold by J. Johnson, London.

―――. Preface to *A Philosophical Inquiry Concerning Human Liberty,* by Anthony Collins. Birmingham: Thomas Pearson, 1790.

―――. *Letters to the Right Honourable Edmund Burke, occasioned by his Reflections on the Revolution in France &c.* 3d ed., corr. Birmingham: Thomas Pearson, 1791.

―――. *An Appeal to the Public, on the Subject of the Riots in Birmingham. Part II. To which is added a Letter from W. Russell Esq. to the Author.* London: J. Johnson, 1792.

―――. *An Answer to Mr. Paine's Age of Reason, being a Continuation of the Letters to the Philosophers and Politicians of France, on the Subject of Religion; and of the Letters to a Philosophical Unbeliever.* Northumberland Town, America, 1794; London: J. Johnson, 1795.

Pulos, C. E. *The Deep Truth: A Study of Shelley's Skepticism.* Lincoln: University of Nebraska Press, 1954.

Punter, David. "1789: The Sex of Revolution." *Criticism* 24 (1982): 201–17.

Ramus, Peter [Pierre de la Ramée]. *The Logike of the Moste Excellent Philosopher P. Ramus Martyr.* Newly translated, and in divers places corrected, [by Roland MacIlmaine] after the mynde of the Author. London, 1574.

―――. *Peter Ramus of Vernandois, the King's Professor, his Dialecticae, in two bookes. Not onely translated into English, but also digested into questions and answers for the more facility of understanding.* By "R. F[age], Gent." London: W. J[ones], 1632.

―――. *Via Regia ad Geometriam. The Way to Geometry. Being necessary and usefull for Astronomers, Geographers, Land-meaters, Sea-Men, Engineres, Architecks, Car-*

penters, Paynters, Carvers etc. Written in Latin by Peter Ramus, and now translated and much enlarged by the learned Mr. William Bedwell. London:
Thomas Cotes for Michael Sparke, 1636.

———. *Avertissements sur la réformation de l'université de Paris* (1562). Pp. 115–63
in L. Cimber et F. Danjou, eds., *Archives curieuses de l'histoire de France depuis
Louis XI jusqu'à Louis XVIII,* 1st ser., vol. 5. Paris, 1835.

Reid, Thomas. *Essays on the Intellectual Powers of Man.* Cambridge and London:
MIT Press, 1969.

———. *An Inquiry into the Human Mind.* Ed. Timothy J. Duggan. Chicago and
London: University of Chicago Press, 1970.

Reid, William Hamilton. *The Rise and Dissolution of the Infidel Societies in this Me-
tropolis, including the Origin of Modern Deism and Atheism; the Genius and Conduct of those Associations; their Lecture-Rooms, Field-Meetings, and Deputations;
from the Publication of Paine's Age of Reason till the Present Period. . . .* London:
J. Hatchard, 1800.

Richardson, Alexander. *The Logicians School-Master: or, a Comment upon Ramus'
"Logicke."* London: John Bellamy, 1629.

Roberts, J. M., and R. C. Cobb, eds. *French Revolution Documents.* 2 vols. Oxford:
Blackwell, 1966, 1973.

Robison, John. *Proofs of a Conspiracy against all the Religions and Governments of
Europe, carried on in the secret Meetings of Free Masons, Illuminati, and Reading
Societies.* 2d ed. London, 1797.

Roddier, Henri. *J-J Rousseau en Angleterre au XVIIIe siècle.* Études de littérature
étrangère et comparée, no. 21. Paris, 1947.

Ross, Marlon. *The Contours of Masculine Desire: Romanticism and the Rise of
Women's Poetry.* New York and Oxford: Oxford University Press, 1989.

Roudinesco, Elisabeth. *Théroigne de Méricourt: A Melancholic Woman during the
French Revolution.* Trans. Martin Thom. London and New York: Verso,
1991.

Rous, George. *Thoughts on Government; occasioned by Mr. Burke's Reflections &c. In
a Letter to a Friend. To which is added a Postscript, in Reply to a Vindication of Mr.
Burke's Reflections.* 4th ed. London: J. Debrett, 1791.

Rousseau, Jean-Jacques. *The Miscellaneous Works of Mr. J-J Rousseau.* 5 vols. London: T. Becket and P. A. De Hondt, 1767.

———. *Eloisa; or a Series of Original Letters Collected and Published by Mr. J-J
Rousseau, Citizen of Geneva.* Trans. from the French; a new ed., to which is
added the sequel of *Julia; or, the New Eloisa.* 4 vols. London: H. Baldwin,
1784.

———. *Émile.* Trans. Barabra Foxley. 1911; rpt. London and New York: Dent
and Dutton, 1974.

———. *Reveries of the Solitary Walker.* Trans. Peter France. Harmondsworth:
Penguin, 1979.

———. *The Confessions of Jean-Jacques Rousseau.* Trans. J. M. Cohen. 1953; rpt.
Harmondsworth: Penguin, 1981.

Roussel, Jean. *Jean-Jacques Rousseau en France après la Révolution, 1795–1830;
lectures et légende.* Paris, 1972.

Runciman, W. G. *Confessions of a Reluctant Theorist.* Hassocks: Harvester, 1990.

Sabin, Margery. *English Romanticism and the French Revolution.* Cambridge and London: Harvard University Press, 1976.

Said, Edward. "Traveling Theory." Pp. 226–47 in idem, *The World, the Text, and the Critic.* Cambridge: Harvard University Press, 1983.

Samuel, Raphael, ed. *Patriotism: The Making and Unmaking of British National Identity.* 3 vols. London and New York: Routledge, 1987.

Schiller, F. W. J. von. "An Essay on the effects of a Well-Regulated Theatre." *German Museum* 1 (1800): 382–90.

———. *Works of Friedrich von Schiller.* Trans. Sir Theodor Martin, R. D. Boylan, and others. 10 vols. in 5. London and New York: Aldus, 1902.

Schilling, Bernard N. *Conservative England and the Case against Voltaire.* New York: Columbia University Press, 1950.

Schor, Naomi. *Reading in Detail: Aesthetics and the Feminine.* London and New York: Methuen, 1987.

Schouls, Peter A. *The Imposition of Method: A Study of Descartes and Locke.* Oxford: Clarendon, 1980.

———. *Descartes and the Enlightenment.* Kingston and Montreal: Queens University Press, 1989.

Scruton, Roger, "Safer Unstated." *Times Literary Supplement,* 9–15 March 1990, p. 252.

Semmel, Bernard. *The Methodist Revolution.* New York: Basic, 1973.

Shaftesbury, Anthony Ashley Cooper, Third Earl of. *Characteristics of Men, Manners, Opinions, Times.* Ed. John M. Robertson. 2 vols. in 1. New York: Bobbs-Merrill, 1964.

Shapin, Steven, and Simon Schaffer. *Leviathan and the Air-Pump: Hobbes, Boyle, and the Experimental Life.* Princeton: Princeton University Press, 1985.

Shapiro, Barbara J. *Probability and Certainty in Seventeenth-Century England: A Study of the Relationships between Natural Science, Religion, History, Law, and Literature.* Princeton: Princeton University Press, 1983.

Sharratt, Peter. "Peter Ramus and the Reform of the University: The Divorce of Philosophy and Eloquence." Pp. 4–20 in idem, ed., *French Renaissance Studies, 1540–70: Humanism and the Encyclopaedia.* Edinburgh: Edinburgh University Press, 1976.

Shelley, Percy B. *Shelley: Poetical Works.* Ed. Thomas Hutchinson; corr. ed. G. M. Matthews. London, Oxford, and New York: Oxford University Press, 1971.

———. *Shelley's Poetry and Prose.* Ed. Donald Reiman and Sharon B. Powers. New York and London: Norton, 1977.

Siedentop, Larry. "Thatcherism and the Constitution." *Times Literary Supplement,* 26 January–1 February 1990, pp. 88, 99.

Sieyès, Émmanuel Joseph, Abbé de. *Déclaration des droits de l'homme en société.* Versailles, 1789.

———. *Quelques idées de constitution, applicables à la ville de Paris en juillet, 1789.* Versailles, 1789.

————. *Vues sur les moyens d'exécution dont les réprésentans de la France pourront disposer en 1789.* [?Versailles], 1789.

————. *What Is the Third Estate?* Trans. M. Blondel; ed. S. E. Finer. New York and London: Praeger, 1964.

Simpson, David. "Putting One's House in Order: The Foundations of Descartes' Method." *New Literary History* 9 (1977): 83–101.

————. *Irony and Authority in Romantic Poetry.* London: Macmillan, 1979.

————. *Wordsworth's Historical Imagination: The Poetry of Displacement.* London and New York: Methuen, 1987.

————. "Coleridge on Wordsworth and the Form of Poetry." Pp. 211–25 in Christine Gallant, ed., *Coleridge's Theory of Imagination Today.* New York: AMS, 1989.

————. "New Brooms at Fawlty Towers: Colin MacCabe and Cambridge English." Pp. 245–71 in Bruce Robbins, ed., *Intellectuals: Aesthetics, Politics, Academics.* Minneapolis: University of Minnesota Press, 1990.

————. "Public Virtues, Private Vices: Reading between the Lines of Wordsworth's 'Anecdote for Fathers.'" Pp. 163–90 in idem, ed., *Subject to History: Ideology, Class, Gender.* Ithaca and London: Cornell University Press, 1991.

————, ed. *The Origins of Modern Critical Thought: German Aesthetic and Literary Criticism from Lessing to Hegel.* Cambridge: Cambridge University Press, 1988.

Smith, Hilda L. *Reason's Disciples: Seventeenth-Century English Feminists.* Urbana, Chicago, and London: University of Illinois Press, 1982.

Smith, Olivia. *The Politics of Language, 1791–1819.* Oxford: Clarendon, 1984.

Smollett, Tobias. *Humphry Clinker.* Ed. James L. Thorson. New York and London: Norton, 1983.

Southey, Robert. *The Life of Wesley and the Rise and Progress of Methodism.* Ed. J. A. Atkinson. London and New York: Frederick Warne, n.d.

[*Spectator:*] *Selections from the Tatler and the Spectator of Steele and Addison.* Ed. Angus Ross. Harmondsworth: Penguin, 1982.

Spence, Thomas. *The Rights of Infants and Strictures on Paine's Agrarian Justice.* London, 1797.

————. *The Restorer of Society to its Natural State, in a Series of Letters to a Fellow Citizen.* London, 1801.

Sprat, Thomas. *History of the Royal Society.* Ed. Jackson I. Cope and Harold Whitmore Jones. London and St. Louis: Routledge and Kegan Paul and Washington University Studies, 1959.

Stedman Jones, Gareth. *Languages of Class: Studies in English Working-Class History, 1832–1982.* Cambridge: Cambridge University Press, 1983.

Stepan, Nancy. *The Idea of Race in Science: Great Britain, 1800–1960.* London: Macmillan, 1982.

Stephens, James. *Francis Bacon and the Style of Science.* Chicago and London: University of Chicago Press, 1975.

Stigler, Stephen M. *The History of Statistics: The Measurement of Uncertainty before 1900.* Cambridge: Harvard University Press, 1986.

Surel, Jeannine. "John Bull." Pp. 3–25 in *Patriotism*, vol. 3 (see Samuel).

Swift, Jonathan. *A Tale of a Tub, to which is added the Battle of the Books and the Mechanical Operation of the Spirit*. Ed. A. C. Guthkelch and D. Nichol Smith. Oxford: Clarendon, 1958.

Taylor, Thomas. *A Vindication of the Rights of Brutes*. London, 1792.

Thelwall, John. *The Rights of Nature, Against the Usurpations of Establishments*. 2 vols. London, 1796.

———. *Sober Reflections on the Seditious and Inflammatory Letter of the Rt. Hon. Edmund Burke to a Noble Lord; addressed to the serious Consideration of his Fellow Citizens*. London: H. D. Symonds, 1796.

Thomas, Keith. "Women and the Civil War Sects." *Past and Present* 13 (April 1958): 42–62.

———. *Religion and the Decline of Magic: Studies in Popular Beliefs in Sixteenth- and Seventeenth-Century England*. 1971; rpt. Harmondsworth: Peregrine Books, 1978.

———. "The Puritans and Adultery: The Act of 1650 Reconsidered." Pp. 257–82 in Donald Pennington and Keith Thomas, eds., *Puritans and Revolutionaries: Essays in Seventeenth-Century History Presented to Christopher Hill*. Oxford: Clarendon Press, 1978.

Thompson, Benjamin. *The German Theatre*. 6 vols. London: Vernor and Hood, 1801.

Thompson, E. P. *The Making of the English Working Class*. 1963; rpt. Harmondsworth: Penguin, 1976.

———. *The Poverty of Theory and Other Essays*. New York and London: Monthly Review Press, 1978.

Thompson, L. F. *Kotzebue: A Survey of his Progress in France and England, preceded by a Consideration of the Critical Attitudes to him in Germany*. Bibliothèque de la revue de littérature comparée, no. 51. Paris, 1928.

Towers, Joseph. *Thoughts on the Commencement of a New Parliament, with an appendix containing Remarks on the Letter of the Rt. Hon. Edmund Burke, on the Revolution in France*. Dublin, 1791.

Trahard, Pierre. *La sensibilité révolutionnaire*. Paris, 1936.

Turner, James G. "The Properties of Libertinism." Pp. 75–87 in Robert Purks Maccubbin, ed., *'Tis Nature's Fault: Unauthorized Sexuality during the Enlightenment*. Cambridge: Cambridge University Press, 1987.

Ulmer, William A. *Shelleyan Eros: The Rhetoric of Romantic Love*. Princeton: Princeton University Press, 1990.

Van Duzer, Charles H. *Contributions of the Ideologues to French Revolutionary Thought*. Baltimore: Johns Hopkins University Press, 1935.

Vartanian, Aram. *Diderot and Descartes: A Study of Scientific Naturalism in the Enlightenment*. Princeton: Princeton University Press, 1953.

———. "La Mettrie, Diderot, and Sexology in the Enlightenment." Pp. 347–67 in Jean Macary, ed., *Essays on the Age of Enlightenment in Honor of Ira O. Wade*. Geneva: Droz, 1977.

Vickers, Brian, ed. *Shakespeare: The Critical Heritage, 1623–1801*. 6 vols. London, Boston, Henley: Routledge, 1974–81.

Viswanathan, Gauri. *Masks of Conquest: Literary Study and British Rule in India.* New York: Columbia University Press, 1989.

Voisine, Jacques. *J-J Rousseau en Angleterre à l'époque romantique: les écrits autobiographiques et la légende.* Études de littérature étrangère et comparée, no. 31. Paris, 1956.

Volney, Constantin François Chasseboeuf, Comte de. *Volney's Ruins: or, Meditations on the Revolution of Empires.* Trans. under the immediate inspection of the author from the 6th Paris ed. New York: Dixon and Sickels, 1828.

Voltaire, François Marie Arouet de. *The Elements of Sir Isaac Newton's Philosophy.* Trans., rev., and corr. by John Hanna. London, 1738; facs. rpt. London: Frank Cass, 1967.

Walzer, Michael. *The Revolution of the Saints: A Study in the Origins of Radical Politics.* 1965; rpt. Cambridge and London: Harvard University Press, 1982.

Warburton, William. *The Works of Alexander Pope, Esq. in Nine Volumes . . . Together with the Commentaries and Notes of Mr. Warburton.* London, 1751.

Weber, Max. *The Protestant Ethic and the Spirit of Capitalism.* Trans. Talcott Parsons. New York: Scribner's, 1958.

Webster, Charles. *The Great Instauration: Science, Medicine, and Reform, 1626–1660.* London: Duckworth, 1975.

Wellek, René. *Immanuel Kant in England, 1793–1838.* Princeton: Princeton University Press, 1931.

Westminster Review 1 (January 1824): 1–18. Review of James Shergold Boone, *Men and Things in 1823.*

Wilkes, John. *An Essay on Woman.* Aberdeen, 1788.

Will, George. "Literary Politics." *Newsweek,* 22 April 1991, p. 72.

[Williams, David]. *Letters to a Young Prince, on the Present Disposition in Europe to a General Revolution.* London: H. D. Simmons, 1790.

Williams, David. "The Politics of Feminism in the French Enlightenment." Pp. 333–51 in Peter Hughes and David Williams, eds., *The Varied Pattern: Studies in the Eighteenth Century.* Toronto: A. M. Hakkert, 1971.

Williams, Eric. *From Columbus to Castro: The History of the Caribbean, 1492–1969.* 1970; rpt. New York: Random House, 1984.

Williams, Gwyn A. *Artisans and Sans-Culottes: Popular Movements in France and Britain during the French Revolution.* London: Edward Arnold, 1968.

Williams, Helen Maria. *Julia, a Novel; Interspersed with some Poetical Pieces.* 2 vols. London: T. Cadell, 1790.

———. *Letters Written in France, in the Summer of 1790, to a Friend in England, containing various Anecdotes relative to the French Revolution; and Memoirs of Mons. and Madame Du F———.* 2d ed. London: T. Cadell, 1791.

———. *Letters Containing a Sketch of the Politics of France, from the thirty-first of May, 1793, till the twenty-eighth of July, 1794; and of the Scenes which have passed in the Prisons of Paris.* 2d ed. 4 vols. London, 1795–96.

———. *Sketches of the State of Manners and Opinions in the French Republic, towards the Close of the Eighteenth Century, in a Series of Letters.* 2 vols. London: G. G. and J. Robinson, 1801.

Williams, L. Pearce. "The Politics of Science in the French Revolution." Pp.

291–308 in Marshall Clagett, ed., *Critical Problems in the History of Science.* Madison: University of Wisconsin Press, 1959.

Williams, Raymond. *Culture and Society, 1780–1950.* 1958; rpt. Harmondsworth: Penguin, 1971.

———. *Marxism and Literature.* Oxford: Oxford University Press, 1978.

———. *Politics and Letters: Interviews with New Left Review.* 1979; rpt. London: Verso, 1981.

———. *Keywords: A Vocabulary of Culture and Society.* Rev. ed. New York: Oxford University Press, 1983.

Willich, A. F. M. *Elements of the Critical Philosophy; Containing a Concise Account of its Origin and Tendency; A View of all the Works Published by its Founder, Professor Immanuel Kant; and a Glossary for the Explanation of Terms and Phrases. To which are added Three Philological Essays, chiefly translated from the German of John Christopher Adelung.* London: T. N. Longman, 1798.

Winstanley, Gerard. *"The Law of Freedom" and Other Writings.* Ed. Christopher Hill. Cambridge: Cambridge University Press, 1983.

Wolfe, Don M., ed. *Leveller Manifestoes of the Puritan Revolution.* New York: Thomas Nelson, 1944.

Wolfson, Susan J. "Feminizing Keats." Pp. 317–56 in Hermione de Almeida, ed., *Critical Essays on John Keats.* Boston: G. K. Hall, 1990.

Wollstonecraft, Mary. *Thoughts on the Education of Daughters; with Reflections on Female Conduct, in the most Important Duties of Life.* London: J. Johnson, 1787.

———. *A Historical and Moral View of the Origin and Progress of the French Revolution; and the Effect it has produced in Europe.* London: J. Johnson, 1794.

———. *Posthumous Works of the Author of 'A Vindication of the Rights of Woman.'* 1798; facs. rpt., 4 vols. in 2, Clifton, N.J.: Augustus Kelley, 1972.

———. *A Vindication of the Rights of Woman.* Ed. Carol Postan. New York and London: Norton, 1975.

———. *"Mary" and "The Wrongs of Woman."* Ed. James Kinsley and Gary Kelley. Oxford: Oxford University Press, 1980.

[Wollstonecraft, Mary]. *The Female Reader; or Miscellaneous Pieces in Prose and Verse; Selected from the best Writers, and dispersed under proper Heads; for the Improvement of Young Women.* 1789; Facs. ed. Moira Ferguson. Delmar, N.Y.: Scholars' Facsimiles and Reprints, 1980.

———. *A Vindication of the Rights of Men, in a Letter to the Rt. Hon. Edmund Burke, occasioned by his Reflections on the Revolution in France.* London: J. Johnson, 1790.

Wood, James. "Literature Its Own best Theory?" *Times Literary Supplement,* 7 June 1991, p. 14.

Wordsworth, William. *The Poetical Works of William Wordsworth.* Ed. E. de Selincourt. 5 vols. Oxford: Clarendon, 1940–49.

———. *The Prose Works of William Wordsworth.* Ed. W. J. B. Owen and Jane Worthington Smyser. 3 vols. Oxford: Clarendon, 1974.

———. *The Prelude: 1799, 1805, 1850.* Ed. Jonathan Wordsworth, M. H. Abrams, and Stephen Gill. New York and London: Norton, 1979.

————. *The Borderers*. Ed. Robert Osborn. Ithaca and London: Cornell University Press, 1982.

Wright, John W. *Shelley's Myth of Metaphor*. Athens: University of Georgia Press, 1970.

Young, Arthur. *The Example of France a Warning to Britain*. Dublin, 1793.

————. *Travels During the Years 1787, 1788, and 1789; undertaken more particularly with a View of ascertaining the Cultivation, Wealth, Resources, and National Prosperity of the Kingdom of France*. 2d ed. 2 vols. London and Bury St. Edmunds, 1794.

————. *An Inquiry into the State of the Public Mind amongst the Lower Classes: and on the Means of turning it to the Welfare of the State; in a Letter to William Wilberforce, Esq., M.P.* London, 1798.

INDEX